JOHNNY'S GIRL

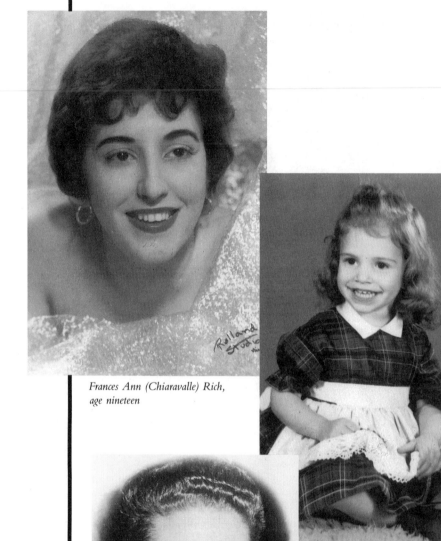

Frances Ann (Chiaravalle) Rich,
age nineteen

Kim Maureen Rich, 1962

Johnny Rich, 1956

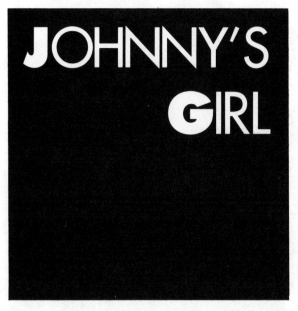

JOHNNY'S GIRL

*A DAUGHTER'S MEMOIR OF
GROWING UP IN
ALASKA'S UNDERWORLD*

KIM RICH

WILLIAM MORROW AND COMPANY, INC. • NEW YORK

It is the policy of William Morrow and Company, Inc., and its imprints and affiliates, recognizing the importance of preserving what has been written, to print the books we publish on acid-free paper, and we exert our best efforts to that end.

Library of Congress Cataloging-in-Publication Data

Rich, Kim, 1958–
    Johnny's girl : a daughter's memoir of growing up in Alaska's underworld / Kim Rich.
        p.   cm.
    ISBN 0-688-11836-4
    1. Rich, John Francis, 1933–1973. 2. Criminals—Alaska—Biography. 3. Rich, Kim, 1958– . 4. Daughters—Alaska—Biography. 5. Criminals—Alaska—Family relationships—Case studies. 6. Organized crime—Alaska—Case studies. I. Title.
HV6248.R45R53 1993
364.1′092—dc20
[B]   92-19973
                 CIP

Printed in the United States of America

First Edition

1 2 3 4 5 6 7 8 9 10

BOOK DESIGN BY DEBBIE GLASSERMAN

FOR JOHNNY AND GINGER

ACKNOWLEDGMENTS

I owe a great deal to so very many. There are countless individuals who gave generously in helping me write this book. I don't know if I can ever find the words to adequately express my deep gratitude. I know that Johnny and Ginger would thank all of you too.

For many of you, please regard your presence and comments on the pages of this book as my thanks. Many of you assisted in other ways, and I will try to express my appreciation here.

I wish to thank the *Anchorage Daily News,* Howard Weaver, my colleagues, and McClatchy Newspapers, Inc. I want to especially thank my former editor and close friend Gary Nielson for helping me put my story on paper for the first time.

I wish to also acknowledge the generous support of the law firm of Birch, Horton, Bittner and Cherot. Thank you so very, very much. And thank you, Jeff Lowenfels, for your boundless optimism and for believing my newspaper series, "Family Secrets," could be so much more.

This book would not have been possible without the faith and commitment of Rafe Sagalyn and his staff at the Sagalyn Literary Agency; the vision of my editor at William Morrow, Paul Bresnick; and the tireless assistance lent to this book by Mark Garofalo. Many thanks also to Wendy Goldman. I particularly want to thank Michael Dolan for his friendship and for helping to guide my sometimes ragged prose into something more meaningful.

I have been blessed with the companionship and generosity of many, especially: Bill Shoemaker, David Shoup, Scott Sidell, and Rebecca Burns. I am deeply grateful to each of you for your emotional and financial support during these last few years.

From the day I entered journalism, I have benefited in so many ways from the guidance, counsel, and friendship of Mike Doogan, who is also my mentor and the best reporter/editor/columnist I'll ever know. Thanks for believing in me from the beginning.

Late in the preparation of the book, I also received the strong support and encouragement of William Large, without whom the final stretch would have been unbearable. Thanks, W.B.

I wish to also acknowledge Richard Murphy and the entire *Anchorage Daily News* photography staff, especially Fran Durner (thanks for the wonderful pictures!), Bill Roth, and Jim Lavrakas. I also owe many thanks to my editor and friend, Bill White, and thank you Pat Dougherty for continuing to find a place for me at the *Daily News*.

Others who have lent their assistance to this book include: Sheila Toomey, Anders Westman, Stan and Susan Jones, Sandra Saville, Cheryl Kirk, Hal Spencer, Don Hunter, Patti Epler and Mark Headlough, David Hulen and L. J. Campbell, Sharon Palmisano and staff, Len Frazier, Nan Elliot, Eric and Beate Zinck, Gail and Jan Sieberts, Janice Ryan, Marilee Enge and George Frost, Phil Blumstein, Doe Anderson, Plesah Wilson, and Steve Zelner. I am also deeply obliged to Rabbi Harry Rosenfeld of Temple Beth Sholom, Richard and Barb Mauer, Beth Rose, and John Levy for welcoming me into their faith.

I also owe much to Dr. Aron Wolf and Dr. David Samson for assisting me in interpreting my mother's medical records; Allen Blumenthal of the State Bar of California; the staff at Birch, Horton, Bittner and Cherot, especially: Roberta Jasper, Edie Burden, Betty Thomas, Pat Fero, Deb Woods, Jean Blake, Bunny Gehring, Robin Feeney, P. J. Marker, Sylvia Provencal, and Allen Gutierrez. Thank you to my talented Alaska researchers: John Baker, Elizabeth Evans, and Karen Dahl. I especially want to note the contributions of those friends who at various stages read the manuscript and offered their suggestions: Averil

Lerman, Kathy Doogan, Ron Spatz, Andy Ryan, Marla Williams, Ed Nawotka, and Eiven and Mary Pat Brudie.

Many of the Alaska history references are based on the newspaper files of both the *Anchorage Daily News* and the *Anchorage Times,* as well as a number of historical texts, most notably *Alaska: A History of the 49th State* by Claus-M. Naske and Herman E. Slotnick. My research in Alaska was aided by the unselfish donations of time and expertise of the following: United States District Court Judge James M. Fitzgerald; Bruce Merrell and Dan Fleming of the Alaska Collection at the Z. J. Loussac Library; Sam Trivette, executive director of the Alaska Parole Board; Bill Roche of the Alcohol Beverage Control Board; LeEllen Baker and Jo Hall of the Alaska State Courthouse, and all of the clerks at the records counter, including Dana Gallipeo, Debbie Vea, Jack Lenardson, and Terry Evans, and Trish Milby and Marge Smith in transcripts; retired United States Marshal for the Territory of Alaska James Chenoweth; Dean Dawson of Alaska State Archives; the Alaska Mental Health Association; Tom Nelson of the Municipality of Anchorage; Ed Park of the Midnight Sun Street Rod Association; Kerry Hoffman and Anchorage Historic Properties; Nancy Ashwell for her earthquake memorabilia; Jeff Hassler; Greg Carr, Rhonda Scott, and Deborah Spoelman-Knox of Carr-Gottstein Foods Co.; Scott Banks; Bette Cato; Paul Edscorn; Peter Jenkins; Tom Gregoire; Fred Witzleben; Lesyle Langla; Robert Wagstaff; Herb Rhodes; Ed Dankworth; Duran Powell; Perry Green; James Dix; Ron Moore; Augie Hiebert; and Charity and Kenneth Kadow. And as always, bless you Melita Hitchen for all your kind words.

Outside of Alaska, I owe a special thanks to Jo Ann Fleming of the Public Library in Ironwood, Michigan; Elsie Jeffers of Burbank High School in California; and Georgianna Kuebler, director of clinical records at Newberry Regional Mental Health Center in Michigan.

In Connecticut, I wish to thank the Connecticut Society of Genealogy, especially retired executive administrator Jacquelyn Ricker; Beverly Tabak (for everything!!!); David Stoddard; historian David Palmquist; Cathy Velenchik; Lizette Pelletier, assistant archivist with the Connecticut State Library; Sister Helen Margaret Feeney and the Chancery; Elizabeth Went of Catholic Social Services in Hartford; William J. F. Rafferty and Catholic Family Services of Norwalk; Estelle LaChance with Catholic Family and Social Services in Bridgeport; Mary

Solero of Connecticut Adoption Resource Exchange; Mary Keegan and Penny Kollmeyer of Saint Agnes Family Center; Ellen Ryder of the Warehouse Point State Receiving Home; and Hedy Gryszan and Bertha Miller of the State of Connecticut Department of Children and Youth Services.

Parts of this book are based on the recollections and assistance of family members and friends, including Christine Gustafson, Sandra Volley, Pat and John Wilson, Henry Palmer and family, Stanley Crowley, Pat and George Brown, Geri Firmin, John Firmin, Pat Heller; and finally, Mary and Earl Delano, thank you for welcoming me into your home.

I will always be grateful to my mother's family for safekeeping her things for me, and for their willingness to talk about my mother and her illness, which will undoubtedly continue to haunt us all.

Thank you to Lynn and John Rich in Charlotte for standing in as family members; Dr. Jean Persons and staff for their continuous support; Tim McGinnis; Irene Miller; the Lenhardts for hosting me in New York; Bill Weimar and the Volley family for doing the same in Washington, D.C.

Finally, I want to thank those I never got a chance to, the people who filled in for family when my parents no longer could: Mike and Red Dodge and family; Hazel Johnson and the entire Johnson clan; the Rays and the Williamsons of Phoenix; the Bains and Walt Morgan of Anchorage; and Donna Fessler, wherever you are.

I miss you Guy Woodward, Jeanne Fortier, Jack Palmer.

CONTENTS

The teenage girl picked up the telephone, dialed the newspaper, and asked to speak to a reporter. She was furious. She wanted to know why, in a three-paragraph article about his disappearance, the reporter had taken pains to mention her father's gambling arrests.

Her father had been missing for almost a month. She thought the reporter had been unfair in writing about the arrests at a time when many believed he was not only missing but dead.

"Why do you guys always have to write about the gambling?" she asked. "Why do you always have to make him sound like a bad guy?"

The reporter said he believed her dad's gambling had something to do with his disappearance. The girl told the reporter he was wrong.

That call to the *Anchorage Daily News* took place September 20, 1973. I was that fifteen-year-old girl. My mother had died the year before. If my father was dead, I was an orphan.

Now resting on my desk is a copy of the newspaper clipping that prompted my call. In the three years I've spent researching and writing this book, I've wondered many times how I would have handled the story if I'd been the reporter. More important, how would I have handled a call from the daughter of a man who had been murdered?

It was a hot story. On an August night in 1973 my father, one of Anchorage's most notorious underworld figures, didn't return home from a visit to a local topless bar. Everyone knew my dad. Since the late 1950s, he had operated illegal gambling houses and run prostitutes all over Anchorage.

"State Troopers and city police have joined forces to hunt the whereabouts of John F. 'Johnny' Rich Jr.," began the newspaper story.

"Rich, who inexplicably disappeared Aug. 22, is the owner of Cindy's Massage Studio at 605 W. 29th Ave., the 736 Club, and Alaska Firearms Distributors.

"He was reportedly last seen in his brown 1971 Cadillac near the Pacific Auction on Old Seward Highway. A long-time Anchorage resident, Rich has had a number of convictions on misdemeanor gambling charges."

I was my father's only child, raised amid the denizens of Anchorage's nightlife—pimps, con men, gamblers, prostitutes, heroin addicts, strippers. I spent most nights home alone, staying close to the television for company while my father was out working the clubs.

I saw firsthand the ravages of "the life": It broke my mother's spirit and triggered her collapse into insanity. Cops and hoodlums beat down the door of our home in the middle of the night. My father taught me to be tough and fearless. He also taught me to speak my mind.

As I look back to that telephone call, which I made years before becoming a journalist myself, it's not surprising to me now that at only fifteen, I would tell a reporter how to do his job. If his mention of my father's arrest record hadn't bothered me so, I also might have pointed out that he was wrong to call my father's Cadillac "brown." The dealer had labeled it "bronzit," but it always looked gold to me.

I remember the car well. The last time I saw my father alive, he was driving it.

That Sunday morning was bright and sunny. I was working my summer job at one of the Twin Tesoro gas stations on Gambell Street near our house when my father drove up in his Cadillac.

In the summer of 1973, any street in Anchorage as busy as Gambell had a Tesoro station at nearly every major intersection. The Twin Tesoros were in Fairview, the closest Anchorage comes to having a ghetto.

In Italian, *tesoro* means treasure; the stations and their setting were assuredly not.

Like all the Tesoro stations in town, the Twins were simply strips of raised concrete, each topped by gas pumps bracketing a glassed-in cashier's booth at the center. The booths, about the size of walk-in closets, weren't comfortable, but the glass doors on either end let an attendant work all the pumps. A tall counter divided the booth in half and held a small cash register and a charge card machine. Narrow shelves, drooping under dozens of cans of oil, lined the walls below the banks of windows. Everything was painted white—the counter, the walls, even the wooden stool where I'd sit when business was slow. One of my assignments was to keep the booth clean. I was forever spraying industrial cleaner in a losing battle against the oil and dirt that collected on everything.

But I loved my job. I was popular with the customers, especially the men—they got a kick out of a girl working at a gas station. I didn't think anything of it.

There was no Tesoro uniform; the manager liked red and white, so I always wore a clean white shirt with my blue jeans and red baseball cap. I worked weekday afternoons and weekends—I usually signed up for the six A.M. to two P.M. shift. I liked Sunday morning, when business dragged and I could listen to the radio. Most other times, the place was a madhouse.

My father was alone in his Cadillac. He wanted a fill-up.

"You want to go to Big Lake?" he asked as he poked his head out the driver's side window, smiling broadly.

He was teasing me. He knew I was the only one working and it was hours before quitting time. It wasn't even nine A.M. yet. Even though he'd probably only had a couple of hours' sleep, there he was with the boat hooked up and ready for the fifty-mile drive north to his favorite lake.

When I was younger, I spent nearly every summer Sunday with him at Big Lake zipping around in his speedboat, the one with red and orange flames painted on the bow. We'd spend the day hitting all the lakefront bars. Since I'd entered my teens, however, there'd been fewer "family days," as my father used to call our Sunday outings. I was more interested in hanging around with my friends than with him.

He'd sold the speedboat several years back and moved on to a Chris-

Craft. The new boat was more conservative-looking—green, with room for six—and was better equipped for sport fishing, my father's new hobby. Besides, it suited him at that point in his life. He had turned forty in the spring and he was slowing down.

He may have been going fishing, but as always, he could have been on his way to a night on the town dressed in dark trousers, open-collared shirt, and brown cotton waistcoat. The only clue that he was headed for a boat-loading ramp was what he called his "boat shoes"— the canvas tennies with the broad rubber sides.

I hadn't had a chance to go out in the new boat. He'd owned it only a few weeks, but I don't think there was anything he was more proud of, except perhaps for me. I knew that even then, despite everything that had gone on between us. For some time, relations between us had been strained.

"Why can't you be like other dads?" I'd yell at him. In a tired voice, he used to tell his friends, "You raise them just so they can grow up to hate you." That wasn't true; I loved my father, but for a long time, there just hadn't been much about him that I liked. We could hardly talk about anything without arguing and without my reminding him that I despised much of what he represented.

But that Sunday morning there was no argument. I was glad to see him. He was in a good mood and seemed happy.

I told him I couldn't join him.

"It's your loss," he said.

"Yeah, yeah, I know," I said.

After I finished gassing up his car and collecting his money, he leaned out the window a second time.

"You still my girl?" he asked.

"Sure," I answered, as I always did.

"You know I love you," he said, then leaning out even farther, he said, "Give your dad a kiss."

I leaned down and kissed him on the cheek.

He smiled again just before he rolled up the window and drove off, waving as he left the lot. How often I've wished I'd gone with him.

Five days later, sometime after five in the afternoon, I was visited at the same gas station by a man and a woman I'd never met before.

I was sitting in the station's booth listening to Led Zeppelin sing "Stairway to Heaven." I spotted the couple, walking side by side, the moment they rounded the corner of the station's asphalt lot. I remember thinking how they looked like real estate agents or bankers in their businesslike clothing, both carrying briefcases, faces dead serious.

He was wearing a tweed sportcoat, a tie, and brown slacks. She was matronly, with a tight coif of graying hair and clad in a skirt and jacket. I remember thinking how handsome he looked with his shaggy curly hair and mustache. There was something about her I didn't like; she reminded me of the brusque secretaries at the school office.

They walked up to the booth and I stepped outside to greet them. They smiled—his was wide and ingratiating; hers was strained. He spoke first, saying he was Duncan Webb, my father's new lawyer. He introduced the woman as his assistant, Caye Mason.

"Your father's in trouble," Webb said. "He's about to lose everything he owns."

Webb explained how somebody—he didn't give a name—had placed a lien against my father's assets. He then handed me a typewritten letter:

> Dear Miss Rich,
>
> Please be advised that I represent Mr. John Rich for purposes of managing his business interests and investments as described more fully in the attached copy of "Power of Attorney" dated August 22, 1973.
>
> This letter is to introduce Ms. Kay [sic] Mason who will instruct you in the procedure for payment of the lease on the property at 736 East 12th Avenue, Anchorage, Alaska. I will be in touch with you within the next few days to answer any questions you may have.
>
> Thank you for your cooperation in this matter.
>
> Very truly yours,
>
> Duncan C. Webb

Webb said my father had gone to Seattle to straighten out his business affairs and would be home in a few days and that he'd asked Webb to look after things in his absence. He took out a legal-size piece of paper, the top half of which contained a long, dense paragraph filled with jargon I didn't understand. At the bottom, however, I recognized one thing: my father's signature.

Webb said the paper was a "Power of Attorney" that gave him the ability to act legally on my father's behalf. He kept insisting he was protecting my father's interests and that he needed my cooperation. He said my father had sent him.

I felt confused. What was this stuff about lease payments? My cooperation? What exactly was a power of attorney? Webb kept talking, saying he needed me to let him into our house to inventory its contents to protect everything from being confiscated. I thought of my father's new boat, his Cadillac, some furniture we'd just bought—things Webb said we were about to lose.

My mind was racing. Who was trying to take my father's property? Why hadn't my father told me about this? Nothing added up. My father hadn't left town in nearly ten years. Why would he leave now? Why would he change lawyers? I knew his lawyer; my father liked him. I was frustrated that my father wasn't there to explain what was going on.

I hadn't seen my father since the Sunday before. But I was accustomed to having him disappear for days at a time, immersed in some poker game. I'd learned long before not to worry if I didn't see him every day. Yet, for all his casual attitudes about schedules and morality, my father lived a guarded life. He had many acquaintances, but few close friends. He was extremely secretive about his affairs. I was never, under any circumstances, to let anyone into our house unless I checked with him first. I was to trust no one, not even his best friends.

I didn't know what to make of Webb and Mason. They leaned toward me, body language demanding a decision. I asked why Al Bennett, my father's friend and roommate, wouldn't let them in.

"Al said to ask you," Webb said.

I didn't want to disappoint them. I've always tried to please, and maybe that's why my father was constantly repeating his warnings to me. He knew I was too trusting.

Webb pressed me for an answer. Nothing seemed right, but I relented. On the back of the envelope containing the letter addressed to me I wrote, "Al, let them in. Kim."

Webb and Mason left to return to our house, less than a half block away. Moments later, Al came running over.

"What the hell did you let them in for?" he yelled at me from across the gas station lot. "Wesley Ladd is with them!"

My heart froze. Webb hadn't mentioned Ladd. I didn't know much about Ladd except that he was my father's enemy. Before I could say anything, Al spun around and left.

I might have been more worried if I weren't accustomed to odd events and people coming and going from my father's life. I coped with my father's erratic life by separating it as much as possible from my own. At the end of my shift I wanted to buy tickets for an upcoming concert, the last big bash of the summer, featuring three bands—Spirit, the Chambers Brothers, and Stories. I called a taxi; it was only a short drive to the ticket outlet. I had the driver wait, then asked him to take me home.

As the cab neared our house, I saw my father's car pulling out of the driveway. I told the cabbie to catch him, but the Cadillac quickly disappeared into traffic. I was disappointed, but I was also elated and relieved. *He hadn't left town. He must have run into the lawyer at the house and everything would be all right.*

I paid the cabbie and walked across the gravel driveway toward our house. The exterior porch door was bolted. When Al opened it, he was carrying a rifle.

"What the heck is going on?" I asked.

"I'll explain in a minute, just hurry up and get in here," Al said as he grabbed me by the shoulder and hustled me into the house.

He told me what Webb and Mason had said—the same story I'd heard. It seemed plausible until Al mentioned that they were driving my father's Cadillac and they had his keys. My father had a large key ring, like the kind janitors carry, jammed with dozens of keys. I never realized how well I knew him until that moment. My father never let anyone drive his Cadillac; he would never have handed over all his keys. *Oh, God,* I thought. *Something is wrong. Something is really wrong.*

Later I learned that as Webb and Mason were talking to me, my father had been dead for two days. The gun that killed him sat in the glove compartment of his car. His murderer was behind the wheel.

Fourth Avenue, Anchorage's main street, February 1964 COURTESY U.S. ARMY CORPS OF ENGINEE

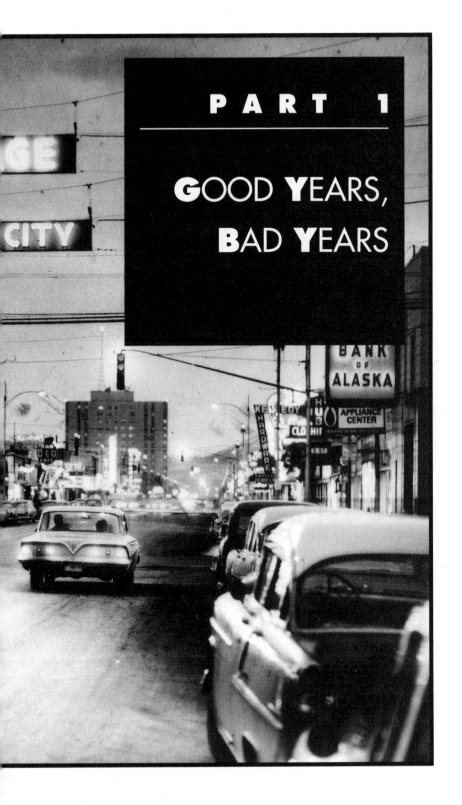

PART 1

GOOD YEARS, BAD YEARS

Johnny and Ginger, San Francisco, 1956

CHAPTER ONE

JOHNNY AND GINGER

I have been told that I am the daughter of two black sheep. It must have seemed that way, especially to those who knew Johnny Rich and Ginger Chiaravalle in the summer of 1956, when they met in Los Angeles.

A casting agent could have named my father—he was of medium build, lithe and handsome, with dark, curly hair that he combed back in neat waves. He wore custom-tailored silk suits and smoked Lucky Strikes. He was urbane, sophisticated, and worldly. And there were so many compelling mysteries about him, not the least of which was a tattoo—his Social Security number—engraved on his left bicep.

When they met, she'd taken to enhancing a beauty mark on her left cheek, in the style of Marilyn Monroe. My mother was exquisite, with pronounced cheekbones and heart-shaped lips she painted cherry red. She dressed in skintight pedal pushers and cashmere sweaters, a true fifties beauty.

My parents—she'd adopted the Ginger; her parents had christened her "Frances"—seemed to be custom-made for each other. They were both on the run, lean, hungry, and ambitious, with pasts that were better forgotten.

No one knows where they met, but after only three weeks they moved into an apartment on Country Club Drive. On August 21, 1956, they were married in a civil ceremony in Santa Monica. My father was twenty-three; my mother, twenty-two. She broke the news to her family in a brief phone call, simply telling them, "We're in love."

The only relic of their brief courtship is a postcard photograph of them taken in Las Vegas in 1956 at the Horseshoe Club and Casino in front of the club's landmark, a giant horseshoe containing a million dollars in greenbacks. At the bottom, my mother wrote, "Here we are with a million dollars in actual cash."

Whatever sparse contact my mother had with her family became even more strained over her marriage to a man she said was Jewish. But Johnny Rich wasn't a Jew. I don't know where my mother got this idea, but I grew up believing I was half Jewish. No one ever asked him, but my father's friends believed it. He certainly looked the part, they say—dark hair, olive complexion, fierce temper, quick wit, the appearance of money—more than enough to convince those given to stereotypes that he was Jewish. He used Yiddishisms like "schmuck."

One of the few times anyone ever saw him drunk was after Israel's 1967 Six-Day War with Egypt. People assumed he was celebrating because he was Jewish. But years later, a friend of his said Johnny's jubilation might have also been fostered by his inclination to cheer for the underdog.

While he lived, my father's past seemed to me to be forbidden ground. Growing up, I knew no one from his side of the family; no aunts, no uncles, no cousins; there was never even the occasional card, letter, or phone call from a grandparent. So I hunted for my heritage among strangers. As a child attending a Christian summer camp, I told a counselor I was Jewish. She smiled broadly and said, "The Jews are God's chosen people." I liked the sound of her answer. Later, the answers weren't that easy. In high school I asked a teacher what it meant to be Jewish. She claimed there was no Jewish race; one was a Polish Jew, a French Jew, a German Jew, or *whatever* Jew. When I met my first New Yorker, I asked him the same question. He answered with another question: What kind of Jew? Conservative? Orthodox? Reformed? I stopped asking. But I never stopped believing I had a Jewish father. Neither did my mother's family. Years after my parents were dead a relative drew a family tree on a sheet of kraft paper that covered her dining room table. On my mother's side, branches jutted off from each member, with space for a spouse's name. My father was identified only as "Jewish Man."

For a long time, my father's FBI rap sheet was all I had by way of a family history. My father never talked about his childhood except for an occasional reference to being raised in boarding homes. My father's silence about his past became my personal mysteries. It would take me years to learn the answers I needed to know; that my father's childhood was anything but a simple story to tell. But there were always stories about where Johnny Rich had come from and he never seemed to discourage any of them. The most frequent rumor made him out to be the estranged son of a wealthy East Coast family. It's easy to see where people might have gotten this impression.

My father was a man of exact manners and expensive tastes. He nurtured a lifelong love affair with huge, finned American luxury cars. Predictably, he loved Cadillacs best. "Land yachts," he called them, and there was an unbroken string of Coupe deVilles and Eldorados that came and went from his life. His last car, the '71 Coupe deVille, delivered him to his murderers.

His jewelry was like his cars: large and expensive. His favorite piece of jewelry was a three-and-a-half carat diamond ring that he wore just about everywhere. But unlike many of his business associates, my father would never wear a diamond pinkie ring. That would be too crass, too cheap, too ordinary-looking. My father despised anything ordinary.

He was a congenial man, well liked by many. Yet, he carried an air of superiority that signaled to others that he'd come from some dignified, you–can't–touch–me roots. He had no patience for indolence, stupidity, or even clumsiness, causing people around him, including myself, to be guarded and cautious. "The world is full of morons," he'd tell me. "Stupid" and "sucker" were words I grew up hearing again and again.

I have two photographic images of my father—a photo taken when he was a teenager and a videotape recorded twenty-one years later. The photo and the tape were found at opposite ends of the United States, yet both tell the same story.

The videotape shows my father in an Anchorage courtroom where he'd been called to testify. He is dressed in a suit and tie, looking fit and trim for a thirty-nine-year-old man who never exercised and who'd spent much of his life in smoke-filled nightclubs. On the tape, his eyes are wary, full of contempt and distrust. A much younger Johnny Rich gives the same signals in the eight-by-ten black-and-white glossy photograph taken when he was eighteen, sitting among paunchy older men wearing well-cut double-breasted suits with white carnations in the lapels. Most of the men are lifting champagne glasses. The occasion is an uncle's wedding reception in 1952 at the Ocean Sea Grill in Bridgeport, Connecticut. By far the youngest man in the group, my father sits in the foreground, wearing a light suit and a floral patterned tie. In the background is a row of padded booths with the tables covered in white linen and the remnants of a meal—half-empty plates, overflowing ashtrays, beer bottles, and whiskey glasses. His right hand, dangling a cigarette, rests on the back of the chair of the man next to him who offers the camera a raised eyebrow and drooping eyes. Everybody else is letting themselves go, but not my father. His smile is barely a smirk. He's just a teenager, yet the distance and cynicism in his eyes make him appear older than everybody else in the picture.

In both video and photograph, my father seems very much alone. He is no more with the men in the wedding party than he is with those in the courtroom around him.

My grandfather, John Rich, Sr.—whom I found nine months after I began my search for my father's roots—keeps a copy of the 1952 photo under a pane of glass in a Miami Beach apartment where he has lived off and on since 1945. The photo is his one memento of his only child. He had another snapshot showing my father at age three. In the picture, he wore a sailor suit and was sitting in a boat on a pond. The photo disappeared long ago.

"He looked cute as a pennywhistle," my grandfather recalled with a wide smile when I asked about the vanished picture.

The sailor photo had accompanied one of the infrequent letters his son's mother had sent, chronicling the boy's progress. News of my father's birth had come in one such letter.

"You've got a son," Helen Galenski wrote from Hartford during the late spring of 1933. "A nice boy. He looks like you."

Helen waited several months before sending the letter/birth announcement, since my grandfather had been jailed for fathering her boy born out of wedlock. Originally he faced three criminal charges: seduction, carnal abuse of a minor, and attempting to procure an abortion.

My father's first brush with the law occurred before he was even out of the womb. His conception is chronicled in a group of yellowing sheets of paper stored in a box titled "Record Group–3" in the Connecticut State Archives in Hartford. The records note how, in October 1932, a pair of police officers arrived at a small barbershop at 1766 Seaview Avenue in Bridgeport with a warrant for the arrest of one of the owners, John Alexander Rich.

The police were called after Helen was caught attempting to take a dose of quinine tablets, which John Rich, Sr., had delivered to her, and which Helen believed would end her pregnancy:

Under the heading "SEDUCTION" begins the list of charges brought against my grandfather:

> State's Attorney . . . accuses JOHN RICH of the crime of seduction of a minor female, and charges that between the 15th day of September 1932 and the 18th day of October 1932, at Bridgeport, said JOHN RICH did seduce and commit fornication with one HELEN GALENSKI a minor female of the age of 17 against the peace. . . .
> ATTEMPT TO PROCURE ABORTION . . . and said State's Attorney further accuses JOHN RICH of the crime to attempt to procure an abortion, and charges that between the 15th day of September 1932 and the 18th day of October 1932, at Bridgeport, said JOHN RICH did unlawfully give or administer to one HELEN GALENSKI a certain drug, and did advise her to use certain means or instruments with intent to procure upon her a miscarriage, against the peace. . . .

My father was born John Francis Galenski on May 5, 1933, at St. Agnes Home for Girls, a forbidding five-story brick building surrounded by lush lawns in West Hartford. St. Agnes gave young mothers fake names to protect them and their families from the dishonor of unwed motherhood. The girls gave birth in the facility's own labor and delivery rooms or, years later, at nearby St. Francis Hospital. Their birth certificates were stamped "CF" for "Closed File" and forever sealed, never to be opened or revealed except by a court order. When I tried to get a copy of my father's birth certificate, I was turned away.

Even my father had never seen his own birth certificate. As an adult, he won a trip to Sweden but had to cancel because a distant relative refused to tell him where he was born. Since he wasn't able to get a birth certificate, he couldn't get a passport. For some reason, he thought he was born in New Britain, not far from Hartford. But he wasn't born there. His mother was.

My grandmother's full name was Anna Helen Galenski, but she always went by Helen, and occasionally her last name is referred to in documents in its Polish feminine form, Galunska. The first time I ever saw her maiden name was after I'd gotten a copy of my parents' marriage license. It was such an unusual name that I was able to find living relatives in the Hartford phone directory without much effort.

Everybody I talked to, both distant and close family members, recalled mainly one thing about Helen, and that was her illegitimate son. But by the time the strikingly attractive daughter of Polish immigrants committed what was then considered the shame of shames, the limbs on her family tree had long been fractured and broken off by an earlier family scandal.

Born in 1915, my grandmother was one of six children, three boys and three girls, born to Leona and Stanislaw Galenski. The family came from a town in eastern Poland that had once been controlled by Russia. My great-grandfather Stanislaw had emigrated from eastern Poland in 1909. Helen's mother came to America, via Hamburg, Germany, on October 12, 1912, on the S.S. *Patricia*. Stanislaw was a large, rounded man who spoke fluent Russian and Polish and found work in the tool factories around Hartford. In his spare time, he played the violin.

In 1920, when Helen was six, her mother died, and her family fell apart. Helen's brother Stanley told me that their mother had "died of internal bleeding." Stanley believes that my great-grandmother died an accidental death, having been beaten by her husband.

"He used to beat all of us," Stanley said as he recounted the afternoon more than seventy years earlier when he walked in the door and found his father beating his mother. She was bleeding badly and was taken to a hospital, where he says she died later that day.

Stanley said church officials came to the house not long afterward and took the children away. Helen, Stanley, and most of the other siblings refused to have anything more to do with their father. Those who were old enough took off on their own; the rest were scattered all over the place, except for the youngest, who remained with Stanislaw.

I asked Stanley how he felt about his father.

"An awful hatred" was all he said. The last time he saw his father was shortly before the old man's death. He'd heard he was dying. When Stanley walked in the door, all he could think to say to his father was "You touch me and I'll kill you."

The church found a home for Stanley with the Crowley family of Pawcatuck, Connecticut. Helen went to live in Bridgeport with her newly married older sister.

Long before I'd spoken with Stanley, I'd heard from others how Helen had also hated her father. All anyone seemed to know was that a rift developed between my great-grandfather and the children of his first marriage when he later remarried a local widow.

Mary Delano, the daughter of my great-grandfather's second union, remembers a different version of events. Mary had always been told that Stanislaw was forced to farm the children out to orphanages and relatives because he was unable to care for them himself once his first wife was dead. She remembers a story about how he even went to the church for assistance, but was told to have the children adopted.

Mary is a sweet, kind woman who has sent me photos and records of my great-grandfather, who died in 1950. She told me how her mother had three children from her earlier marriage when she and my great-grandfather married. They eventually had several kids of their own, including Mary. She remembers my great-grandfather as a wonderful father, a hard worker, and a dedicated family man, who while strict, never laid a hand on any of them. She loved him very much.

In trying to determine what happened, I thought about Mary and a lot of other things. I have thought about the possibility that my great-grandfather probably didn't mean to kill his wife. Or that her death may not have occurred that way at all. No records can be found of the incident. My great-grandmother died at a hospital in Hartford; her death certificate is vague, listing "interstitial obstruction acute" as the cause. If any estate existed, it was never probated. Maybe Helen's brother Stanley remembers things wrong. Maybe he's right. Then I recalled what one relative said when told I was writing a book: "What you're doing is digging in things a lot of people consider dead and buried."

My grandmother, Helen, had an uneventful childhood. She worked at her older sister's butcher shop and grocery store at 126 Deacon Street. Just down Deacon, in the 200 block, lived the bustling household of Leonardo Ricci, his wife Rosina, and their ten children, among them, my grandfather.

There were many Riccios and Riccis in Bridgeport, all of whom emigrated from Castelfranco, Italy. There were so many, they formed their own Castelfranco Men's Society. Leonardo had come sometime around the turn of the century, later sending for a bride from his hometown. He worked for the railroad before hiring on with a silver company, spending thirty-three years coming home with his handlebar mustache tinted green from the factory's polishing agents. But about 1923, around the time their son John Alexander was twelve, Leonardo, like many of his fellow Castelfranco immigrants, had shortened the family's last name to Rich.

It was only a distance of two blocks between the Szwolkon butcher shop, owned by Helen's sister and her husband, and the Rich home, but in the checkerboard neighborhoods of Bridgeport, the American melting pot was more ideal than reality: Poles and Italians didn't mix. Evidently, that didn't matter to Helen in the summer of her seventeenth year, when she began to take notice of John as he'd stroll past the store.

"She'd see me and smile," my grandfather recalled of the tall, slim Helen when he first began noticing her in the summer of '32. He remembers how friendly she was and how she began striking up conversations with him as he'd walk by. He also remembers that Helen's family didn't approve.

"I guess they [my grandfather's family] were of the Italian extraction and of course, if you weren't Polish, forget it," said one family member.

When my grandfather met Helen, he, along with two of his brothers, ran the barbershop on Seaview Avenue. At the "Rich Barbershop," a shave cost fifteen cents and a haircut a quarter. But the shop's advertised services weren't its main draw. A sports news wire, set up in a backroom that displayed the latest results from the region's horse tracks, was the shop's real reason for existing. My grandfather called the shop a "blind": a front for an off-track betting operation. "You weren't supposed to know what was going on in back," he said. During Prohibition, barbershops such as the one my grandfather and his brothers ran were common throughout Bridgeport.

John Rich, Sr., got his taste for the gambler's life as a youth. To help support his family, he hooked up with a blind man selling pencils and shoelaces on street corners. Pretending to be his son, and accompanied by an older man hired as a chauffeur, the trio spent the summers traveling up and down the Eastern Seaboard. During racing season, they spent weeks at a time in Saratoga Springs, New York, hustling the crowds who flocked to the track.

"I learned a lot," he said. "They had gambling there and everything. Craps games everywhere. In Bridgeport, they had it too, but this was big. This was where all the high-class people gambled. There were all these movie stars in the clubs, Lucille Ball, Don Ameche. Everybody hobnobbed with each other. Everybody was friendly, everybody was nice in them days."

It was also at the tracks where my grandfather says he met some of the best-known bookmakers of the day, and they were all kind to the blind man and the kid, figuring it was bad luck if they didn't give generously.

My grandfather says he dated Helen only a few months. But their seeing each other created so much trouble at home that Helen eventually moved out of her family's house. She went to Catholic welfare authorities asking to be placed in a foster home, claiming she'd been abused. Helen and John would meet after she got off work in a nearby park. He said they made love only a few times.

The abortion and carnal abuse charges were dropped when my grandfather agreed to plead guilty to the single charge of "seduction."

Court records say John Rich, Sr., was sentenced to six weeks in jail; he says it was six months. However long, it was enough time to sever his relationship with Helen.

My grandmother did considerably longer time for her offense, spending nearly two years in Catholic homes for wayward girls—the House of the Good Shepherd and St. Agnes in Hartford. The homes, run by nuns who referred to the girls as "the unfortunate ones," were a refuge of last resort for the young women who were often turned out by their families and had no place else to go.

Nearly two hundred children were kept at St. Agnes, which also took in children under the age of four who were orphaned or abandoned by families who could not afford to care for them. As such large facilities go, St. Agnes, the only Catholic home of its kind in the state, wasn't a bad place. It was clean, well staffed, and even included a nursing school, but it was an institution nonetheless. To further protect the mothers' identities, they were housed in a separate section of the building where few visitors were allowed.

Mothers who delivered at the facility were encouraged to give their infants up for adoption or to grant custody to the church or other social work agencies, which would then place in foster homes. Helen stayed in the homes until my father was sixteen months old. She resisted attempts to adopt her baby and even tried to keep him, but eventually was forced to relinquish care of my father to state authorities after an uncle she'd gone to live with refused to let the baby stay.

John, Jr., remained in state custody until he was ten, and Helen married Zigmunt "Ziggie" Wolanski, the blue-eyed son of Polish immigrants.

Helen and Ziggie met in Hartford through mutual friends. Ziggie was smitten right away. "She was nice in the beginning. A pretty woman. Pretty woman all right," he said.

Six months after meeting, they were married in December 1942. The following September, Helen brought my father home and in January 1943, Ziggie adopted him and my father became John Wolanski.

Soon after my father moved in, the new family went to stay with Ziggie's parents in Gardner, Massachusetts. From the beginning, Helen's expensive tastes in clothing and entertainment—something my father would inherit from his mother—grated on her in-laws' nerves.

"She lived very high. So it created problems all around, I think," said Genevieve Binkauski, Ziggie's sister. "She liked to buy nothing but the best. This was her way. She just looked prim and proper. The high-heeled slingback sandals, that type of thing. Nylons, the dresses, always very dressed up."

Within a few months Helen grew restless in Gardner and packed up and left, leaving both Ziggie and my father behind. Ziggie caught up with her, but my father remained with Ziggie's parents, for a while. They enrolled him in school that fall.

"He was a nice little boy. A very neat little boy. A little rascal. I'd call him perfectly normal. Doing little things as he pleased. But he was a very good boy with us. That's why we didn't mind having him with us," said Genevieve.

Not long after leaving Gardner, Helen and Ziggie opened a dry cleaning shop in Windsor, outside Hartford. Ziggie also sold real estate on the side and before long, they opened a second shop and became one of the first dry cleaners in the area to offer overnight service. Ziggie's thriving business eventually employed a half dozen people, and like many fathers, he hoped that his son would one day take over. His hopes were dashed when my father began getting into trouble.

My father was around eleven when the money started disappearing. First five dollars here and ten dollars there from the cash register. Then there were reports of fights at school and rumors of more petty thefts.

As my father's list of delinquencies grew, so did the fights at home between Helen and Ziggie over how to discipline him. For a long time, Ziggie said Helen refused to believe my father was guilty of anything. Then he and two other boys robbed a grocer, and Helen, Ziggie, and my father had a showdown.

Standing in the living room with Helen, Ziggie asked my father about the robbery. He denied taking part in it. Ziggie forced him to empty his pockets; out came $110 in small bills.

"At first Helen couldn't believe it," Ziggie said. "Then we found that big money and she found out the truth. That knocked the hell out of her."

After the store robbery, Ziggie had my father placed in a privately run juvenile detention facility. Not long afterward, he and Helen separated. Ziggie is vague about what went wrong, except to say that all their troubles began when my father came into the home. "She was all right until the boy come," he said. "I treated him like I treat anybody. I took him for good or bad. Turned out to be bad. The only sour apples in my life. Him and Helen."

After they split, Ziggie left town, spending a few years driving a truck and working for a carnival. In 1951, a divorce was granted in a court hearing held in Ziggie's absence after Helen ran a series of notices in the newspaper. In a letter written to the court agreeing to the divorce, Ziggie's bitterness is evident:

> To Whom it may concern: I Z. B. Wolanski the husband of Anne Helen Wolanski authorize my wife to petition and allow her to receive a divorce on ground of incompatibility only.
>
> I shall not contest it for her. The sooner she receives divorce the better it will be for both of us.
>
> I hope that someday she will realize that marriage is sacred and not used for personal gains and deceits. Signed Z. B. Wolanski
>
> P.S. God Bless her and I still love her.

I don't know how long my father remained in the boys' home. No records of his incarceration can be found. But by the time he was sixteen, he had gotten his first job with a traveling carnival, which he listed as his source of employment on his application for a Social Security card in 1949.

For at least a couple of seasons, my father lived the carny life, working the rides and manning the sucker bets. On the midway, he learned the art of "cake cutting," or shortchanging customers, using "sticks"—carnies posing as customers pretending to win a big prize—and "gaffs"—concealed devices such as magnets used to ensure that the house always won. It was while working as a carny that my father had his first adult run-in with the law.

At the top of his FBI arrest record is a 1950 arrest listed under the name "John Francis Ritch" for assault with a deadly weapon in Charlotte, North Carolina. The "deadly weapon" was a broken beer bottle he'd waved at somebody during a drunken brawl when he was seventeen and in Charlotte with the carnival. The charge was dismissed.

During one of the carnival's winter breaks, my father went to Bridgeport to meet his real father. He was told he could find him in New York City.

At the time, John Rich, Sr., was in Manhattan selling televisions for an outfit that ran radio ads urging listeners to guess the name of a song. Since the test was far from difficult, everybody "won" a hundred-dollar discount toward the purchase of a new television set. As a sideline John Rich also worked as a bookie in the Garment District.

"I liked the boy. He was handsome," my grandfather said of their first encounter. "He was smart as a whip. Took after me."

The feelings must have been mutual. It was shortly after their meeting that my father began calling himself "John Rich, Jr."

The elder Rich was in New York between frequent trips to Miami. In the thirties and forties, Miami was the crime syndicate's winter capital, and mobsters and gamblers from New York, Philadelphia, Kansas City, Cleveland, St. Louis, Chicago, and Detroit came through the city on a regular basis.

Despite bans on gambling, Miami had a history of corruption. As many as two hundred bookies, including my grandfather, worked the lobbies of the hotels lining Collins Avenue where giant tote boards displayed the latest race results and speakers blared the action, live from the tracks. Casino-style gambling could be found in numerous posh bars and restaurants.

My grandfather did many things in his life—he served as an army medic in World War II, he sold cars and jewelry, he owned a piece of a Miami Beach restaurant—but mostly he was a bookie, part of organized crime's outer circle of functionaries who aren't actually part of a crime family, but who do business with them—running numbers, taking phone calls, peddling vending machines, laundering money. My grandfather knew the guy who knew the guy who knew the *real* guys. He remembers when Miami was filled with undeveloped lots and views of the beach were unobstructed by concrete and steel. He speaks fondly of the mornings spent at Wolfie's restaurant watching the stars stroll in after they were finished performing at the local lounges.

He recalls the times he'd spot Meyer Lansky walking his dog along Collins Avenue and the mobster would offer a friendly "Good morning, Mr. Rich." That acknowledgment meant as much to my grandfather as it would to a junior executive offered a friendly nod in the hall by the company CEO.

My grandfather turned down a job offer in Las Vegas, he said, opting instead to stay in Miami to care for his ailing mother. He was in on trips to Cuba to meet with dictator Fulgencio Batista to help set up casinos, and had to leave Havana early after hearing reports that Fidel Castro and his rebel army were closing in. In my grandfather's eyes, men like Lansky, Lefty Clark, and Fat the Butch were businessmen and nothing more.

I once asked him if he worked for racketeers. He laughed. "Everybody thinks the Italians were racketeers."

When my father met his father, John, Jr., was looking to buy a car. So my grandfather got a job for him with a friend in Bridgeport who owned a Ford dealership. Within a few weeks, the owner was raving about the young man who was an instant success with the customers and knew everything there was to know about cars.

"I'm going to have him running the place in a couple of years," the owner said. But my father wouldn't wait that long. Within six months he was on the road, headed for California.

As his mother had remained distant from her family, my father did the same, only occasionally writing or calling home. Only once did he meet Helen's second husband, an accountant named Julian Fickett, whom she married a year after divorcing Ziggie.

"She'd hear from him every once in a while from different parts of the country. Just a note and maybe a telephone call or something like that and that would be the end of it," Julian said. "She may not hear from him again for a year or two. She never knew where he was half the time. He appeared to be a wheeler-dealer. He was going to make a million dollars in the next ten minutes. One of those types. I call them ten-cent millionaires."

The last time my father saw his mother, he announced that he was headed for California. He would never see her again. One late Sunday evening, February 18, 1962, Helen and Julian were walking home from a friend's house when she slipped on ice, slammed her head on the pavement, and went into a coma. She never recovered, dying on April 7, 1962. My grandmother was forty-six.

I have only a few things of my mother's: some photos and a cedar box of costume jewelry. The bottom of the box is lined with stray beads and rhinestones fallen from necklaces and pins that have seen better days. My mother's sisters sent the jewelry to me during my freshman year in college. The necklaces were tangled into a big knot inside an old plastic bag. I spent hours straightening out each and laying them out on the floor.

The black beaded necklace is long enough to twirl. The pearl choker with the imitation diamond at its center is pure Grace Kelly. I look at a line of small beads that could have been sliced from a desert rainbow of crimson, gold, and jade, and think she must have worn it with something exotic, maybe middle eastern.

I almost gave the necklaces to charity; they seemed outdated and old-fashioned. But a friend recognized their value and took them from me, saying she'd keep them until I wanted them. She was right. A few years later I asked for them back.

I rarely wear my mother's jewelry, but I take it out occasionally to look at it and roll the beads between my fingers. I also have the silver and diamond engagement ring my father gave her. It was broken in half a long time ago. No one knows what happened to her other diamonds and a strand of real pearls my father had also given her.

The last time I saw my mother was in 1967. I was nine. For the preceding three years, she'd been in and out of mental hospitals and nursing facilities—cold places with white walls and white linoleum floors that smelled of rubbing alcohol and disinfectant. I didn't look forward to seeing her. My mother was a stranger, someone who cried often. Her eyes seemed to search mine for answers and help, but I never knew what to do. I resented the way she looked at me and I was both repelled and frightened by her.

Those last years weren't at all the way it had been when I was younger, when she'd stoop down next to me, hugging me cheek-to-cheek, telling my father to take another picture. Sometimes she'd put a 45 by Chubby Checker on the phonograph and we'd do the twist. I've never forgotten those early dance lessons, the way she'd point one toe out, swinging her hips and tossing her head back with a laugh.

I believed her that Christmas Eve when we stood at her bedroom window and she told me she'd just seen Santa on his sleigh and if I looked hard enough, I'd see him too. I can still see her running from the kitchen when our Pekinese bit me on the lip. She dabbed frantically at the blood with her shirttail, yelling at my father to get the car, then holding me on her lap on the trip to the emergency room. I can still recall the night I came down with the three-day measles and my parents returned home early—one of the few times I remember them being home at night. As I lay on the couch, my mother wrapped me tightly in a blanket to break the fever. She smelled of perfume, hair spray, and cigarette smoke.

But when I got older things changed. For much of my life, I couldn't remember how I'd felt about her. I'd tell people I never really knew her, and I believed myself.

When I ask someone from her family about her, they don't say much. Few photos of my mother hang in any of her relatives' homes; few can be found in family scrapbooks. One close relative even asked if I was going to use real names in writing about my mother.

Distant family members find it easier to talk about her, perhaps because they weren't around to see her change. When her closest family members remember her, it's often with confusion, shame, and envy.

"Oh, she had the figure," her sisters say. They're happy to describe the gorgeous clothes and jewelry my mother bought in Alaska—the minks and the diamonds, especially—but anything more of her eludes them, except for their acknowledgment that she always had big ideas.

My mother wanted to be a movie star. As a girl she kept a scrapbook in which she carefully pasted photographs of her favorite actors and actresses, making meticulous notes under each picture. She especially loved John Agar and Shirley Temple. She'd spend hours leafing through the book, dreaming of Hollywood, my aunts say.

I have a hand-tinted studio photo of my mother taken right after high school. In it she's leaning toward the camera, bare-shouldered and surrounded by billows of gold fabric. She's wearing small hoop earrings. Her short, auburn hair is combed into soft curls that sweep down on her forehead, her lips are bright red, her skin glowing, with her cheeks tinged pale pink, her almond brown eyes wide open. The picture is the sort once used by aspiring actresses and models to land jobs. In it, she's all glamour, softness, and full of youthful innocence. This is how she must have looked to my father when they met.

Baptized Frances Ann Chiaravalle, my mother was born March 15, 1934. She was the baby of the family, the fourth child born—after Sandra, Anthony, and Lena—to Crayia, whom everybody called Marietta, and Pellino (Paul). She was named for her mother's mother, Francesca, who died during the Spanish influenza epidemic of 1918. Her middle name, Ann, was Paul's mother's name.

My mother's parents had grown up in Gagliano Aterno, Italy, a tiny village about seventy-five miles and three hundred years from Rome. My mother's father, like many men in the region, worked as a miner, first in Italy, then in Germany, before taking a steamship to New York on the eve of World War I. He made his way west, spending time in Minnesota before moving to Michigan's Upper Peninsula. There, he opened a small store and saloon in Jessieville, a mining town near the UP's far northwest corner. When the war ended, he sent for Marietta Paolone, his best friend's sister.

Jessieville was a company town, built by and for the iron ore mines that dotted the UP's landscape. There was so much ore in the ground that on a rainy day, the dirt roads turned to what seemed like streams of liquid rust. Jessieville was a link in the chain of mining and logging towns spread across the densely wooded hills where the Upper Peninsula touches northern Wisconsin. The towns marked the proximity of an ore lode to be mined or a forest to be clear-cut. Each town was as tightly controlled as the next, and all of them designed by mining company architects in the same grid of plain, square wooden houses and redbrick churches and schools, a no-frills, functional setting to house workers and their families.

Jessieville had no mayor or city council, but did have its own fire department, library, post office, hospital, grocery store, roller skating rink, taverns, and even a streetcar line to Ironwood, the region's commercial center.

With 27,000 people and a cluster of stores and banks, Ironwood, built by the Milwaukee, Lakeshore and Western Railway, was named, at least according to one account, for the two abundant resources hauled away by the ton in the railroad's cars. The people of Jessieville and Ironwood were descendants of Italian, Finnish, Serbian, Polish, and Welsh immigrants who came in the late 1800s to dig in the mines and cut down the forests. The area offered work and a place to raise families away from the cities of the East and Midwest. Besides the subterranean skills they'd honed in their homelands, most brought their languages, customs, and religions, all of which remained fresh despite their emigration to America.

These deep ethnic roots made Ironwood and Jessieville towns where the traditions of God, work, and family ran as deep as the ore veins worked by their inhabitants. At one time Ironwood had three flourishing Catholic parishes, as well as Episcopalian, Lutheran, and Methodist congregations. Even today, front porches often feature statues of the Virgin Mary.

But life in Ironwood had a price, and this was obvious to me the day I revisited my mother's hometown. As I stood at the side of a dirt road marked by potholes, I began to understand why she left. Dense, gray clouds hung low in the sky, the air was damp and cool, and all around, heavily wooded hills rolled off into the horizon, seeming to lead nowhere. It was March and the snowbanks were still three feet high. Ironwood's winters are bitter and long, lasting from October to April, sometimes bringing as much as two hundred inches of snow. There was a palpable sense of decay and conformity, with house after look-alike house lining the street, each painted drab white or dirty gray, matching both the overcast sky and the melting snow at my feet. Whatever opportunity existed in Ironwood for the immigrants of my grandparents' generation was long gone by the time I returned. It had been gone even by the time my mother was born.

My mother's birth occurred as her family's fortunes began to falter. The Depression and its blizzard of IOUs closed her father's grocery, and he had to hire on as a clerk in a hardware store.

My mother's father was a resourceful man. During Prohibition, he and his neighbors set up stills to make beer, wine, and whiskey. Her father would wrap bottles of moonshine in brown paper sacks and pack them into wooden grape boxes for the kids to sell in the "Flats," a line of houses along the dirt road connecting Ironwood to Hurley, Wisconsin.

Ironwood was where the miners and loggers went to church. Hurley was where they went to sin. Since the early 1900s, the six blocks of Hurley's Silver Street had offered girls, gambling, and liquor. Some joints, like the First and Last Chance Bar and the Club Blue Note, stayed open around the clock. The talk in Ironwood was that Hurley sometimes hosted gangsters from Chicago. Ralph Capone, Al's brother, lived near Hurley, and family legend has it that an uncle of mine once tended bar for him.

In the early 1930s, a police raid nabbed my mother's father and seven other men. Convicted of bootlegging, he did three months in Jackson State Prison. Marietta told the children he was away at college.

My mother's father was older than Marietta and far more sophisticated. Every Sunday after dinner, he'd head for the taverns, never saying where he was going. He'd bring home matchbooks bearing saloon names, show them to the children, and say with a laugh, "It's a good thing your mother can't read English."

Like many women from the old country, Marietta was deeply religious. She decorated the house with crucifixes, statues, and candles, as well as pictures of Jesus, the Holy Family, and assorted saints. For her, every day was a saint's day, each with its restrictions. On one day you couldn't wash clothes, on another you couldn't work in the garden, and so on all down the calendar. The family belonged to St. Ambrose parish, where the children made their first Holy Communions and later were confirmed. They attended Catholic elementary school, walking several miles at Marietta's order although the local public school was less than five minutes from the house.

My mother's sisters are reluctant to talk about my mother's childhood other than to say that as the youngest, she got away with everything. Where they'd been denied access to school dances and basketball games, my mother was given permission to go. She was the baby and she was spoiled, but she became the undoing of Marietta's nights. She was restless and convinced that she was too good for Ironwood.

A note from my mother's first grade teacher is perhaps more revealing:

> Frances Cairavalli [sic] was tested March 28, 1940 and received a rating of 95.8 which is normal. Frances is a nice child with a sweet disposition. She mixes well with the children and is well liked. Frances enjoys art work and is quite artistic in this line. Her musical ability is fair. Frances is rather slovenly in her appearance and is not so well cared for. She tends to follow the examples of other children and lacks initiative. Frances possesses a fair conversational ability and should get along quite well in first grade work.

Lena and Sandra never strayed far from Ironwood, but as soon as she was old enough to think about such things, my mother could talk of nothing except leaving. Her ticket out of town came in 1951, the summer after her junior year in high school.

Her brother Tony had moved to Burbank, California, and gotten married. He returned to Ironwood with his wife, Luce. They bought a new car in Pontiac and were heading back for the West Coast. My mother begged Marietta to let her go with them, promising to finish high school in Burbank. Her sisters say Marietta assented. My mother would later tell a friend that she'd run away from home.

That autumn, she roomed with Tony and Luce and enrolled at Burbank High School, where academics were clearly not a priority. Her highest grade was an 82 in "Family Living." But then who can blame her? There were so many distractions: the beach, boys, and Hollywood.

A transfer student, she didn't leave much of a mark. But a yearbook photo shows an angelic girl wearing hardly any makeup, a cashmere pullover, and around her neck a single strand of pearls, like the other senior girls. Friends who signed her yearbook refer to my mother as being "dizzy" and having a "terrific" sense of humor. A good-bye from best friend Carol Nelson says all there is to know about what it was like for my mother, a small-town girl let loose in a big city. She went a little wild:

> I'll always remember the time I met you at Delores' party. Boring wasn't it? All the time in Hollywood. All those marines, sailors, and etc. . . . at the skating rink, too. Remember the time we borrowed the car from the car lot? Fun, huh? I'll always remember the Sundays at my house and the Saturday nights when you a !!!! ! You know what I mean. I only wish I could have come back with you. We really could have shaken old Jessieville up . . . Remember Tommy and Bob and the rabbit country up at Stough Park? We sure had fun graduation night . . . mom really liked you and I'm glad . . . you're cute with your peroxide hair. Love Carol.

After graduation, my mother headed east, first to Chicago, where Sandra and her husband Joe lived for a time. Shortly after arriving, she and a girlfriend stopped at a Voice-O-Graph booth and made a 78 rpm record:

> Hi Mom, this is Fran. I'm calling from Chicago. I was downtown looking for a job, but didn't find anything yet. So how's Dad? What's he doing now? Boy did I have a nice trip, ah, ride on the plane. Sure went fast. Well, I guess I'll stay in Chicago for a while. Ironwood doesn't bother me anymore. I wish you'd move out closer, but I guess you're close enough now. So how's baby Chuck, does he talk yet? Well, the recording's probably full and I don't know what to

say. I'm with Pat Brown, we're down here together. Yeah, she's in Chicago too. We're looking for Evelyn, but her phone number's not in the book. So get me out of here so I can go see her. Well, I'm going to go to Montgomery Ward's and see if I can get a job and start paying Tony back. Does the baby talk yet? Oh, it's so funny, I think I'm talking on the telephone and I'm waiting for you to answer. This doesn't make sense. Well, I guess I have to say good-bye. We're going to call up Marjorie now and talk to her. Well, lots of love and don't worry about me, I'm always good.

She never found work in Chicago and returned to Ironwood briefly, before moving with girlfriends to Milwaukee. There, she stayed awhile, finding work as a waitress, a movie usher, and a clerk—all the time aspiring to be a model. It was in Milwaukee that she had her starlet portrait taken. Like my father, my mother lived at the edge of her family until the summer of 1956, when she returned to Los Angeles.

When my mother met my father, he was selling Cadillacs. He owned one of his first Caddies, a '48—the torpedo-shaped coupe that introduced the tail fin. Finished in black lacquer, fitted with a big V–8, whitewall tires, and automatic windows, it was the kind of car people noticed. In addition to selling cars, my father engaged in other, uncertain business that caused him to travel often between Los Angeles and San Diego. In both cities, he was picked up frequently by the police, first as a burglary suspect in each town in 1953. (In those days, simply being a suspicious character could land you in the clink for three days without charges being pressed, a handy method for dealing with undesirables.) In March 1954, he was picked up again in each city, charged with failure to register with the Selective Service for the Korean War.

The charges were always dropped, but to the Chiaravalles, my father was guilty of being plain no good.

Shortly after marrying, my parents moved to San Francisco, where they opened a little restaurant in the Tenderloin called Cindy's Corner. In her usual attempt to document everything, my mother taped the restaurant's operating permit and sanitary inspection certificate in the family album, below a message in big bold letters: "First Business."

My father's travels had taken him to San Francisco on many occasions. Rounders, gamblers, con artists, and thieves worked the area strip bars and pool halls, many of which offered card games in some back-room or dice games at the bar—usually rigged with loaded or mag-netized dice. It was in these clubs that my father further developed the skills he'd learned while working with the carnival.

During the first two years of their marriage, neither of my parents maintained close family ties and they seemed to be constantly on the move. A photo booth snapshot taken during their early days in San Francisco shows them in a cheek-to-cheek pose and is marked "Johnny and Ginger, San Francisco 1956."

Ginger was my mother's nightclub name, to match her new career working as a part-time stripteaser and "B-girl" in Tenderloin "B-joints." There, "B-girls" (high-priced cocktail waitresses) earned com-missions on overpriced drinks that they persuaded lonely men to buy for them.

My mother's family had no idea she'd worked as a stripper until I told them.

"There was little association with us after she married," my mother's sister Lena said. "You are talking about your mother as a person I never knew. I always felt that she was too young to leave home anyway."

I'd learned that my mother was a stripper from my father. I'd asked him about her work when I was a teenager.

"She was working as a telephone operator when I met her," he said. "I turned her into a stripper."

By February of 1958, my parents had left San Francisco and moved back to Hollywood. On February 24, I was born at Hollywood Pres-byterian Hospital.

They named me Kim after the actress Kim Novak. I don't know where they got my middle name, Maureen. My parents had my picture taken within the hour, and in a yellow cloth-bound book, titled "Happy Days with Our Baby," my mother wrote, "A cute little baby girl, just what we wanted—a pixy-looking baby. Looks like her daddy."

My mother documented every stage of my infancy. She kept every-thing—the hospital's instructions on using formula, a lock of hair, my hospital ID bracelet, cards from "Your Loving Husband," and one from his mother, Helen.

She also chronicled my growth in detail. At one month I smiled; at two months, I played with a rattle and ate my first cereal. At three months I rolled over. I didn't take my first step until I was a year old, but at eight months I said my first word: "Daddy."

With roll after roll of black-and-white film, she photographed me, filling two scrapbooks with photos, grouped by birthday party or Christmas, each carefully labeled with the date and event. She sometimes came back later to add additional detail: "Kim 1 month old. Born Feb. 24, 1958—Monday 3:03 P.M.—Hollywood Calif." She may have been Ginger to the nightclub crowd, but next to each picture of me, with her or with my father, she was "Mommy" and my father wasn't Johnny, but "Daddy." "Daddy" was lucky if he made it into the photo album; if he did, it was usually in a photograph with me. The only member of the family photographed as often was Tuffy, my father's scruffy Pekinese. If there was a picture of the baby on the bed, there was a picture next to it of Tuffy in the same spot.

Most of the photos are well composed—there are long shots, close-ups, and wide-angle views—and the whole scrapbook carefully assembled. When I was two months old she had me baptized Roman Catholic at Our Lady of Solitude, an event she once again captured in a half dozen black-and-white photographs.

My father wore his best white shirt and dark blue suit; my mother, a white suit with a mid-calf skirt and a short-waisted jacket with white buttons and a wide, rounded collar. She carried a black patent leather handbag and a pair of white dress gloves, looking like she could have been a senator's wife. Her Uncle Anthony and his wife Agatha were my godparents.

Agatha was always fond of my mother. She, Anthony, and their daughter Lizabeth are some of the only relatives my mother kept in close contact with while in California. They are also the only family members, aside from nephews Chuck and Paul, in the album.

I was in my late twenties before I saw Agatha again. Anthony had been dead many years. Agatha was in her nineties; we met at Lizabeth's house in Burbank. Sitting at the dining room table with Lizabeth and me, she clutched my hand, never taking her eyes off me and calling me her "special goddaughter" in Italian, her native language. I asked about my baptism. Speaking in Italian, with Lizabeth translating, she recounted a dream she had had the night before the ceremony in which a statue of the Madonna carved in black stone appeared to her. The following day, when she stepped into Our Lady of Solitude, there was a statue similar to the one in her dream.

"It was a good sign," she said. "You were going to be blessed."

The same month of the baptism, my parents bought their first house in Monterey Hills, a subdivision south of Pasadena. It was a modest ranch design, one of thousands scattered like so many building blocks around L.A.; but to my mother, it was a dream come true. She documented every detail of every room, photographing the refrigerator, the sliding glass doors, the back patio, the parquet floor, the drapes, the fireplace, even the built-in shelves. It was a handsome house, sleek and airy—a world removed from the dark miners' homes of her youth.

My mother deeply cherished her little piece of the American dream. But for Johnny Rich, the quickest route between any two points was always an angle. As one of his friends once told me, "Many, many of his ideas were just harebrained ideas. I mean they were crazy. He was always thinking. Always scamming. He was looking for shortcuts. Nothing was long-term in John's life. It had to be quick."

Less than six months after we'd moved to Monterey Hills, my father saw his next move. My mother never had a chance to furnish her new house.

Frances as "Renee," seated front with other B-girls in Anchorage, 1958

CHAPTER TWO

THE LAST FRONTIER

Long after the rest of America had been subdivided, there remained Alaska—distant and wide open, where the boomtown spirit still lived. A place with few laws, fewer rules, and even fewer ties to the past, nothing to hold you back or hem you in. The sheer size of the place seemed to give license to the meaning of big dreams.

My parents had such dreams, and that's what drove them from L.A.'s orange-juice warmth to Anchorage's icebox in the fall of 1958.

An old-timer once told me that Anchorage had a saying about new-comers: They were either misfits or on the run. Nobody came for the weather, and few came because they'd been successes somewhere else. Aside from a few adventurer types, bush pilots, entrepreneurs, or the rare federally appointed government leader, many of Anchorage's founders were end-of-the-roaders who'd run out of money, luck, and highway. In the late 1950s, Anchorage wasn't a place most people aspired to; it was where they ended up, where they went to start over. In Anchorage, as in any Alaskan town, people didn't ask where you were from or why you'd come.

It must have seemed the perfect place to my parents.

The move couldn't have been easy, especially for my mother, who flew north several weeks ahead of my father and me. I imagine she must have wondered what she'd gotten herself into the moment she stepped off the plane and surveyed a snow-covered landscape not unlike the one she'd left behind in Michigan.

None of my mother's family knew that my parents were planning to move. One of my aunts called California to talk to my mother, and my father simply said that she was in Alaska. Only my father's father spoke with my dad before he left.

"He said it was a new place," my grandfather recalled. "The place to get something going."

Before leaving California, my mother left a note for my father in my baby book. "John," she wrote, "keep record of shots baby receives in this book. There is a record page in the middle of the book. Keep record of baby's progress for me. Pictures once a week. Keep negatives, mark them."

In the same book, under "Long Trips," she wrote that my first plane ride was "from Los Angeles to Anchorage, Oct. 1958, with Daddy."

We came at the start of winter, which, in Alaska, arrives in October without benefit of an Indian summer. September ends and bang, you're looking at six months of snow and ice and rain and dark. Not the day-long darkness that comes above the Arctic Circle, but dark enough.

During the winter, Anchorage is sort of a reverse Camelot. The sun doesn't rise until mid-morning and by mid-afternoon, it's gone. There were already several inches of snow on the ground when my father walked off a Pacific Northern Airlines plane carrying me into the terminal at Anchorage International Airport—a fancy name for a narrow, two-story facility that serviced only a handful of airlines.

Anchorage International got its name because of the transpolar flights between Europe and Asia that used the airport to refuel. The pole-hopping flights had started only the year before, but city officials already were calling Anchorage the "Air Crossroads of the World." Strictly speaking, it was true, and there certainly were more paths crossing in the air over Anchorage than on the ground around it. The town had only two highways, one north and one south, both narrow bands of cracked, potholed pavement.

In those days, Anchorage was six hours by plane from Seattle (now only three) and five time zones removed from the East Coast (four these days). The town's two newspapers—the *Daily Times* and the *Daily News*—carried an eclectic assortment of stories that month, reflecting both the unique nature of Anchorage and its strong ties to the rest of the country. There were stories about whale hunters in Barrow, the Yankees beating the Braves in the World Series, and advance coverage of an impending visit by Richard Nixon. The vice-president would arrive a month ahead of undeclared presidential rival Senator John Kennedy of Massachusetts.

The town's three movie theaters were packing them in with movies that reflected Anchorage's frontier spirit—*White Wilderness, The Lone Ranger and the Lost City of Gold,* and *Rio Grande.*

In the year of Alaska's statehood, Anchorage was nothing more than a rough-edged community of some fifty thousand people. Other than the highways in and out of town, there were few paved roads. Most streets were dirt or gravel; in dry weather, Anchorage huddled under a giant dust cloud. As in any frontier town, amenities were scarce. Most houses had private wells; city water mains didn't extend much beyond the town's narrow city limits, which ran only ten blocks north to south, and twenty-one blocks east to west. City water was a chancy proposition; now and again it ran brown, and the health department sometimes warned residents to boil it before drinking. Telephone service was spotty, and the party line persisted in Anchorage long after the rest of America had private lines. But then, as now, Alaska was the "Land of Opportunity," a place where there was little competition.

In Anchorage, you could start your own utility company, found a bank, own the first Chinese restaurant, open a nightclub, or build your own little criminal empire. In every endeavor, there was little government regulation to get in your way or question your background. If your past did catch up with you, the police were more than happy to buy you a "blue ticket," the term used to describe the one-way passages they'd purchase to send shady characters back to wherever they'd come from.

My parents' piece of this northern frontier sat at the edge of town, off a narrow dirt road, aptly named Post Road, that led to two military bases. There, in a one-story, nothing-fancy bar, my mother found her first job in Alaska, and her second alias. To the lonely soldiers at the Stagecoach Lounge, Frances/Ginger Rich was known as "Renee."

Anchorage always had a lively nightlife. Couples danced at clubs like the South Seas, the Trade Winds, and the Club Paris. A western-leaning crowd took to the Silver Dollar, the Palomino, and Fort Starns. There were Alaska theme clubs such as the Union Club, which advertised itself as the place "where you'll find the sourdoughs," and the Chee-chako Bar. (*Cheechako* is a word used to describe people new to Alaska. It is *not* complimentary. The Cheechako Bar still exists.) Performers such as Billie Holiday and T. Bone Walker played gigs in Anchorage, as did local groups such as Tex Johnston and his Hollywood Cowgirls. But in 1958, the hottest bars in town were B-joints.

The Stagecoach, just outside the city limits, was pure B-joint—bar, jukebox, tables, chairs, dance floor. Up the street was the cavernous Last Chance, then a B-joint but once the first night spot in town to book real strippers, accomplished dancers who could make their tassels twirl to the grinding tune of a live band. In its heyday, the Last Chance had been the hottest Saturday night in Anchorage, with packed houses of three hundred turning out to see national acts like fan dancer Sally Rand. Other popular B-joints were the Guys and Dolls Club, Club Reno, the Pink Garter, and the Club Open House. All were open twenty-four hours a day and all were shadowy, if not entirely illegal.

Like my mother, most B-girls used phony names. No one knows why she chose Renee. Like my mother, most of the girls came from L.A. or San Francisco, where they'd already tasted the life. A bartender who went by the name "Big Sam" is said to have made recruiting trips to the West Coast, where some believe he found my mother in Los Angeles. I don't remember Big Sam, but he, his wife Cindy, and their toddler son Billy attended my first birthday party and are pictured in one of my mother's scrapbooks.

Sam, as well as other recruiters, touted Anchorage as the kind of on-the-edge place where the men outnumbered women three to one, and a good-looking girl could make big money. Once a boomtown, always a boomtown.

Anchorage was an accident of schedule and setting, created not to take advantage of natural bounty like the gold, fish, timber, and wildlife that spawned other Alaskan towns, but because it was a useful stop on the way to other places. The city's site was a mosquito-infested swamp, home to only a few perpetually frustrated prospectors —until 1915.

That year, the Alaska Railroad was laying tracks to link the ice-free port of Seward to the south with the interior city of Fairbanks, nearly seven hundred miles north. The railroaders needed a base camp where they could anchor barges carrying laborers and materials. They picked a bowllike recess off Cook Inlet that had quiet waters and easy off-loading. Their anchorage became Anchorage, and what it lacked in natural resources, it made up for in scenic beauty and relatively mild weather.

The city lies between Knik and Turnagain arms, each a branch of Cook Inlet. The Chugach Mountains tower to the east, and all around are ranges—the Talkeetna, the Kenai, and the Alaska Range with its active volcanoes. The view across the inlet is of Mount Susitna, called "Sleeping Lady" for the profile she presents. On a clear day, Denali, or Mount McKinley as it was dubbed by whites, looms in the north like an enormous ghost pyramid. Not only breathtakingly beautiful, the mountains block storms from the south and north, and the result is a climate temperate by Alaskan standards.

The same qualities that endeared Anchorage to the railroad lured the armed forces, which made the city a key supply center. Anchorage's real growth began with World War II, and continued through the Cold War. In 1943, the Japanese army invaded and occupied Attu, the tail end of the Aleutian Islands, shocking the U.S. into arming the Territory of Alaska to prevent an invasion. After the war, Alaska's proximity to Russia maintained that state of alarm with the U.S. showering down dollars by the hundreds of millions to build docks, roads, army and air bases, Nike missile sites, and radar outposts. North of Anchorage, the military built Fort Richardson, an army encampment, and Elmendorf Air Force Base.

When the troops arrive, they bring a lot of company. In the thirties, Anchorage had been home to slightly more than four thousand people who worked mostly for the federal government, a handful of domestic and international airlines, and in some minor industries—a little banking, construction, and retail. But by the time peace returned in 1945, the population was around twelve thousand—not a huge number, but an explosive growth in so brief a time, far more than the meager city government could manage.

Between the paranoid bustle of the Cold War and the city's boom-town tradition, Anchorage grew haphazardly. An architect might have labeled the look "neotemporary." Most businesses occupied boxy one- and two-story structures lacking in any architectural value.

Housing was scarce and expensive. Pockets of snug little well-built bungalows housed the few families that could be considered "old money"—the descendants of railroad bosses, early bankers, and large retail store owners. A few neighborhoods featured new ranch-style homes, handsome cottages, or a Cape Cod–design home here and there. The rest of Anchorage lived in the charmless, flat-roofed housing that pops up near every military base, or in a wild array of instant homes: log cabins, abandoned Quonset huts, trailers. Near the military bases, there was a row of shacks called "Starvation Alley," built by nailing together old airplane engine crates.

In military fashion, the railroad bosses laid out Anchorage on a grid—numbered streets running north to south, alphabetized streets east to west. From 1st Avenue, on a small bluff above Ship Creek, the original city limits extended south to 10th Avenue and east to Eagle. Between 9th and 10th avenues sits the sixteen-block-long and one-block-wide Delaney Park Strip, originally an airfield. Eastward from A the streets again are in alphabetical order, but instead of letters they're named for native animals and Alaskan towns and villages—Barrow, Cordova, Denali, Eagle, Fairbanks—all the way to Orca, which borders Merrill Field, Anchorage's small-plane airport.

In parceling out urban lots, the railroad had barred "gambling, pros-titution, or the manufacture and sale of liquor," but the city fathers had no such delusions. Their original layout incorporated a red-light district. During its earliest days, 4th Avenue, the main street, was a parade of wooden boardwalks running past the wood-framed false fronts of sa-loons, cigar stores, and pool halls.

Separated by large wooded areas, most of the city's neighborhoods grew up around former homesteads. The first roads to these areas were often hacked out by tractor, and kept their distinctive curves as the city grew up around them. No matter how much Anchorage grew, how-ever, you could get in your car downtown and drive in any direction (except west toward the water) and be in wilderness in half an hour.

But despite the crazy-quilt look, Anchorage was an All-American City, or so it was proclaimed in 1956 and trumpeted by a neon sign strung across 4th Avenue. One reason for the designation might have been residents' dogged insistence on making Anchorage over into a facsimile of all the little towns and big cities they'd left behind.

That effort extended to Anchorage society, which had its own aristocracy consisting of military officers and their wives and a handful of businessmen with social or political ambitions.

During its earliest years, Anchorage resembled a backlot set for a frontier town. Long before my parents and I arrived, Anchorage had cast off its frontier facades and boardwalks, substituting glass and steel buildings, concrete sidewalks, and parking meters.

At the east and west ends of downtown stood matching fourteen-story office and apartment buildings—optimistically described as "skyscrapers"—which dominated the city profile. One was named the McKinley Building, after the mountain that dwarfed it. During the Depression, a suitably New Deal–looking city hall went up, complete with a big clock hanging above an arched doorway. Across the street was a corner drugstore with a luncheon counter. And like many American towns with less dramatic horizons, Anchorage had a Ben Franklin five-and-dime and a Super Piggly Wiggly grocery.

Yet, despite its aspirations, Anchorage in the late 1950s was in spirit the closest thing to a Wild West frontier town in twentieth-century America.

All through the days of territorial status, Anchorage's minuscule coterie of police, prosecutors, and judges (the city's one prosecutor and one judge were responsible for all of south central Alaska, a region encompassing approximately a third of Alaska's 591,000 square miles) made Anchorage a carnival of vice, which convinced a small band of local hoods to think they inhabited a twilight world where the law could never intrude.

At the Stagecoach, the 1950s version of a dance hall saloon, drinks were $2.50, and a bottle of watered-down champagne cost $20 to $1,000. B-girls made $50 to $100 a night for getting men to buy them drinks by whatever means necessary—dancing, flirting, or trips to the "Blue Room," a dimly lit cubicle at the rear furnished only with a small couch. The Blue Room was where the girls led enthusiastic patrons who had bought the thousand-dollar bottle of bubbly. The blue lighting not only heightened the excitement; it kept customers from seeing the bucket under the couch where sponges muffled the sound of a girl emptying her glass. Few customers left the Blue Room with virtue or bankrolls intact.

Diane Davis, a former exotic dancer who used to perform in Anchorage under the stage name "Lady Diane," told me that my mother was considered one of Big Sam's better finds.

"She was something to see when she was all dressed up," Diane said. "When Renee dressed, I mean she *dressed*. She used to have those little mink tails. Just sharp as a tack. Whatever she imagined she could be, she could be that. There was a lot of businessmen, you try to tell them she's a B-girl or something, they wouldn't believe it. 'No, she's from a high-class, rich family from back East,' they'd say."

Diane said my mother was fond of cigarette holders like the one Audrey Hepburn carried in the movie *Breakfast at Tiffany's*. And like the party girl Hepburn portrayed, my mother exuded a combination of innocence and sophistication that customers in the B-joints found irresistible.

"She'd just sparkle," said Diane. "You couldn't be around anybody who liked to party better than her. She was real glamorous. She had class. She was a princess and she acted like one and people treated her like one. Your mother lived in an imaginary world and her world was a happy place. Everybody loved her."

Some customers, like a married cook named Ernie, paid cabdriver Chic Phillips up to twenty dollars a pop just to take him to the Stagecoach, where he shelled out even more money to spend hours sitting next to my mother at the bar.

My mother and Chic were close friends. She trusted Chic, a tall, lean Oklahoman who'd come to Alaska in the late 1950s after his marriage failed. Chic's southern manners and easy smile put her at ease.

"She was attractive and she knew it, but she wasn't stuck up or nothin'," Chic said. "You see, all the guys liked her. They thought she was pretty and all. In them days, you didn't find a pretty girl everywhere. In them days the pretty ones were few and far between."

Since most B-joint customers were GIs or construction workers in town for the weekend, few had cars. Cabdrivers could make a hundred dollars or more a night ferrying guys between bars. There was enough business to keep three cab companies hopping all night. Cabdrivers, like bartenders, would get a cut of the action for customers they'd bring in. Chic would get a two-dollar tip for every twenty-dollar bottle of liquor my mother sold. For Chic, guys like Ernie were gold mines.

"I said, 'Ernie, every time you drink a bottle of wine, I get two dollars,' " Chic once said to his best customer. But Ernie didn't care. "I take care of you," he told Chic. "You take care of me. Don't worry about it."

The truth about B-joints was that while the money for selling drinks was sometimes good, many girls—my mother among them—pumped up their pocketbooks by engaging in prostitution. Nobody I talked to wanted to come right out with it, but it was clear in my mother's medical records, in statements that she herself had made that selling drinks wasn't the only way that she made her living.

A tamer version of the B-joint champagne routine meant teasing customers into buying drink after watered drink, then agreeing to meet them somewhere before dodging the chump and going home to sleep. Another scheme was the occasional shopping spree.

Most of the customers were lonely guys who were just as happy to spend time with women in a store as in a bar. My mother and Midge took a couple of eager fellows on one such memorable outing. In less than an hour they'd ravaged the women's department of one store. My mother grabbed whatever looked like it would fit her. But more important to her was picking out clothes for me.

"Every chance she got, she'd get clothes for you," Midge would later tell me.

That day, as during other shopping sprees, my mother hurried about, fearing that her fisherman would sober up, causing his interest and generosity to vanish. By the time they reached the jewelry counter they had a half dozen outfits, and were about to leave when my mother spotted the rhinestones. She threw her hip against the display case, propped her elbow on the counter, and batted her eyes at a row of necklaces.

"Buy us some jewelry, honeee?" she purred.

"Okay, but if it's more than a hundred dollars, I'm walking out," one of the fishermen said, holding out a crisp C-note.

My mother snatched the bill and went to find a sales clerk. Midge herded the men toward the door, where my mother caught up with them a few minutes later. She was wearing one of the necklaces. She didn't offer any change and the man didn't ask. But his hundred-dollar chunk of costume jewelry had carried a ten-dollar price tag, which Midge says my mother had seen the moment she looked down. My mother pocketed the rest of the money.

While my mother worked the Stagecoach, my father found work tending bar at night and by day selling cars at Westward Motors, following the Alaskan tradition of doing what you had to do to get by. Despite the constant booster chatter of the chamber of commerce, the territory had a thin, unpredictable economy, propelled by the boom-and-bust cycles of the fishing, mining, and logging industries. In Anchorage, most of the money flowed from the military and the federal government, and if you weren't a soldier or a bureaucrat, you did what my father did until you found something better. Even Walter Hickel, two-time governor of the state and U.S. secretary of the interior in the Nixon administration, did a stint of bartending in Anchorage.

Between stints working the car lot, my father even took up commercial fishing for a couple of summers, working a flat-bottomed, thirty-two-foot boat, the *Gray Goose*, with two hired crewmen. Some of my earliest memories are driving around with my father in a pickup truck while he marketed halibut to local restaurants and supermarkets. My father is said to have loved fishing, but near the end of his second season the boat's engine broke down and he and his crew ended up rowing it into the harbor. One of the men on that trip remembers how defeated my father looked when he realized what it was going to cost to fix the boat. That ended my father's fishing career.

Bartending, selling cars, and fishing were, however, just sidelines for Johnny Rich. Within a few weeks of moving in, my father launched what would become his enduring career in Alaska.

Among local gamblers, my father quickly became known as one of the better steermen in town. A "steerman" hunts for "pigeons," unsuspecting amateurs who could be steered into fixed games with professional card players.

Gambling was nothing new in Anchorage. Throughout territorial times, nearly every local club had its one-armed bandits and cash-payoff pinball machines. There was so much gambling that some enterprising locals even proposed legalizing it and turning Anchorage into a Las Vegas of the north until federal law banned the cash-payoff machines (attempts to legalize gambling in Alaska would surface repeatedly in subsequent years). Despite being against the law, in the late 1950s gambling could be found all over town in a half dozen or more small, after-hours gambling joints that opened when the bars closed.

They were ordinary houses outfitted with bars and gaming equipment and sometimes a billiards table. Early on, my father ran one of his own, in addition to organizing poker games at other locations.

My father studied at the feet of some of the town's more established con men. They were from the old school, with a business code echoing that of underworld types everywhere: Mind your own business, keep your mouth shut, and trust no one. They ran nightclubs, numbers rackets, and girls; they cracked safes and fenced stolen property. They wore their shirts open at the collar, sported diamond pinkie rings, and called women "dolls." Many liked to pretend they were "mobbed up"—associated with big-city organized crime.

My father cruised bars like Club China Town, the Penguin, the Pink Poodle, and the Green Dragon, working the rooms, nodding to the musicians, barmen, and waitresses, flirting with the girls, and watching for guys who were spending heavily and drinking to match. He used the promise of women, booze, money, and even porno flicks to lure players.

Friends remember him as suave, funny, and even kind, all the marks of a good hustler. As one gambler told me, "Part of poker is to be a good psychologist and figure people's moods and needs."

"Johnny would go a thousand miles out of his way to help somebody," another friend said. "But as soon as they were back on their feet, he would turn around and try and cheat them out of every dime."

Like a politician, my father came alive in the middle of a crowd. He rarely drank; instead, to stay sharp and to get through games that could last for days, he'd gobble amphetamine tablets bought from a bent pharmacist, a hundred pills for five dollars.

Once my father spotted a mark, he'd strike up a conversation and steer the talk around to poker, then set the hook and call his partners.

They'd arrange games on a moment's notice in my father's gambling houses, in hotel rooms, or the backrooms of bars. They'd work in pairs or in threesomes. One guy would deal, another would cut the deck; the third would win the crooked hand, separating the pigeon from his cash.

"If we put money in the pot," said one of my father's former gambling partners, "we made sure we had the best odds of getting it back or we didn't put it in."

I spent a week interviewing this man, who for years worked as a professional card cheat. He retired years ago and asked that I not use his name because of the life he's built for himself since then.

The men used elaborate signals during games. A touch on the nose meant "It stinks, get out"; a hand on the heart told the dealer the cards looked good. Words took on shady meanings: "play" meant ace; "auto" was for a deuce; "try" stood for three; "funny" meant four; "fine" stood for five or six; "lucky" meant seven.

Sometimes the con got more complicated. For a while, my father used a "stinger"—a wireless electrical device strapped to his legs. His partner, carrying a device that activated the stinger, would sit the game out, positioned to see the other players' hands and using a predetermined code that would send a series of mild shocks to my father, telling him what the others were holding.

"John and I spent probably twenty, twenty-five hours just developing a code and memorizing it and practicing it so he would know exactly what I was sending him," the former partner said.

From the collaborators' perspective, the games were a form of theater; every player had his role, based on ability, talent, and experience. Some knew how to deal seconds—cards from underneath the top card—without anyone being the wiser. Others were masters at stacking the deck. And there was always a guy who was good at working with marked cards.

A team stayed together as long as six months, or until word got out that they had suspiciously hot hands; then that unit would break up and its members would align with others in the set. "You might be with them a month, six months, a year, then you move on and run with someone new for a while. That's how I met your father. One guy and I couldn't work together anymore so he had told John about me and John said, 'Bring him around, I want to meet him.' "

Occasionally my father and his partner rented a hotel banquet room and put on a Monte Carlo night—blackjack, poker, and craps, with the cards marked and the dice loaded. Sometimes they took their act on the road to a nearby resort, advertising a raffle featuring expensive door prizes, such as a brand-new Cadillac.

My father rationalized cheating by adhering to the basic belief that honest men don't gamble. Anyone who'll bet you a quarter will steal you a quarter, gamblers like to say.

"I never sat at a poker table with a truly honest man," his former partner told me. "A truly honest man won't sit at a poker table because he doesn't want something for nothing. Now the guy that sits at the table believes that he's better than the people he's sitting down with. If he didn't think he could win, he wouldn't be there. I've seen people who were supposed to be square shooters that use signals, they steal money out of the pot. I've seen people who didn't do anything but mentally play the game and they were good players. But any time you sit down with somebody and you can play the game better than them, what is it? You're taking the advantage. What is cheating? It's taking the advantage."

My father's world was one of shadows and suggestions. No one wrote anything down. People did "favors" for each other, often on the vaguest of hints. He and his partners were free with their cash—any one of them could borrow thousands from another, with the understanding that if someone didn't pay up, he was out on the street with a bad reputation. Sometimes my father stored cash, hidden in secret compartments built into door frames, at the homes of his most trusted friends. He kept a hidden cash register at home. The talk was always small, especially when the deals were big. Occasionally, he and his pals packed pistols or tear gas guns, but mainly they got by on attitude. Many perpetuated their own myth of being attached to the Mafia, including my father. Few knew it to be false.

"He wasn't what a lot thought he was," his old friend said. "As far as the cops were concerned Johnny was just a lowlife gambler and someone just to run out of town. The public in general feared him because they felt that he was part of organized crime. Then those of us that were in the inside knew that he was nothing but a professional steerman, and that's probably all he would ever be."

· · ·

I doubt that my parents initially intended to stay long in Alaska. People's reasons for moving to a place often aren't the same reasons that keep them there. But by our first Christmas—one my mother so carefully documented in a half dozen or so color snapshots in the family photo album—Alaska had become home.

In the living room corner of a tiny, one-bedroom apartment my parents rented on 5th Avenue, my mother had placed a small fake Christmas tree on the coffee table, which she'd draped in white tissue. The funny little tree, with its rod-straight limbs jutting in all directions, was decorated in red ornaments, streams of icicles, and an aluminum star lit at the center with an orange bulb. Along the border of the table, she hung a few brightly colored Christmas cards; underneath the tree was a pile of gifts, mostly for me, including a rounded, stuffed Humpty Dumpty doll and a tall, black-and-white stuffed penguin. The penguin was practically bigger than I was and part of what I'm sure was meant to be an Alaskan theme Christmas, even though penguins live at the South Pole.

(The only two penguins I can remember in Alaska were two imported by a local nightclub owner. The owner's idea was to stick them in a swimming pool outside the Penguin bar, where customers could watch them frolic in the water. While they were building the bar's pool, the penguins stayed with the club owner in his outdoor swimming pool, one of only three outdoor pools in Alaska. The bar owner was also the proprietor of the short-lived Alaska Swimming Pool Company, the exclusive Alaska distributor of Esther Williams Swimming Pools. With the summers only three months long and the temperature rarely above 70 degrees, outdoor pools are not in great demand. But the club owner didn't care. He had lived in Alaska for years and he and his wife wanted a heated swimming pool in their backyard.

(The owner had a deal with the California swimming pool company that if he bought three and sold the other two, he could get a discount on his own pool. He sold the other two and put the third in his yard. I remember my parents taking me to see the penguins. They seemed happy enough when I was there. But they wouldn't live long enough to see their new home at the bar. They became sick and died.)

That first Christmas my father started what would become a family tradition—he bought my first fur parka, a white rabbit coat with a white wolf ruff and a pink satin lining. My first parka was too large for a ten-month-old, but they propped me up in it anyway, with the sleeves acting as ballast, to take a picture.

Christmas 1958 also marked the beginning of the end of the city's freewheeling days. In January, the territory would become a state, finishing a decades-long struggle.

Statehood had been an elusive grail as long as it seemed that Alaska couldn't generate enough revenues to support a state government and all that it entailed. The main industry that did flourish—salmon canneries—fought fiercely against the arrival of federal regulation and taxation. And there was the issue of adding two members to the Senate, which would threaten the national balance of power between Democrats and Republicans.

Two things altered the equation: the discovery in 1957 of oil on the Kenai Peninsula south of Anchorage, and a powerful statehood movement in Hawaii.

Admitting Alaska, with guarantees of later admitting Hawaii, would likely maintain the partisan balance in the Senate. And set as it was in an accessible part of the state, the Kenai oil field held out the same promise of wealth and prosperity that gold had sixty years earlier, heightening chances that Alaska could develop a stable economy.

"WE'RE IN" declared a seven-inch banner headline in the *Anchorage Daily Times* the day the Senate voted to admit Alaska. Celebrations were held in communities all across the state. Nearly half of Anchorage—an estimated twenty-five thousand people—converged on the Park Strip to be treated to a gigantic bonfire made from forty-nine tons of scrap lumber and a forty-nine-gun salute followed by *fifty* small planes that flew overhead. (The extra plane was thrown in for Hawaii as a friendship gesture, symbolizing the two territories' joint effort to gain statehood.) There were so many fireworks explosions that night that the local police called the revelry the biggest celebration in Alaska since V-J Day.

"It's full speed ahead into a new era," wrote the Odsather Simpson Insurance Co. in one of the dozens of ads local businesses took out in the newspapers to celebrate. The O.K. Rubber Welding Co. called statehood a "Dream come true for me and you." Outside of Alaska, the occasion was noted by the likes of evangelist Billy Graham, who predicted that in twenty-five years, Alaska would become the nation's "greatest state." Others used the event to heave yet another blow in the battle against communism. Senator Estes Kefauver (D-Tenn.) called admission of the forty-ninth state "worth a dozen Sputniks." He explained, in an odd twist of rationale, that "it will help us in our troubled world relations. . . . Admission of Alaska as a state offers sharp contrast with Russian treatment of its satellites."

In Texas, no longer the biggest state in the union, the author of the Texas state song was busy trying to come up with a replacement for the song's third line, which called Texas the "largest and grandest" of them all. The admission of Alaska as a state was a sensitive issue in Texas. One Texan, stopped on the street, told a newspaper reporter how "Alaska isn't really as big as Texas—not when you melt all the ice." Notwithstanding such sentiment, to show its heart was in the right place, a group of Texas businessmen proposed flying to Alaska on a "Friendship Flight" to welcome the new state. The nation's smallest state—Rhode Island—sent its own goodwill ambassador, Linnea La Pointed. The "just turned 13"-year-old youngster (as she was described by the press) traveled to the state capital in Juneau and shared a milk shake with acting state governor Waino Hendricksson.

Not everyone liked the idea of giving up the hardscrabble but independent status of territory. Alaska's first U.S. senator, Democrat Ernest Gruening, tried to reassure statehood opponents in a recorded radio program that the admission of Alaska to the Union would revive the "pioneering spirit in America . . . the people who went to Alaska followed the oldest American tradition, the westward quest for greater freedom and greater opportunity."

But towns where the frontier ethic still reigned opposed the change, as did many of Anchorage's less bourgeois residents, including my father. "There was a lot more money in town before statehood," he once told me. But he had other reasons to be less than happy about this turn of events. He could also see the handwriting on the statehouse wall: Everything he'd hoped to escape by leaving California—squares, rules, laws, cops, judges, jailers—was following him. Still, despite whatever reservations he might have had about statehood, in January, he and my mother made a down payment on a house.

My dad and me, Easter Sunday, 1960

CHAPTER THREE

FIREWEED LANE

Not far from the center of Anchorage, and named for the fuchsia weed that grows abundantly in Alaska, sits Fireweed Lane.

In the forties, Fireweed was called the "burned-over" district for all the fires lit by the competing madams whose bordellos once lined the narrow dirt road. But by the late fifties Fireweed Lane was quiet and suburban, lined with empty lots and small businesses. Then it was in the suburbs—block after block of tree-filled neighborhoods dotted with modest, wood-frame houses, one of which was 604 E. Fireweed Lane, where we moved in the early spring of 1959.

On the first page of my mother's family scrapbook there's a photograph of me with my father and Tuffy. The three of us are in bed, with me sitting up next to my father, who's lying down with one arm around Tuffy, who's at my feet, and his other arm propping up his head. In the picture, I'm squealing as my father tickles me by nibbling on my shoulder. Below the picture my mother wrote, *"Kim, John, Tuffy . . . 604 E. Fireweed Lane . . . 1959, Anchorage."*

Below this photograph is another, showing the front of our house, with me as a toddler in a pink sundress and bonnet, standing at the doorway. Underneath it is a caption that makes it clear for whom the house was really bought—*"Kim's Home in Anchorage."*

A stand of birch trees, encircled by a dirt driveway, stood in the front yard and there was a forest of birches across the street where I used to play. Next door was the Party House Bar, where I was welcome even as a small child. My parents were good friends with the couple who owned it. I'd often go over to drink Shirley Temples while sitting on a barstool staring at a special wine bottle that the bartender would set out to entertain me. It was a novelty bottle with a tiny spring-driven ballerina inside. You wound a key at the base and she'd pirouette, one leg bouncing out to the side. In the shadows of the barroom, the twirling ballerina seemed magical to me.

All of my earliest and best childhood memories begin and end in the funny little white house with its shingled roof and red brick trim along the lower half. Just down the street was Kiddy Land, a small amusement park not unlike those found in many American cities. There, my mother would take me to ride its merry-go-round, little boats that went in circles, and a miniature train that took a five-minute spin through a dense forest of black spruce trees.

A couple blocks south of our house was the Bun Drive-In, where every Friday and Saturday night, kids from Anchorage High congregated in the parking lot in souped-up Chevys and stripped-down Fords. My father would take me there for hamburgers, and I was mesmerized. The Bun was a real drive-in, complete with carhops—girls with names like "Putt Putt" who wore red pants, white shirts, and red lipstick, and who brought you french fries, hamburgers, and soda pop delivered on plastic trays clipped to the door windows. The main attraction of the Bun was a nightly radio program called *The Coke Show,* broadcast live from a tiny booth tacked atop the building. The star of *The Coke Show* was a rail-thin deejay named Ron Moore who called himself "The Royal Coachman."

The Royal Coachman was a genuine teen idol who wore gold lamé jackets and ruffled satin shirts with *RC* embroidered on the front breast pocket. He drove the "Royal Coach," a black 1958 Cadillac with painted gold hubcaps and musical notes embroidered on the seat covers. On the driver's door was *RC* in tall, gold letters. Blushing teenage girls, dressed in tight pink cashmere sweaters and strapless gowns, crowded around Moore during sock hops held at The Royal Pad, a teen club where they danced to the sounds of The Royal Tones. In their hands, the girls clutched their "Ron Moore Fan Club" cards.

The house on Fireweed Lane was a realization of my mother's dream of having a home of her own. A small living room was just inside the front door. My parents' bedroom was off the left end of the living room; my room was at the opposite end. Directly across from the front door was a wide opening to the kitchen; behind that, a small dining room. A hall off the kitchen led to the bathroom and the spare bedroom.

Along with the house we lived in on Fireweed Lane, my parents bought a similar-looking house, only smaller, that was next door. I rarely was allowed inside the second home, and only years later learned why: My father used the house as an after-hours gambling joint. They took out a $21,000 bank loan to cover the purchases and eventually had to borrow $5,000 more to make both homes habitable. The interior of our house was originally covered with cheap, smoke-stained paneling; the floors, with dingy brown carpet. My father pulled down the paneling, ripped up the rugs and kitchen floor, and replaced everything.

My mother handled the home decorations, collecting every modern gadget and gizmo she could find, turning the house into your typical, early-sixties American home: television, stereo, brass starburst wall clock, electric toothbrush, salon-style bonnet hair dryer, electric polisher for my father's shoes.

Inside was an Asian motif, an interior look popular at the time. She chose red and white as her color scheme, vibrant colors expressing the optimism she must have felt. There was a white Naugahyde living room set, the big, blocky kind with square arms so wide you could sit on them, and bright red carpeting. Behind the couch was expensive black-and-gold woven wallpaper, a bamboo cone chair, a walnut buffet with shelves to hold her *Reader's Digest* Condensed Books collection, a miniature ceramic Chinese junk, and figurines of Siamese dancers in ceremonial dress. On the wall hung black-and-white prints of Chinese carvings. She had a seamstress make floor-length silk drapes in a black, peach, and gold pattern of kindred design. The dining room continued the red-and-white theme, adding red tiles halfway up the walls and above that, white, gray, and black checked wallpaper with alternating rows of descending cherry boughs. On the windows were white ruffled curtains, behind which my mother placed small potted plants.

This room was where my mother hosted my elaborate birthday parties, stringing it with colored balloons and strips of matching crepe paper. There were always a half dozen or more children sitting around the table wearing paper cone hats, playing with party favors, and digging their fingers into tiny paper cups my mother filled with jelly beans and wrapped in ribbon. In the center of the table would be a layered cake decorated with a plastic doll dressed in a hoopskirt that matched my new party dress. I was always seated at the head of the table, looking like the little princess my mother believed me to be. I reigned over these parties, snapping orders at my friends and fighting with them over who got what party favor.

I was the center of my parents' world. My father used to say they'd found me on the doorstep and had named me Kim, as in "Es-Kim-O." They called me "Kimmy" or sometimes, "Kimmer." I had my mother's big brown eyes, my father's curly hair and wide smile. Because of my feisty disposition and a habit of demanding that I get my own way, my father nicknamed me "The Little Monster."

Despite the life my parents led away from home, they were determined I'd be raised like any other little girl. My mother created a child-size world for me within the house: I had my own miniature table and chairs, a tiny toy grand piano, a rocking horse, and shelves stuffed with toys. She painted my room pink, adding a matching pink satin bedspread and a pink ruffle outlining a rounded mirror that hung above my dresser. On the dresser, beside a big pink piggy bank, she'd placed a small statue of the Virgin Mary.

There were trips to Sunday school and church on Easter that my mother chronicled in a series of posed, colored snapshots pasted into her scrapbook. Here's Kim with her hand on the door getting ready to leave; here she is with "Daddy"; there's Kim with Toy. (Toy, the teenage daughter of one of my mother's B-girl friends, was the first in a series of live-in babysitters my parents hired to look after me when they went to work at night.)

At Christmas, my mother hosted holiday parties, inviting all their friends—people with names like Big Jimmy, Little Jimmy, Tequila, Slim, Pots 'n' Pans Johnny, and Mexican Ray. They were bar owners, barkeeps, strippers, B-girls, prostitutes, gamblers, and pimps. Men like Red, a tall man with red hair and a large hooked nose, became unofficial uncles to me, bringing me gifts at Christmas and on my birthdays.

Every Christmas, my mother and I would set out a plate of cookies and milk for Santa on top of a cardboard fireplace she'd set up in the living room and from which she'd hang our stockings. Every Christmas morning I'd awaken to find dozens of gifts, each stamped with a sticker that read, *From Santa.* There were dolls and stuffed animals, including one year a life-size stuffed standard black poodle.

The poodle was my father's idea. He loved purebred dogs. Once he got me up in the middle of the night to show me a Pomeranian penned up in the dining room—a gift for my mother. She was still sleeping but he wanted to show me first. We decided to call her Nugget because she was the color of gold.

Besides Tuffy the Pekinese (listed as my favorite playmate in my baby book), there was a black toy poodle named Pierre. Tuffy was booted out of the household when he later bit me on the upper lip, leaving a scar. My best friend, and for years my constant companion, was Yukon, a big white purebred Samoyed husky. His full name was "Duke of the Yukon." My father joked that he shortened the name to Yukon because if he stood around in the yard yelling "HEEERE, DUKE OF THE YUKON," two guys in white coats would come take him away.

Years later, I would sometimes look at Yukon's pedigree papers—a pamphlet that folded out to reveal three sides listing his ancestors back a dozen or more generations—and realize that I knew more about where Yukon had come from than about my own father.

Despite the newfangled appliances and the contemporary decor, our house was like every other house in Anchorage—a little removed from the world. When I watched *Walt Disney's Wonderful World of Color* on Sunday night, it was the program that had run three weeks before in the Lower 48, just like every network program in Anchorage. Shows arrived on film that went first to Hawaii, so we saw Thanksgiving specials around Christmastime and Christmas shows in late January. Even the news arrived late; the CBS evening broadcast had to be flown in from Seattle so Anchorage could see Walter Cronkite at eleven

P.M.—unless the plane was late, in which case the show ran the next morning.

The Buckeroo Club, on the other hand, was original Alaska. Produced in Anchorage, the half-hour show featured two men dressed in cowboy boots, hats, and shirts who introduced cartoons. Local kids appeared as guests on the show and sat on bleachers in the studio. The Buckeroos always asked for your name and what you wanted to be when you grew up. My mother sent me to be on the show once and coached me to say "a nurse." But when my big moment came, impressed by their cowboy getups, I said, "a cowboy." This sent my parents and several of their friends, who were watching the program at home, into fits of laughter.

My mother told her family little about life in Alaska, except to write letters bragging of her new home, its new furnishings, and her new red Corvair and my father's white Cadillac convertible. But her family had their suspicions.

When my mother's father died in 1960, she went home for the funeral. There, she let a few clues slip; she stepped off the plane wearing a mink stole, jewelry, and the sort of clothes a girl couldn't buy working a day job. She stayed two days, long enough to get her father in the ground, but when Lena pressed her to spend a little more time in Ironwood, she said, "I have to go back. If I don't, I might not find my house or car. Johnny just might gamble it all away."

The only other part of her life she talked about was a small hotel that my father had begun managing shortly after we moved into the house on Fireweed Lane. She described the Safari as a wonderful place which my father planned on expanding into a fancy high-rise with shops, cafés, swank restaurants, and a nightclub featuring Las Vegas–style entertainment. My mother even said she planned to open her own gift shop in the lobby.

But even my memories of the Safari don't live up to the billing my mother gave it. The plain, two-story hotel, located downtown in the 4th Avenue bar district, may have had all the potential in the world, but when my father took over running it, the Safari was little more than a scrubbed-up flophouse for street drunks.

. . .

Fourth Avenue offered the full spectrum of Anchorage's urban culture. The stretch ending at L Street sported the best restaurants and shops, yielding gradually to less exalted establishments until you got to the far east side with its low-rent clubs and all-night cafés. The balance shifted at around E Street. The Safari, and its twelve-dollar-a-night rooms, was near the corner of 4th and A, deep in the heart of the bars popular with visiting fishermen, construction workers, and Alaska Natives.

The Safari was, as its advertising claimed, centrally located. On either side were the Denali Theater, a legitimate movie house incongruous in that setting, and Sam's Liquor and the Scandinavian Club Bar.

Above the hotel's front door hung a green awning on which a local sign painter using white enamel had lettered *The Safari* in his idea of Arabic script. Inside, the Safari was far less exotic. A small lobby with a check-in counter sat just inside the front door. A hallway led back to the first floor's half dozen rooms. Behind the desk, a small flight of stairs led to the second-floor rooms. The lobby furniture consisted of a couch and some end tables and a door leading to a small gift shop next door. The walls were painted an institutional green and the floors covered in drab linoleum. But my father kept the place neat and clean, spending all of his free time trying to spruce it up.

The owner of the Safari was one of my father's earliest friends in Anchorage, a flamboyant local bail bondsman who went by the name "Duke."

Duke's real name was Charles Knuth, and he was known for favoring double-breasted pinstripe suits, a white Stetson, and spit-polished black cowboy boots. A Chicagoan, Duke had been in Alaska since the mid-fifties, when he'd been released from prison after serving eleven years for armed robbery, according to newspaper accounts. He claimed he did the time as a favor for friends in the Mafia who paid him for his trouble.

Duke's balding head was a common sight in my father's world. He was polite and courteous in the way that men who have power can be. His bail bond operation had offices in Anchorage, Fairbanks, Juneau, and Kenai, with representatives reportedly as far away as Seattle and Tokyo, as well as sidelines like the Safari and Splash & Dash car wash.

Like my father, Duke drove only Cadillacs; his was bronze with a license plate reading DUKE.

In dress and attitude, my father and Duke were alike, and after meeting, they became inseparable. Duke became a mentor for my father, and my father became Duke's trusted aide.

"Duke liked to talk to Johnny because Johnny knew what was going on around town," said Fred Adkerson, another local bail bondsman.

Duke preferred not to spend his evenings on the street, so he relied on my father to be his eyes and ears in the Anchorage underworld. For his part, my father got some cash and sometimes a percentage of the recovered bond. Like any pair of businessmen in similar circumstances, neither he nor Duke ever wrote anything down about their transactions.

A fearless and relentless pursuer of bond jumpers—once he flew to Puerto Rico to grab a stray customer—Duke was a frontier baron who ran his fiefdom on a very personal basis. If a client couldn't make his payments, he could always indenture himself to a stint wiping down cars at the Splash & Dash.

Bail bonding is the grease that makes the criminal justice system work, and bondsmen must walk on either side of the street. Sometimes, as Duke tended to, they stray too far into the shadows.

(Long after my father was no longer running the Safari, in December 1968, Knuth was murdered. My father was stunned by the news, especially since the killing took place at Duke's house, which was next door to the apartment we were living in at the time.

(Two days after Christmas, a lone gunman entered Duke's lavishly decorated ranch house and shot Duke three times, one bullet fired into his forehead at point blank range. The case has never been solved, but police suspect that the killer was someone Duke had bailed out of jail. Another local bail bondsman named Ron Waters had met a similar fate two years earlier. Waters was strangled in a triple-locked basement across the street from the police station. He was found with a coat hanger around his neck. Waters's killer was never found either. Police don't like to talk about either incident. The murders led to a saying used around town about bail bondsmen: "The pay is good, but the retirement plan stinks.")

·　　·　　·

The Safari was more than just an ordinary hotel.

The east end of 4th Avenue was popular with the city's prostitutes, and two offenses on my father's police record give a clearer picture of what actually went on there. Twice during the early sixties my father was arrested on the quaint-sounding charge of "renting a room to an unwed couple." The first time I saw this, it took me by surprise. Just when I'd gotten used to the idea that my father was a professional gambler, I realized he was also in the business of running whorehouses.

I learned my father's view of his activities in occasional conversations. In his view, prostitution, as long as nobody was being forced into anything, was perfectly acceptable. He'd say things like "Variety is the spice of life." In his eyes, gambling and prostitution were all recreational activities—businesses, as legitimate as any other. He truly believed this, even when it came to my mother.

For a long time, I viewed my parents as people living outside the mainstream. But they weren't, really. Like many second-generation Americans, they had left the ethnic neighborhoods of their parents for the perceived security and conventions of the suburbs. They possessed everything that was valued in post–World War II America: They were attractive; they had money, or at least the appearance of money; and they had started a family.

A woman then was judged for her beauty and was encouraged, through popular media, folklore, and myth, to marry a millionaire, or at least marry a man who *looked* like a millionaire. A man was judged by the car he drove and the beautiful wife by his side. He was also judged by his power, his ability to control his surroundings, and how far he climbed up the ladder of success. In the corporate world of the fifties, as among gamblers, every step up meant that somebody— most everybody else—was left behind. The ladder has always been more of a pyramid. Far more populated the bottom, and my father understood this.

My parents' goals were no different from those of others of their generation; only their means were. For them, places like the Stagecoach and after-hours gambling dens were an apparently easy way to make it, to achieve the American Dream. But there were real hidden costs, which wouldn't remain hidden for long.

Me and my mom during one of our few visits after she had been hospitalized. This one took place in June 1964. She had been released temporarily to attend a friend's wedding.

CHAPTER FOUR

THE HIDDEN COSTS

I have a faint memory of traveling to Southern California twice with my mother sometime before the age of five.

I remember one of the trips as a collection of unrelated events—walking onto the plane and giggling as a couple of stewardesses tugged at the hood strings of my rabbit fur parka, calling me a little Eskimo; watching my Uncle Tony put Christmas lights on the bushes outside of his house in Burbank and wondering why there was no snow; sitting on the living room floor, watching President Kennedy's funeral procession on TV. And somewhere in the back of the house, hearing my mother cry.

The trips, I would learn years later, were my mother's attempts to leave my father. Unknown to me at the time, by 1963, my parents' marriage was all but over. It would take a lot of sorting to understand what had happened, but in the end, there were two reasons. The first was the ghosts from my mother's past that had come back to haunt her. The second was my father's infidelities.

His first affair occurred in 1961. While my mother was out of town for a few weeks, my father began romancing a black exotic dancer named Tammy Townsend.

. . .

Her real name was Mildred Townsend, but at the Club Oasis, where she was a headliner, she was known simply as "Tammy." She was a stunning five feet two, slender, with fine features, big brown eyes, and a headful of tinted red hair.

Out of all my parents' friends, Tammy is one of the few I remember from my early childhood and with whom I'm still in touch now. Even as a kid, I remember thinking how beautiful and kind she was. She has always been a thoughtful, gentle woman who speaks unabashedly about leaving her poor Mississippi home as a teenager, hoping for a better life working as a nightclub dancer. There weren't a whole lot of opportunities for a poor southern black woman in the 1950s, so she did what she could.

Tammy spent much of her life dancing, retiring some years ago not because she had to—even into her fifties, she's as striking as ever—but because she wanted to devote more time to civil rights issues, work on political campaigns, and serve in the administration of one Anchorage mayor.

Most of what I thought I knew about Tammy was that long after my parents had divorced, when I was around twelve, she and my father dated. She took me to my first rock concert (The Jefferson Airplane), and it was she to whom I went when I began menstruating. I would rather have died than talk to my father about such things. But Tammy and my father had known each other long before then.

Tammy was only nineteen when she met my father, during her first night in Anchorage on February 22, 1961. She'd arrived from L.A. for a six-week engagement at the Club Oasis. The Oasis' owner, Frank Evans, had been trying to recruit Tammy out of a club where she worked in L.A. for more than a year. Frank was taken with Tammy's act, which included an opening number in which she entered onstage dressed like Carmen Miranda in a green, layered skirt and matching top, dancing calypso-style to a live band playing "Spanish Harlem." By the end of her fifteen-minute set, she'd be stripped down to a bikini and fishnet stockings (full nudity was strictly prohibited by most state liquor control boards) with a feather in her hair and kicking up her heels to "There's No Business Like Show Business."

Tammy didn't like the idea of working in Alaska during the dead of winter. In order to entice her north, Frank had to offer her $150 a week—double her normal salary—plus a six-week contract that would be paid in full if she decided she didn't like it and wanted to go home. Within a few days, Tammy boarded a plane bound for Anchorage.

She came with two other dancers who worked under the names Margo St. John and Lady Lee. No sooner had they landed at the airport than Tammy wondered what she'd gotten herself into.

"It was really small. Almost like a little house. I could not believe that it was an airport," she recalled. "I thought to myself, 'What on earth have I done?' "

They were picked up by a friend of Frank's who took them to the club where Frank and his wife, Josephine—a large black woman whom everybody called Mama Jo—were waiting to greet them with one of Mama Jo's home-cooked meals. After dinner, the girls were shown to their rooms in the back of the club. At around nine-thirty that night, there was a knock on Tammy's door.

"Why don't you come out and meet the people?" Frank Evans asked.

At first Tammy declined, saying she was tired. But Frank insisted; he wanted to show her off. He'd been bragging for a long time about Tammy to the bar's regular customers, my father being one of them.

"I felt not very at ease," she recalled. She didn't drink, so when she walked up to the bar she ordered her usual, a glass of orange juice. She was sipping it when my father stepped forward and introduced himself.

"Hi, I'm Johnny Rich. Frank told me about you."

My father was a regular at the Oasis as well as at the other all-black nightclubs, including bars that catered to all races, called "black and tan" bars. He frequented places with names like the Mermaid, the Nevada, and the North Starlight Lounge. Within a few months of arriving in Alaska, he was well known in the black community, especially among those in the nightclub and restaurant business.

Many of the blacks in Anchorage, then only a few thousand, had come north to work for the military or the railroad as laborers. The wages were higher and there was more opportunity for them, even though racist neighborhood covenants kept them from buying homes in some areas. The city also had a large native Alaskan population—as well as a strong bias against them. My father had no patience with such rules and routinely walked into places where black patrons were frowned upon and demanded that the waiters and bartenders serve his black friends.

Tammy was taken with his good looks and charm and they spent the rest of the evening talking at the bar. When closing time arrived, my father asked Tammy if he could buy her breakfast. She declined, saying she was too tired. But when she learned that her roommate, Margo, was hosting a party in their room, she decided to go with him. Knowing she wanted to rest, he took her to an after-hours joint where he said she could get a room to sleep.

This was Tammy's introduction to an area of Anchorage known as the "Flats."

The Flats was a woodsy stretch of dirt road along a basin area off Chester Creek, which runs down from the mountains through Anchorage, emptying into Cook Inlet. Along the west side—Westchester—were some of Anchorage's oldest and most established families. The "Eastchester Flats" was another matter, with its rows of wooden shacks housing rowdy bars and raunchy whorehouses.

In a hipster's pun on the nickname of nearby Katmai National Park and Preserve, the Flats was sometimes called "the Valley of Ten Thousand Smokes" because of the neighborhood's marijuana dealers. Less-than-kind police officers were known to call the all-black neighborhood "Cadillac Row," for all the big cars that belonged to the local pimps.

The Flats was enormously popular with soldiers and airmen from Fort Richardson and Elmendorf, and weekend street brawls involving dozens of drunken soldiers weren't uncommon. As with Harlem in the twenties and thirties, the city's white elite liked to make a night of it in the Flats, where the hot spots always had room for city council members, leading lawyers, and politicians.

The Flats ran flat out, twenty-four hours a day, featuring jazz bands, torch singers, and Alaska's best barbecued ribs at places like the Lark, Lucky's Hotspot, the Harlem Club, Brown's Chicken Shack, and the Red Hut. Scattered among the restaurants and bars were tiny gambling dens, like the one my father took Tammy to that morning.

Upon arriving, my father set it up with the club's owner to get Tammy a room upstairs where she could sleep while he hit the gaming room. Several hours later, after she awoke, they went to breakfast and then he took her home.

For the next two weeks, he was at the Oasis every night, waiting for Tammy to get off work so he could take her out.

"Johnny's married," Frank Evans warned Tammy. "You shouldn't be going places with him."

Tammy didn't believe it—my father had said he was single or separated or something like that—until one night when she was in her dressing room between sets and a panicked Margo burst through the door.

"Someone's trying to kill me!" Margo screamed.

"What?" Tammy asked, rising from where she'd been sitting.

"There's this woman out there with a gun!" Margo yelled as she darted about the dressing room, grabbing her robe and shoes.

"What woman?" Tammy asked.

"Johnny's wife. Coming right for the stage, for me!"

"Oh my God" was all Tammy could think to say.

She spun around and headed for the door. From the moment she left the dressing room and walked down the narrow hallway that led to the bar, she heard the sound of a woman screaming above the din of voices and jukebox music. As she entered the club, she spotted my father standing at the door struggling with a small, dark-haired woman who was kicking and cursing.

Tammy hung back until my father had pulled my mother out of the bar. She then asked Frank Evans what happened. He told her how he'd seen my mother come through the front door during Margo's set and head straight for the stage. Frank saw that my mother was carrying a small handgun and he called out for my father. Frank got to my mother first, wrestling the gun from her hands before she had a chance to fire it.

While my father had been seeing Tammy, my mother was under contract, go-go dancing at a club in Kodiak. Occasionally, she and a couple of other girls would make a circuit around the state, hitting a string of clubs in remote towns for two or three weeks at a time. When she got back, somebody told her that my father was seeing a redheaded black dancer at the Club Oasis. Both Tammy and Margo had red-dyed hair.

"They didn't tell her *which* redhead," Tammy said. She refused to see my father anymore until years later.

I am told that the affair shattered my mother, although she'd long had her suspicions about my father's ability to remain faithful.

"She was insanely jealous of him," remembers Chic, her cabdriver friend. "That was one thing that affected your mom more than anything. He was nice looking and he always looked nice. He never looked cheap. Your mom did too, but she was always working. Johnny, he was always prowling around, 'taking care of business.' "

When things were good between them, people talk about how caring my father seemed toward my mother. They mention how he protectively picked her up at the end of her shift at the Stagecoach. When in public, they often held hands and were openly affectionate.

But both were hotheaded and stubborn, always concerned about money. Not whether there was enough, but who was spending it and how. My mother kept a checking account in her name. In those days, many married couples listed everything in the husband's name, but our house on Fireweed Lane was in both names—partly because my mother earned the most money, and partly because she knew my father all too well.

Most of the time, she revealed her fears about my father and other women to Chic when the two would run into each other at the Stagecoach and have a drink together.

"Do you think he loves me?" she'd ask. "Do you think he's seeing anyone else? I know Johnny's cheating."

"No, John's not cheatin' on you," Chic would tell her. "These girls, they just like him. They know he's married. You're lucky to have him."

She'd cry a little bit and then she'd ask, "Do you think he cares about me?"

"Hell, I know he does," Chic would answer. "If he didn't, he wouldn't be with you."

Chic's reassurances weren't enough for my mother. According to court records, she filed for divorce after she learned of my father's affair with Tammy and she made him move out of the house. In a preliminary settlement, he agreed to give her ten thousand dollars in cash and two airline tickets, which she used to fly herself and me to California. The arrangement was brokered by her lawyer, John Hellenthal.

"I tried to tell her that she wasn't getting anywhere with John Rich," Hellenthal said. "It wasn't good for her to continue to be with him because he clearly gave the impression that nothing was going to change him."

Despite Hellenthal's advice, my mother returned from California with me after a few weeks, telling Hellenthal she loved my father too much to go through with the divorce.

Until I'd found the court record of my mother's divorce filing, I'd no idea that things had started to fall apart between my parents that early. No one said anything to me. My mother never announced that my father had moved out. I don't recall seeing him pack. He'd kept such odd hours, he seemed to be around as much as before anyway. Sometimes he'd take me to the Safari with him, where I'd stay for a day or two, again never understanding why he was there and my mother was at home. For a long time, they hid it well, until one afternoon in late December 1962.

I was in my room playing when I heard the muffled shouts of my parents arguing in their bedroom. I stepped out of my room and stared across the living room at the door to their room. It was shut and from behind it, I could hear my father yelling. I'd never heard them fight before. I'd never even seen my father angry except for one other time: I'd evidently said a "bad" word—I don't recall what—but I do remember standing in the bathroom and crying while my father put a bar of soap in my mouth.

I moved only a few inches past my door, afraid to move any nearer. As I stood there, the shouts intensified. My heart quickened and I felt a sinking feeling in my stomach. I could hear my father's voice, alternating between strained and high-pitched, and low and gruff. It sounded almost like a growl. My mother was crying, in between occasional screaming outbursts. I felt paralyzed by what I heard and felt.

I don't know how long I stood there, waiting, anticipating, and hoping it would end before I heard the crash—the sound of glass striking glass, either my mother's perfume bottles smashing into each other or a fist being thrown through the dresser mirror. Then came the distinct, low thud of flesh and bone slamming against the wooden walls, followed by the smack of a fist hitting a cheek. My mother screamed.

Suddenly their door flew open, and my father emerged, his face reddened and puffy; he was dragging my mother by the hair. She was sprawled behind him, her arms pinned underneath her, flopping from side to side like some hooked fish. He pulled her through the living room, headed toward the front door. As he reached the middle of the room, he spotted me in the corner.

"Get in your room. Go on," he yelled.

But I just stood there motionless as I watched my mother's hands reach out, her face streaked in tears.

The reconciliation was short-lived. My mother went back to Hellenthal, this time asking for a restraining order as well as another divorce, and we left Alaska a second time.

The only time my father ever spoke to me of their marital troubles was to blame it all on my mother.

"We had five good years together," he once told me. "Then she began suffering from memory blackouts, sometimes forgetting who I was."

The blackouts were only the first sign of a more deeply rooted problem. Prior to meeting my father, my mother had spent nearly two years in and out of psychiatric hospitals. Few people, including my father, knew the full extent of her hospitalizations and her struggle with a debilitating bout of mental illness.

Her troubles began in 1954 when she'd slipped into a serious depression after the breakup of a love affair with a married man. She was in Milwaukee at the time and had holed up in her apartment, refusing to come out. Her landlady finally contacted my mother's family. The call marked what my mother's sisters refer to as "Breakdown Time."

After the call, Lena says my mother was brought home by a friend. In Ironwood, she got worse, sobbing for hours, then bursting into fits of uncontrollable rage, shrieking and swearing, smashing everything in her path. Once she threw a clothes iron at Marietta, missing her head by inches. Marietta finally took my mother to a doctor, who recommended she be hospitalized for depression. The nearest and best facility was St. Mary's Hospital in Duluth.

The doctors focused first on her vitiligo, an ailment that leaves white patches on the skin and is associated with several conditions, including an overactive thyroid. Thyroid problems ran in the family and my mother had been battling the vitiligo since her teens. The doctors concluded, however, that the condition stemmed from emotional instability. "Psychiatric review brought out considerable hostility, especially toward the mother," noted one physician, echoing the popular view of the time—blaming the family for psychiatric woes.

During her first three-week hospitalization, my mother received counseling and insulin injections—deliberate overdoses that sent her into deep but temporary coma states. After many episodes of what was then the latest cure-all fad in psychiatric care, my mother's doctors concluded that she suffered from an "anxiety state." She was released, but a week later was readmitted after attempting suicide by slashing her wrists.

"She was probably too close to the mother's home," wrote one doctor after she was readmitted. She left the hospital after nine days, only to be brought back less than two weeks later.

This time, she was readmitted for "one or more episodes of aggressive hostility." It was during this last visit to St. Mary's that my mother was subjected to a battery of shock treatments.

Each morning two hospital attendants appeared at her bedside to escort her to a small room down the hall. There, her arms and legs were strapped onto a cart and a pair of electrodes attached to her head. As with all patients who were given shock treatments, the attendants kept an eye on her big toe. If it didn't wiggle the procedure was repeated a minute later.

Her records indicate that she was scheduled for more treatments—a "series" could last as long as twenty days—but her resistance led the doctors to substitute twenty days of insulin overdoses, after which she was released with a diagnosis of "personality disorder."

Home again in Ironwood in early July, my mother continued to deteriorate. In November, she again slit her wrists, prompting her parents to commit her permanently to Newberry State Hospital, a big facility about two hundred thirty miles away. Her medical records state that she "attempted to burn the house down." Lena says that what really happened was that my mother had fallen asleep in a chair while smoking.

At Newberry, my mother refused to cooperate with the nurses and doctors, or obey hospital rules. She finally lost her privileges when attendants suspected her of having sex with male patients. But by Christmas she improved enough to participate in occupational therapy.

After the holidays, though, she was subjected to another twenty days of insulin therapy. The treatments produced "no appreciable change," and a week before her twenty-first birthday, she was "paroled."

My mother immediately left the Midwest and moved to Denver, where little is known of her life except that she called home once telling her family she'd been "cured" at a clinic there. Not long afterward, she moved back to California.

Everyone in my mother's family, including my mother, had hoped that her emotional troubles were temporary. But one of the side effects of shock treatments is memory loss. Lena can still recall the difficulty my mother had in remembering what day it was. She was fortunate. Some patients forgot their own names. But the side effects of her treatment, which even my father noticed years later, were the least of my mother's problems. The psychological difficulties she had experienced in her early twenties were not some postadolescent phase she'd grow out of. When her marriage to my father began to disintegrate, the true, and more terrifying, nature of her mental illness began surfacing.

Friends of my parents remember the way my mother flew into unprovoked fits of rage, or the way she'd begun lying in bed for days at a time, complaining of mind-numbing headaches. Other times, her behavior seemed completely irrational, such as the day my mother's friend Midge found her wandering aimlessly downtown.

Midge was driving by when she spotted my mother walking slowly and dressed in only a light sweater, skirt, and high heels. The temperature was below freezing. My mother seemed nervous when Midge pulled over and called to her.

"Frances, are you all right?" Midge asked.

My mother didn't respond. Midge got out of the car and gently led my mother to the passenger side. Midge then brought her home where she tried to get her to eat, talk, or do anything besides staring into space.

There is some evidence in my mother's medical records that during this period my father tried to get her help, although friends say he had a hard time accepting that my mother was seriously ill.

"John fought that for a long, long time," said one friend. "It was hard for him to admit to that."

He sent her to a psychiatrist, but she refused to heed the doctor's advice. By early 1963, my mother's behavior became completely unpredictable, as she slowly slipped into insanity. Even I wasn't immune to the erratic nature of my mother's illness.

One day we were in the living room and she was sitting on the couch, talking on the phone. I sat at her feet, wrapped in the lengths of the curled white phone cord, and I began tugging on it to get her attention. Then suddenly she slammed down the receiver and began whipping me with the cord. I tumbled away from her and ran for my bedroom. She gave chase, cornering me on the bed where she pounded me with her fists. Then, as quickly as she'd turned on me, she stopped and pulled me to her. Sobbing, she began rocking back and forth and saying, "I'm sorry."

A few minutes later she rose and went back to the phone. This time she called the Alaska Psychiatric Institute and told the switchboard operator she needed help.

"I'm afraid I'm losing my mind," she said, giving only her name.

When the operator asked for her address and telephone number, she hung up. The operator then contacted the state Division of Mental Health, which tracked my father to the Safari. He gave them our address and a social worker immediately came to the house. After meeting briefly with my mother, the social worker made an appointment for her at the state mental health clinic the following week. My father arrived shortly after the social worker to take me with him.

Several days before her appointment, desperate and alone, my mother called and asked to be seen sooner. She was told they couldn't get her in and to contact her family doctor.

On February 5, the day before her scheduled clinic appointment, my mother's doctor admitted her to the emergency room at Providence Hospital.

"I don't feel nothing," she told the doctors upon admission. "I'm like a dummy. I have some pressure in my head and my head is empty. I feel very sick and nobody can help me."

One of the doctors asked about her family's mental health history.

"In my family nobody is crazy but me" was all she would say.

·   ·   ·

I realize now that my mother's photo albums, which she so carefully kept, were not so much a record of my childhood but her attempts to hang on to the pieces of her life she must have always feared would one day slip away again. The photographs are a message in a bottle from her to me. She wanted to make sure that I would remember the years when things were good.

Fourth Avenue in ruins the morning after the Good Friday earthquake of 1964. The Safari Hotel is on the left side of the street, near Sam's Liquor Store.
COURTESY U.S. GEOLOGICAL SURVEY

CHAPTER FIVE

SHATTERED DREAMS

For most who were in Anchorage in the early 1960s, few things in their lives compared with the events of Good Friday, March 27, 1964. There was life before The Earthquake and life after The Earthquake. But for me, the earthquake had virtually no emotional impact. By the time the quake occurred, my life had already fallen apart.

The quake began at 5:36 P.M. and was a monster, measuring 8.4 to 8.7 on the Richter scale—the worst ever in North America. The epicenter was near the headwaters of Prince William Sound, only eighty miles east of Anchorage, striking at the heart of Alaska's population center.

A terrible rumbling was felt throughout an area of half a million square miles. In Anchorage, the earth rippled and pitched like giant ocean waves. Telephone poles slammed from one side of the ground to the other; parked cars bounced as if they'd been placed on trampolines, and tall buildings swayed violently, like palm trees caught in a hurricane-force wind.

Throughout south central Alaska, many people watched horrified and helplessly as their loved ones and coworkers were swallowed by shifting slabs of earth or buried in cascading waterfalls of rubble.

Throughout the ordeal, the sound of glass breaking and groaning timber filled the air. Some thought it was the end of the world. Others were convinced that the Russians had dropped a nuclear bomb on Fort Richardson.

I was at my mother's friend Midge's house sitting on Terry the babysitter's lap, alternating between moments of watching *Fireball XL5,* a silly black-and-white show about puppet space travelers, and breaking into sobbing fits. Terry was the babysitter for me and Midge's two sons, Tony and Bobby. I was miserably unhappy because Midge was taking Tony for a haircut and I wanted to go with them, but instead I was made to stay home with Terry, along with Bob and Vern, a couple of Midge's friends who'd stopped by with a bucket of chicken.

I'd worked myself into a raging fury, kicking, yelling, screaming. Terry did her best to calm me.

We were in the chair that faced the television set. Behind the TV was a small dining area where a picture window looked out onto the parking lot at the front of the duplex. As Midge was sliding behind the steering wheel of her car, it suddenly began rocking in slow motion, looking as if it was going to come through the window. I thought, *Why is Midge trying to drive the car into the house?*

Simultaneously, the whole apartment began rocking in the same slow, sick way. Terry tried to stand, but the floor buckled under her feet and threw her sideways and we fell back into the overstuffed rocker.

While still looking out the window, I saw Bobby ride up from his newspaper route on his bicycle. He threw the bike down and grabbed the car's passenger door. Midge was now standing at the driver's side as they both strained to keep it from bouncing into the building. Tony was inside, caroming around like a human tennis ball. Terry jumped up a second time, this time pushing me out of her lap.

"*Earthquake!*" she screamed.

Everything kept moving. *Fireball XL5* was still on the television—until the set tipped backward and crashed to the floor. Pictures rattled and banged on the walls, swinging like crazed pendulums. The kitchen cupboards flew open, sending their contents crashing to the floor.

Terry dragged me to the front door, staggering like a drunk. Then she handed me over to Bob. Another tremor hit and my head was slammed against the doorframe as we passed under it. He let out a loud laugh when I cried out, "I wish I was in California."

"Yeah, me too, baby," Bob said as he rushed out to the street where the shaking continued.

By the time we'd reached the middle of the road, there was already a wide, deep fissure that disappeared beneath Midge's duplex. Once outside, I heard a terrible snapping noise, like a dozen firecrackers exploding. It was the windows breaking in the McKinley building, only a few blocks directly south of the duplex.

After five minutes, the shaking finally stopped. The first thing I noticed was the McKinley building seemed to be leaning our way, giving me the feeling it could fall on us. We huddled in the street only a few moments before my father came running toward us, looking disheveled and haggard.

My father had been at the Safari, in the middle of taking a shower when the quake started. He jumped out, grabbed some slacks, and ran into the hallway, where he met half a dozen guests headed for the stairs. He ran past them, checking the rooms to make sure everybody was out. As he turned to head back toward the stairs, the floor tilted downward. He began yelling for Yukon. The dog had run out of the room with him, but was nowhere in sight. My father grabbed the stair railing but the stairway walls began to cave in, so he ran back toward his room, where Yukon stood on the bed. He kicked out the window overlooking the back alley, grabbed the dog and heaved him outside, then jumped behind him. By the time he landed on the ground, the two-story Safari had become a one-story building, its first floor sinking into the ground. When the earth had stopped shaking, 115 Alaskans were dead, nine in Anchorage.

Fourth Avenue was a wreck, and none of it was more devastated than the district around the Safari. The ground had sunk twenty feet, swallowing whole buildings and leaving bars, pawnshops, stores, restaurants, and other structures in heaps of cracked glass, smashed timbers, and shattered signs. The Safari was gone, along with the Scandinavian Club, the Frisco Bar, Koslosky's Men's Store, Northern Jewelers, and dozens of other businesses.

The stores that were left leaned against one another like staggering winos. Some had been ripped from their foundations; others looked untouched until you realized that what looked like the first floor was the second, squashed down as if under the palm of an angry giant. The

Denali Theater had sunk below street level, its huge neon sign inches from the ground.

The streets were strewn with vehicles that the earthquake had tossed like jackstraws. Ironically, the destruction spared a banner strung across 4th Avenue to promote a play running at Alaska Methodist University. In big white letters, the words OUR TOWN flapped quietly above the wreckage.

Anchorage's death toll could have been much worse: Most of the town's small, sturdy buildings were located far away from the slide areas; the earthquake occurred late in the afternoon at a time when most people had already left work and were at home, and whatever fires broke out were easily contained, and because it was a holiday, school was out of session.

As darkness fell, teams of civilian and military search and rescue squads, aided by flashlights, began sifting through the rubble on 4th Avenue and in neighborhoods where the homes had been destroyed, looking for survivors and trying to retrieve bodies. Servicemen on the bases began cutting fifty-five-gallon barrels in half and fitting them with plywood tops for makeshift outhouses to be distributed to the badly damaged areas. It was announced on the radio that within a few days, typhoid immunization centers would be set up around town. Everyone was advised to get the shots.

That night, families camped in what was left of their homes or bunked with friends whose houses survived intact. Countless aftershocks shook Anchorage, rattling what was left of everybody's nerves. In between momentary dashes out the front door (in case the roof was going to cave in), families sat close to their radios listening to disc jockeys pass along emergency messages. With most of the phone lines down and those that were up reserved for emergency use only, radio became the only communication link between residents who didn't know if their friends or family members across town were still alive.

In addition to emergency messages and the latest Richter scale reading on the last tremor (there were several that night) came the tidal wave warnings. At one point, the neighborhoods of Bootlegger's Cove, South Addition, and Turnagain were evacuated by a false alarm. The wave rolled in, measuring only three feet. But who wanted to take any chances?

Midge, my father, Tony, Bobby, several others, and I stayed at the home of a friend. There was no electricity, running water, or heat. For us, like many others, it was a cold night's rest as the outside temperature dipped to 20 degrees.

As my father tucked me into bed that night I wondered if the Easter bunny would still come. My father had other worries. The Safari was gone, and although the house on Fireweed Lane had sustained only minor damage, the rest of his life was a ruin. His livelihood—at least, the one he claimed when paying taxes—was gone. My mother, who'd been hospitalized since January, had been diagnosed as hopelessly schizophrenic.

"Everyone here in the building would not condone our morals" was the first thing my father told a social worker who interviewed him the day after my mother had been hospitalized.

The text of the interview is included in my mother's medical records, attached to the back of a dozen or so pages of medical summaries, doctors' comments, and hospital notes. The interview, which took place before the earthquake at the state Division of Mental Health office downtown, was held to determine who would pay for my mother's medical expenses. What my father had to say that day isn't surprising to me.

First, it's noted in the file that he didn't think her medical fees were his responsibility since he and my mother were separated. It would be just like him to try to get out of paying the bill. While he honored his personal debts (in part because if he didn't, he'd lose his cachet among his fellow gamblers), my father thought nothing of cheating institutions, government or social, and even many businesses. The nearly thirty civil suits filed against him in state court during his lifetime for nonpayment of his bills attest to this. Second, his candor about who he was is the one thing I've always admired about him.

He used to rail about hypocrites, people who pretended to be one thing during the day and acted like another at night. It was a word whose meaning he made sure I understood. He'd complain about the hypocrisy of a police force that would raid his gambling parlors but not touch the high-stakes poker games that went on between the town's high-powered businessmen. (The police have told me that those games were for pleasure; my father's were a continuing criminal enterprise. He never recognized the difference.) He'd carry on about the preachers who came to his gambling dens, the so-called "straight" businessmen who sat at his poker tables, and the married men for whom he'd find prostitutes.

I can only imagine the social worker's reaction to a man like my father and the life he described. She noted that my father "looked younger than his years, in contrast to his wife who looked older than her years."

"We have one daughter who will turn six on February twenty-fourth," my father said, outlining the family history. He went on to explain their separate living arrangements and said that prior to her hospitalization, my mother hadn't cleaned the house for weeks. The place was filthy. The trash was overflowing in the kitchen, the sink was filled with dirty dishes, the bathroom was a mess. "It will take a maid two days to clean it all up," he said.

In part, my father gave the kind of answers the social worker wanted to hear. Most of his responses, however, reflect his own conflict and confusion about what was happening to my mother.

Prior to their marriage in 1956 in California, Mr. Rich said that he understood that his wife had attempted suicide by taking a razor blade to herself. For a time she was placed in an institution in Michigan. At the time of their marriage and for a number of years afterward, everything was fine until about three years ago.

Mr. Rich said when they were married she "listened and looked up to me and this was because of all of my experience." He seemed proud of his wife's position as a B-girl and said she was "number one" until the clubs were closed several years ago. For a time, everything in their marriage went fine. He made money. Then his wife became jealous and nagged him, seemingly forcing him into an argument as if she wanted him to hit her. They got along well, he said, until about three years ago when she found him in bed with another woman. As Mr. Rich acknowledged, he had also found her in bed with other men. He told of observing her in recent months in the alley in back of the Safari Hotel picking up a man, and on other occasions when mad about something, taking the car and bumping it into the walls of buildings or garbage cans. She has also made a number of long-distance calls to her family in Burbank, California. Mr. Rich says she is not in the good graces of her family.

He said he does not feel that his wife has been a good mother to their child but feels if the child were taken from her, she would be very upset. He said on several occasions he had gone back to his wife in an attempt to keep the family together. About a month ago when his wife came back from California she had not seemed coherent in her thinking and her personal appearance had deteriorated to the point where he had to ask her several times to take a bath. He said that she does not appeal to him sexually but that he still loves her.

After the interview, my father agreed, at least for the time being, to pay for my mother's hospitalization. In his Cadillac, he and the social worker drove to Providence Hospital to pick her up. She was being transferred to Alaska Psychiatric Institute. At Providence, the psychiatrist who had seen her before concluded that she was not psychotic, but in a "panic state due to her age and loss of ability in her former income business." The B-joints had closed down after the first session of the Alaska State Legislature outlawed the practice of women selling drinks on commission. The doctor determined that it was not medical attention that my mother needed, but psychiatric care.

API, just up the road from Providence, was so new that only about a third of the three-story, multimillion-dollar building was being used— in part because there weren't enough patients to fill all the beds and they had yet to fill all their staff positions.

The nurses at Providence had my mother dressed and ready to go when my father and the social worker arrived. Still taking notes, the social worker rode in the back while my mother sat next to my father in the front seat. She was heavily medicated and kept leaning over against him, asking over and over, "Do you love me?"

"Yes," my father said.

"Will you come back to me if I get better?"

"Yes."

At API, my father walked her through admissions—hers was a voluntary one—and then to her ward.

As my father was driving the social worker back to her office, he stopped by the house on Fireweed Lane.

"Mr. Rich drove me by the home where his wife had lived and told me how he had remodeled the home," she wrote. "He said that he thought that another reason his wife felt the way she did was because several of her friends had had marital problems."

As a final note, the social worker wrote that my father drove a white Cadillac equipped with two radio receivers, "one which he can listen to state and city police calls and the other on which he can contact his hotel."

Despite her psychiatrist's optimism, my mother was a troubled woman. Dr. Virginia Gorton wasn't quite sure how to sum up her condition.

"This 29-year-old white female, married, was admitted to this hospital February 13, 1964," Dr. Gorton wrote. "She was very upset and in many ways resembled a pseudo-neurotic schizophrenic with her paranoia, anxiety, depression, etc. . . . Diagnosis: Psychoneurosis anxiety reaction with depression and hysteria in a basic character disorder individual."

Other doctors were equally uncertain about how to label her ailment. "The onset seems gradual, of several years' duration, initiating with a lack of responsibility, with a desire of having the easy life, alcoholism, prostitution, and finally with psychotic manifestations," another doctor wrote. "Patient started to hear voices three or four months ago."

"Patient spontaneously admitted to being promiscuous for many years. . . . At present she is accusing her husband of neglecting her and therefore, she asked for a divorce. Patient is very much concerned about her child and she is afraid her husband may get the child."

My mother was placed on Women's One, the acute care ward. For the first few weeks, she clung to the staff, repeatedly asking them for reassurance that she had not lost her mind. She was severely depressed, telling the doctors how my father had been running around with other women for years. She explained that she knew her behavior was bizarre. She told them how she'd spent days wandering around the house wearing several layers of coats.

"Is my case hopeless?" she asked in a rare moment of clarity.

At API they didn't believe in shock treatment, electrical or chemical. Because the facility was so new, patients received some of the most progressive treatments available at the time: psychotherapy, group counseling, and, if appropriate, drugs to control behavior. Once my mother had gone through a battery of tests and talked with several staff people, they put her in both individual and group therapy. The hospital sustained only minor damage in the earthquake, and her treatment continued without interruption.

Like my father, she didn't believe in holding back, and it is in her interviews with her doctors that I learned more about the person my mother was, and the illness she suffered from, than anything anybody could have told me. As with many suffering from schizophrenia, her moods during the interviews alternated between being angry and defiant or vulnerable and confused.

She explained how she'd turned tricks for years, sometimes getting as much as fifty dollars a party. The only thing that made her mad was thinking about how she'd given my father so much of the money that she worked for. "I want to divorce him and move to Las Vegas where I can be in my own element," she told one interviewer. "I took care of myself before I met John and I could do so again."

The staff at API did what it could. But after three months, my mother had to be released. Her discharge summary states:

> Her course in the hospital has been a stormy one. Her improvement has been slow and at times seemed to be at a standstill. She has been very ambivalent about her husband and her feelings toward him. She complained of having loss of memory, of losing her mind, and constantly agitating about something or another. She showed no interest in anything other than her own physical needs for a long time. She went into frequent panic states and would upset the entire group.
>
> She was a prostitute much of her life and this seems to be her only interest, even to this date. We made an attempt to get her interested in some sort of rehabilitation but she could not seem to develop any interest. We made an attempt to get her interested in some sort of rehabilitation while on the Day/Night Unit, but she could not seem to develop any interest in this. The patient was taken to the Day/Night Unit May 11, and showed rather steady improvement from that time on. She has made moderate improvement by the time she decided to leave and it is felt that probably she had reached her maximum improvement. We feel that she would have gone back to her prostituting probably right away anyway, and she would return to her husband, so we no longer tried to deter her. Patient was discharged on June 26, 1964.

Not long ago I had a dream that at first made no sense to me. I dreamed that I was in an abandoned house where I walked slowly from one empty room to the next, until I came to a room in the back. There I saw a sight that startled me. Water was pouring down one of the walls as if a pipe had burst. I ran from the room and into another where I met a woman with teased black hair. She was distraught. She kept saying, "I know he'll come back."

Later, I realized what I had dreamed was actually a deeply buried memory. My sleeping mind had dredged up what my conscious mind would not—what it had felt like when my mother had come home from the hospital.

She looked anemic, her hair oily and stringy, and her fingers stained yellow from constant smoking. I felt an overwhelming sense of isolation being near her, and the house that had once brought me such joy felt like a prison.

One day, my mother didn't get out of bed. Hours went by as I waited for her to come out and fix me some breakfast. The morning drained away; by the middle of the afternoon I was so scared and hungry that I finally got up the courage to open her bedroom door.

The room was dark and cold, the shades and curtains drawn. My mother was lying in bed with blankets pulled up around her face. I don't remember what I said to her; I don't remember her answer. I only remember closing the door and quietly walking away. I wanted her to get up; yet I was afraid that she would. I learned at that moment that I could no longer depend on grown-ups to take care of me, so I went into the kitchen, climbed onto the counter, and made myself a bowl of tapioca pudding. I fixed it because there was a colored picture on the box that showed what it should look like. I couldn't read the directions, so I just put the dry mix in a bowl, added water, and stirred it up.

A friend of my parents once told me I didn't grow up—I was *kicked* up. This is true.

On July 2, less than a week after she was released from the hospital, my mother started hearing the voices again, this time telling her to run away.

That morning I noticed two suitcases by the front door. Before I could ask her what they were for, a cabdriver was outside, honking his horn. My mother grabbed the suitcases and told me to get into the cab.

I climbed in the backseat while she and the cabbie ran back in for several boxes. When everything was loaded, she got in the front seat and told the cabbie to take us to the airport. She was holding a Northwest Airlines ticket envelope on which were written the names Mrs. C. Jones and Jane Jones. I still have the ticket stubs. They were one-way to Chicago. I couldn't have known it then, but it would be years before I would see my father or Alaska again.

My mother never would return.

PART 2

TRANSITIONS

The Chiaravalle home in Ironwood, Michigan

CHAPTER SIX

IRONWOOD AND THE FBI

"All that money, and look at them. They're starving," my grandmother said as my mother and I stepped from the cab that had brought us from Ironwood's tiny airport.

My mother was frail and thin. I'd always been a petite child, and was skinnier than ever.

The journey from Alaska had been a grind. After endless hours on the plane from Anchorage, we spent the night in a black vinyl chair at Chicago's O'Hare Airport, straining to sleep under the glare of the fluorescents, before boarding a smaller aircraft for the hop to Michigan.

My grandmother looked that day as she always would to me—like a European peasant wife who had labored without much reward for most of her life. She was clad in a worn, shapeless cotton dress and heavy black leather shoes. Her hair was wrapped in a bun and bobby-pinned to the back of her head. It never failed to fascinate me when she'd unfurl the bun, revealing graying hair that fell below her waist. She had large, sagging breasts above a barrel-shaped waist; her neck was disfigured by a large goiter.

Also on hand to greet the taxi were my mother's sisters—Lena, nick-named "Red" for her strawberry blond hair, and Sandra, whom I'd come to call "Nanny." They were all strangers to me, yet everyone seemed happy to see my mother, despite the circumstances. As much as she'd dreamed of fleeing Ironwood, it was home, and all that home implied: love, loathing, rejection, and acceptance. I find it surprising that of all places, my mother returned to her hometown, but then, where else did she have to go?

The Ironwood to which my mother brought me was a ghost town, left emptier and emptier as the mines around Jessieville had slowly shut down over the years. As the ore veins thinned the miners cut more deeply into the ground, opening tunnels so far into the earth that the ground water rushed in to fill them again and again. As the mines were turning into drowning pools, ore prices were dropping, and it became cheaper to close a mine than to keep it open.

So the jobs fled, and with them the people, who left behind vacant stores, bankrupt businesses, and empty houses. Once Ironwood had been home to nearly thirty thousand; by the time my mother and I arrived, only ten thousand people remained.

Jessieville fared as badly, withering to a mere suburb of Ironwood. The shops, taverns, and movie houses that had thrived in the center of town when my mother was growing up were closed, leaving big empty buildings with decaying false fronts and windows thick with dust. I thought spirits lived in the old buildings that my cousins and I would pass on our bikes, just as I was convinced that ghosts lived in the abandoned house next door to my grandmother's.

Everything in my life changed that summer of 1964. Recalling the journey back to my mother's hometown has never been easy. The memories and the emotions become twisted and tangled, turning up bad, again and again. So much of what shapes who I am today occurred during the three years I lived in Ironwood. It was there that I came to know the same sense of being an outsider that my father had known as a child; the feeling of not belonging and not being good enough, even when you are, and even when no one intends to inflict such emotional injury.

When I revisited Ironwood as an adult, I was surprised at how it looked to me. Naturally, as I had grown, the streets and houses seemed to have gotten narrower and smaller. Other things had shrunk as well; mostly the overriding sense of loneliness that was the hallmark of my memories of the time I spent there. Yet, scattered among the bitter memories are happier ones of what it meant to be a youngster in a small, midwestern town.

In Ironwood, I learned to ride a two-wheeled bike on a stretch of brand-new asphalt; to catch fireflies in glass jars on hot summer nights, and to know the thrill of gliding an American Flyer solo down a snowy hill. A part of every Saturday morning was spent at Naple's, the corner store up the hill, where my cousins and I debated how to spend the nickel, and sometimes quarter, we had managed to pry from sympathetic adult hands. There were the afternoons after school spent screeching my brains out while watching the television matinee horror flicks at my friend Kathleen's house. Or the Saturday afternoons at the downtown theater catching the latest Flash Gordon serial along with the newest Disney movie.

I learned to squabble with my cousins—one minute fighting and the next conspiring with them. I learned to feel like I couldn't live without them, as if we were brothers and sisters.

I attended Newport Elementary School, which sat at the middle of a huge, sunken grassy lot, blocked in on all four sides by house-filled streets. Like many midwestern schools, Newport looked more like a factory—red brick walls, tiny windows, and a tall, blackened smokestack. Within its walls, I learned to read in the first grade, write cursive in the second, and by the third grade, I'd nearly forgotten about my former life in Alaska.

At Newport, I attended school carnivals at Halloween where I did the cakewalk for a penny and bought homemade candied apples for a nickel. I decided I wanted to be a singer and an actress after I appeared in a school production of *Oklahoma!*

But whatever sense of acceptance I might have otherwise developed in Ironwood and at Newport was shattered that first Christmas, when I was taken out of class to attend a party for underprivileged children. The party was sponsored by an organization that meant well, but didn't realize what it felt like to be singled out from the rest of the class.

We got a turkey dinner and gifts and I was assigned to sit with a man I'd never met. He was a nice person who gave me a white, hooded sweater with wooden buttons. But I felt humiliated when I was returned to class in the middle of the day, everyone knowing where I'd been.

"Underprivileged," in my case, meant I was without parents.

. . .

Within days of arriving in Ironwood, my mother was whisked away to spend the next several years being transferred from one mental hospital to another. I can count the number of times I saw her on the fingers of one hand. My father was simply gone, and I didn't know if I'd ever see him again. Ironwood was my mother's and her family's hometown, but not mine. And whatever hurt I'd experienced at school was only compounded that first Christmas at home.

My mother was there, on leave from the hospital. She chainsmoked the entire evening, tossing the butts into the coal stove. My grandmother rummaged around, muttering in Italian, as uncomfortable as I was. I kept wondering, where was everybody else?

After nightfall, Lena's son, my cousin Chuckie, dressed in a Santa suit and carrying a white bag full of presents, walked through the door. Born deaf, Chuckie spent most of the year at private schools but was always home for the holidays. Dressing as Santa was probably his idea. Despite his disability, he was extremely bright, theatrical, and talented, winning scholastic awards and always being written up in the newspaper.

Chuckie refused to acknowledge who was really behind the beard, as he pranced around the room, handing out presents. I quickly opened mine—a Raggedy Ann doll and a pair of flannel pajamas. I still have the doll. Then he left. How I hated to see him go.

I felt as if my lot had been cast with the undesirables. Regardless of why we were left alone that Christmas by the rest of the family, my child's mind interpreted it to me that I was unwanted.

"Of course you felt that way," said a friend of the family when I returned to Ironwood. "No matter what anybody would have done for you, you would have felt that way because your parents were gone."

There was probably little anybody could have done to have made me feel any different. Almost from day one, I began to express my sense of dislocation and abandonment in the way children do: I became a difficult child. I was a bright student and one of the star readers in first grade, but by second grade, I'd developed speech problems and met regularly with a speech therapist. At home, I threw fierce tantrums and screaming fits, running through the house knocking over chairs and smashing everything within arm's reach.

My cousins were always playing pranks, each of which I took straight to heart. Many years later, a friend, who was also a mother of two small children, pointed out that my sense of vulnerability came from the fact that I had no mother; no one I knew could protect me, run to my aid, chastise other children in my defense. Maybe. I had never thought about it that way.

I developed an intense rivalry with my cousin Christine. Before I arrived, she'd been the only princess in the family kingdom. We became like sisters, yet we fought like cat and dog. We were treated like twins, but I was always aware that we weren't equals. One Easter we posed for a picture in front of my grandmother's house wearing pink dresses, both with our hair in "pixie" cuts. Christine's was professionally done, cut in neat little points around her face; mine looked as if someone had taken a bowl to my head. Christine wore a brand new lace dress; mine, made of cotton, was two years old and I knew the difference.

During my first two years in Ironwood, I lived with my grandmother on Kennedy Street in what was once the family store and the house where my mother had been born and raised. "Kennedy Street"— which reminded me of President Kennedy—had no sidewalks or gutters, and was lined with plain, two-story homes with pitched roofs, small windows, and postage-stamp lawns.

My aunt Lena and her husband Charles, parents of Chuckie and Christine, owned a home a few houses away. Charles worked in the copper mines up north. Aunt Sandra and her husband Joe were bartenders; they and their sons, Bobby and PJ (short for Paul Joseph), lived in an apartment built onto the back of my grandmother's house.

If you stood in my grandmother's yard and yelled loud enough, they could hear you down at Lena's, but that short distance was enough to buffer Lena and her family from the pressures Sandra endured living in the same house as her mother. Sandra always resented the block or two that separated her from her sister and the way she seemed to be the one Marietta leaned on. In the heat of a fight, she'd rail in anger at Lena about her house "down the hill."

Lena's was a handsome home, better looking than most on the street, with an enclosed front porch and a big sloping lawn, the site of many family gatherings.

The backyard of my grandmother's house was filled with the vegetable garden she'd tilled since the girls were born. The house itself, nothing more than a large, rectangular box, had a false front. The back half was made up of the two-story, three-bedroom apartment where Sandra and her family lived. Their apartment was a modest but comfortable home filled with furniture, lace curtains, and ceramic knick-knacks decorating every bare shelf or countertop.

My grandmother's house, though, was a cold, barren place. The living room, dwarfed by an eighteen-foot ceiling, was furnished with only a console black-and-white television, a small couch, and beside the coal stove, a straight-backed wooden chair on which my grandmother sat each night, saying the Rosary in Italian. The room, painted beige, had once housed my grandparents' grocery store, which accounted for the high ceiling and huge picture window that looked out over the street.

Walnut cabinets reaching nearly to the top of the ceiling set off a narrow strip of the living room that my grandmother used as our bedroom. My grandparents had once stocked the shelves with dry goods and canned food; now they stood empty, covered with dust or strips of drying, handmade pasta. The shelves were turned to face the smaller room, where my grandmother and I shared a twin bed, sleeping with her head at one end and mine at the other.

The kitchen was off the back of the living room, alongside a small dining room where narrow stairs, with a white painted railing, led to the second floor. A ceramic wall hanging of the head and arms of the Virgin Mary, her hands clasped in prayer, hung over the dining room table.

There were three bedrooms upstairs but my grandmother preferred to sleep downstairs, as she'd done since my grandfather's death. I hated to sleep alone, so I stayed with her.

Upstairs, a door opened onto a wide hall with a bedroom at each end, including one that used to be my mother's, in the closet of which hung the dresses and furs she brought with her from Alaska. To the left of the hall was a sitting parlor where my grandmother kept her overstuffed red velvet sofa, a richly carved china cabinet filled to capacity, and an ornate Oriental rug—all kept neat and clean, but again, since my grandfather's death, virtually unused. The room seemed to wait for company that never came.

I hated being upstairs, especially if it meant going into my grand-mother's bedroom, which she had turned into a religious shrine. Above the bed she hung a color picture of Jesus wearing the crown of thorns, blood dripping down his face. In one corner was a three-foot-tall statue of St. Anthony, her patron saint. The top of the dresser was stacked with red and clear glass votive candles that flickered day and night before miniature pictures of the saints and the Holy Family. She was a Catholic, and her faith was no different from that of any of her other Italian neighbors. But her room gave me the creeps. One cousin even called it the "Little Vatican."

My grandmother was Old World in so many ways. She washed clothes with a wringer washer, cooked on a wood stove, and canned her own fruits and vegetables, putting them on shelves in the cellar. The house always smelled of simmering tomato sauce and boiling noo-dles. She made everything from scratch, rolling out noodles on the counter in the downstairs bedroom and hanging them to dry on a clothesline. She spent her days in the garden, and almost daily, she'd send me with a colander filled with fresh vegetables to take to all the Italian neighbors: some kindly and sweet little old Italian women and others who lived in homes that smelled of dust and mildew.

Every morning she let me watch *Captain Kangaroo,* although it usually made me late for school. She bought me my favorite cereal, Cheerios, and cooked me my favorite Italian dish, gnocchi. She told me about Italy, explaining that the country was shaped like a woman's boot, and taught me the Italian words for lamb, chicken, and rabbit. And nearly every night, in an animated voice accompanied by lots of arm waving, she recited my favorite children's story, "Peter Rabbit."

My grandmother also had less savory stories—like the one about putting ground glass in the spaghetti they'd give enemy soldiers during World War I. For years, you couldn't get me anywhere near a kitchen where glass had been broken.

Every Sunday my grandmother or Aunt Sandra took me to Mass at St. Ambrose. It seemed a grand palace, mysterious and magical, where I would stare up at the smooth ceramic face and glass eyes of a statue of Mary. "She was the most beautiful woman who had ever lived," my grandmother told me. Enthralled by the movie *The Miracle of Our*

Lady of Fatima, I wanted to see her in person. The Lady of Fatima had appeared atop a bush, so I was particularly observant when alone near bushes. For a brief period, I thought if I was devout enough and declared my desire to become a nun, she might come to me.

Mass at St. Ambrose was like the summer storms that shot across Ironwood, all rolling thunder and sheet lightning. The candles, incense, and Latin incantations enthralled and frightened me. God was with us during Mass, Aunt Sandra once told me. So I spent every Sunday morning on the lookout for Him. He was there somewhere—in a pew, maybe, or in one of the stained glass windows, perhaps hiding in a confessional. At Saturday catechism class I learned by heart the Hail Mary and the Our Father, reciting them each night before I went to bed, praying for my mother.

My father became a distant figure who sent gifts on holidays and birthdays. Once he sent a giant stuffed white dog, meant to be Yukon; on another occasion, a transistor radio wrapped in a royal blue shoe bag. For my seventh birthday, he sent a miniature combination filmstrip and record player with a film depicting the story of Ali Baba and the Forty Thieves. I must have watched it a hundred times, amazed and entranced by the story and colorful images, as much as I was drawn to it because I knew the gift came from my father.

Two years would pass before I saw my father again. During the summer of 1966, he came to Ironwood.

"I'M HEEEERE," I yelled at the top of my lungs as I bounded up the exterior steps of my Aunt Lena's house. My heart was pounding as I reached for the screen door and swung around inside, racing through the porch and front entry hall, running full bore into the living room, where I came to a screeching stop the second I laid eyes on him.

My father was sitting in the corner of the couch.

"Come here and say hello," he said as I entered the living room.

I looked to Lena, who stood across the room, for direction. She nodded, and I sat beside him.

"What happened to all your hair?" he asked.

When we'd left Anchorage my hair had hung past my shoulders in curly ringlets. I explained that during the summer I'd gotten it cut because of the heat. He made some small talk about school, then finally asked, "Would you like to come back to Alaska with me?"

I wanted nothing more. Despite all I had been told about him, I held him up as a hero, someone who would rescue me from my Ironwood exile.

It was an article of faith with my mother's family that the blame for her trips to the psychiatric hospitals lay squarely at my father's feet. They never said this directly to me; I heard the stories and plenty more from neighbors. My mother had started it. When we arrived from Alaska she'd told her family everything: the gambling, my father's hustles, and her whoring. Some of her stories were true, some delusional, and others were fantasy. She claimed that my father got her loaded on drugs and put her on the street to turn tricks, that she'd seen him shoot a man, and that he'd threatened to kill her. The stories spread through the neighborhood like groundwater in a drowned mine, eventually circling back to me. I began to question my love for my father until that day he showed up. Then I knew how I really felt.

He did meet my mother's relatives' expectations in one way. As the story goes, they swear they spotted my father packing a small pistol tucked under his jacket, but no one actually saw him take it out. I can't imagine what he thought he was doing with a gun, if he was really even carrying one. Knowing what my mother's family thought of him, it wouldn't surprise me that they would imagine such a thing.

He and my mother had divorced the September before. Child custody was easy. Despite my mother's history of emotional instability, the courts at that time almost invariably sided with the mother. The financial side was less easy. My father thought my mother's family was trying to steal her money; they thought he was trying to leave her with nothing.

A letter written during their divorce negotiations in May 1965, which Lena saved and gave me, shows that whatever was going on, my father was in deep financial trouble. The letter also offers a unique insight into my father's character.

I once had a police officer tell me that he always thought my father was a bright man who was also a hard worker. "I can't help but think if John may have been able to get a stake and not gamble it away, he probably would have been a successful businessman," the officer said.

The letter is an example of what the policeman was talking about. It shows that my father had good business sense, a quality he rarely capitalized on. Throughout the letter, he expresses himself clearly and his thoughts are well organized. Yet, recognizing my mother's emotional state, he also strives for a personal tone where it counts.

Dear Frances:

Enclosed herewith please find three pieces of paper which require your signature. This loan of $33,000 is to consolidate money already owed to different banks on the property. At this time there is a total of $15,600 owed to the First National Bank, a total of $12,700 owed to the Alaska Mutual Savings Bank and a total of $1,800 owed to the National Bank of Alaska. To pay the water assessments and to get city water put on both pieces of property is going to cost $2,900 which brings the total to $33,000.

The mortgages are delinquent at this time. The reason being that Bob Wilson has not paid me any rent for three months. As soon as I put water in the big house I have a construction company that will lease the property. This will make it possible for us to save the property and in a few years either [sic] be able to sell it. If I do not complete this loan the property will definitely be repossessed by the banks. I think that this big loan is a godsend. I cannot begin to express the urgency of these papers coming back immediately because the Alaska Mutual Savings Bank would like nothing better than to repossess this property causing us to lose every last thing.

If you need to verify with the First National Bank that this money is to pay off all of these outstanding loans you may call Mr. Wayne Young at the First National Bank of Anchorage. If you call him please, but please, do not call collect and do not in any way pester this man concerning the loan because I do not want the bank to back out of making this big loan now. They are a little edgy about making this loan to us due to the fact that my credit rating at this time is very bad.

In about 45 days if you wish to I will send you the money to come to Alaska.

Sincerely and love,

John Rich

P.S. Do not under any circumstances if you call the bank or anyone up here let them know anything about our marital difficulties because as far as the bank is concerned you just went to Michigan to take care of your mother for a few months. If they think there are any marital difficulties between us this loan will be killed instantly.

. . .

During the first day of his visit, everybody was on their best behavior, including my father, who did his best to charm and win over the family. He drove my cousin Christine and me around town in a Mustang convertible he'd rented, taking us out for ice cream and candy.

My mother was even happy to see him, despite everything that she had said about him. She was home on a temporary leave from the hospital when he arrived.

Even my grandmother was a gracious host, letting my father stay at the house and putting him in her bedroom, perhaps hoping that the array of crucifixes and Sacred Bleeding Hearts would work some change.

For dinner that night, Lena recalled that my grandmother made chicken and had everyone over. The next morning, my grandmother was in the living room when Lena stopped by.

"What's the matter?" Lena asked. "Why are you so angry?"

My grandmother said my mother was serving my father breakfast in bed. Incredulous, Lena went upstairs and found my mother on the edge of the bed, smiling as she watched my father eat from a tray in his lap.

"Isn't he handsome?" my mother asked.

Lena turned and stomped out of the room without saying a word.

By the evening of the second day, when my father prepared to leave with me, all hell broke loose. My mother's family had not told my mother of my father's plans to take me back to Alaska. When she heard, she stole the keys to his rented car and drove it to the Ironwood police station. There, she got an officer to call her lawyer, who agreed to meet my mother and a policeman at Lena's house.

I felt bewildered by what was going on as I stood in Lena's living room while my father and the others met in the front entryway. The talk seemed serious. After a few minutes, my father came over and told me I'd have to stay.

He left without incident that night on a flight back to Chicago.

I'd always wondered why my father came and went from Ironwood without a fight. It became apparent to me why many years later when the 150 or so pages of his FBI file arrived in the mail. A quick read made it clear that the last thing my father needed that summer's night in 1966 was more trouble with the law. My father was in the thick of a host of legal troubles, and he didn't need to make matters worse by aggravating law enforcement officials in Michigan.

Five months before he'd gone to Ironwood, he'd been arrested for running a poker game in the house on Fireweed Lane. It was his second gambling arrest in Alaska; the first, which was eventually dismissed, occurred a couple of months after the earthquake, when he was picked up in a raid at another gambling parlor.

For the Fireweed Lane bust, my father posted the five hundred dollars' bail to cover the three counts of illegal gambling and one of unlicensed sale of liquor and assumed his lawyer would quickly dispense with the rest. But the case dragged after him, gradually putting him in the sights of the Federal Bureau of Investigation, which opened a file on him and put him under surveillance. Within a month, agents were sending reports and memoranda to offices in Seattle and Washington, D.C., all asking the same question: Was Johnny Rich a member of the Mob?

"On 1/29/66, officers of the Alaska State Police conducted a raid at 604 Fireweed Lane, Anchorage, Alaska," begins a March 11, 1966, FBI memo at the front of his file. "This location is a gambling house operated by RICH and during the course of the raid, numerous individuals were arrested and charged either with gambling or illegal sale of liquor."

It was really only a matter of time before the FBI got involved. My father had been warring with local police departments since his youth, and in Anchorage, things were no different.

My father hated cops. They were the obstacle that got in the way of everything he tried to do and he'd felt shadowed by them all of his life. His feelings were somewhat justified—sometimes they *were* after him—but then he also had a knack for attracting their attention.

By the mid-sixties, he'd been arrested sixteen times; some were his earlier California arrests, two were from his days managing the Safari, and the rest were for gambling. Most of the time the charges were later dropped, as had occurred in Los Angeles and San Francisco. But then some of the charges were never meant to stick in the first place.

"That was one of the problems with Johnny's relationship with the police in the early years. He always had this very adversarial position," remembered Charlie Audino, now retired, who once walked the 4th Avenue beat where the Safari used to stand.

Audino was first introduced to my father when he came to Anchorage with the army and he and a couple of GI buddies paid a visit to the Safari, a place he described as the closest thing to a Tijuana whorehouse he'd ever seen. "If you wanted, you could wander the halls and whoever was working the desk would open the doors and let you check out the women in there."

Among local cops, my father was known as someone who was trying to act like an Italian gangster. "He'd work harder to steal a nickel than earn a dime," said Audino.

It didn't help matters that my father was also hotheaded and easily goaded into confrontations.

"Johnny was very paranoid—extremely paranoid about the cops," Audino said. "According to him, the cops were always after him. So he used to have a police scanner in his car and one in the whorehouse. Everyplace he went, he had a scanner."

My father, though, almost seemed to enjoy the legal games that followed his arrests. He liked the challenge of trying to beat the rap, and he became well acquainted with the criminal justice system.

I learned this as a teenager one afternoon when my father and I stood looking out the kitchen window of one of his gambling parlors watching a crew of police officers unload a flatbed truck piled high with furniture they'd confiscated in an earlier raid. Police and prosecutors had tried to have a judge order the furniture destroyed, but my father had won the round of legal maneuvering that resulted in the police being forced to return everything they'd taken.

My father stood at the window with a satisfied-looking smirk on his face, enjoying his little victory, watching the officers, several of whom were in civilian dress, clamor around on the back of the truck, crawling over chairs, tables, and sofas, acting like ordinary moving men.

I stood by his side, getting madder and madder. They were treating the furniture like junk, throwing everything off the back of the truck like so many bags of trash. Except for obviously fragile items like ceramic lamps and pictures, they heaved every piece of furniture off the truck onto the dirt driveway below, each setting off a small dust cloud when it landed.

Finally I blurted out, "Can't you do something? Do we have to let them just throw the furniture around?"

My father just shook his head.

"That's exactly what they want me to do," he said. "They want me to get mad and slug a cop. Gambling is just a misdemeanor offense. I pay my fines and it's over. But slug a cop—now there's a charge that'll stick."

One way to get at someone like my father was to entice him into swearing and then arrest him for obscenity, Audino said. Two such charges appear on my father's FBI rap sheet; the first occurred in 1962.

A cop had followed my father home one day, and when my father pulled into his driveway, he jumped out of the car and yelled at the cop, calling him a son of a bitch.

Not only did the officer arrest him for obscenity, but he slapped him with a concealed-weapon charge for a gun he found tucked under my father's jacket (carrying a gun in plain sight is legal in Alaska).

My father's outburst against the officer came as a result of an incident a few days earlier, when he'd found that someone had snapped off the scanner aerial from his Cadillac. He was sure a cop had done it, and openly accused two of them. The officers retaliated one day by parking their squad car near the Safari and talking as if they were going to rip off my father's new replacement aerial, then roared with laughter when my father came boiling out the backdoor.

It was the same technique they used to harass him at his gambling houses. They'd park nearby and talk into their radios, pretending to be preparing for a raid, then sit back and laugh as everyone came bolting out the door, jumping into their cars and speeding off.

"We'd do anything to get a reaction," Audino said. "He was more or less somebody we used to enjoy screwing with, but as time went on he wised up quite a bit."

The latter seemed to be the case the day my father appeared before District Court Judge Richard "Rip" Collins for his trial on the obscenity and concealed-weapon charges. His lawyer was Joe Josephson.

Josephson was not long out of law school, full of ideals and determined to win his first big criminal case. He'd met my father while working in John Hellenthal's law office. Josephson went to work for Hellenthal after a three-year stint in Washington, D.C., working as an aide to Alaska U.S. senator and renowned statesman E. L. "Bob" Bartlett. Josephson liked my father, both men were the same age, and when Josephson decided to open his own practice in 1961, my father became one of his first clients.

"He always aspired to respectability," recalled Josephson. "In a way he liked the notoriety, but I think in another way I would read him as wanting to be a respectable person. I always had this feeling that if he could figure out a way to live at the standard he wanted to live at as a respectable citizen, he would have done it."

For his first big case, Josephson hired an expert witness, an English professor from Alaska Methodist University, to establish the literary merit of the phrase "son of a bitch." He intended to have the professor testify at length, perhaps filling up the entire morning session. His plans were dashed when Judge Collins didn't bite. He told Josephson he didn't need any professor telling him what was obscene and what wasn't. He refused to let the expert testify and found my father guilty, leaving the concealed-weapon charge yet to be tried.

Just before noon, the arresting officer began his testimony by trying to describe how my father had been carrying his .38 revolver. Judge Collins was having a hard time following the witness and adjourned for lunch, asking that my father return that afternoon with the leather jacket he'd been wearing the day he was arrested.

After lunch, the police officer returned to the stand. Judge Collins ordered my father to the front of the courtroom for a demonstration.

"Is this the jacket Mr. Rich was wearing?" Judge Collins asked the officer.

"Yes, it appears to be so, Your Honor," he replied.

"Would you zip the jacket, Mr. Rich, in the way the zipper was the night in question?"

My father obliged.

"Does that look like the way the zipper was?" Judge Collins asked. "Yes it does, Your Honor," the officer said, with a puzzled look on his face.

"Mr. Rich, would you march to my right?" Collins asked. My father did so. "Now would you march to my left."

"Well," Judge Collins said, "it's evident to me that the butt handle of the gun can be seen by the naked eye. I'm acquitting Mr. Rich of the concealed weapons charge."

And that was that.

Josephson felt victorious. As he stood packing papers into his briefcase, he had fantasies of himself being the next Clarence Darrow. *This courtroom stuff is easy and I'm a very gifted advocate,* he thought to himself.

As he and my father were walking out of the courtroom, my father turned to Josephson.

"What a crazy lunch hour I had," he said.

"What do you mean?" Josephson asked.

"I had to run over to Northern Commercial Company and find the identical jacket, one size smaller," my father said. "I almost couldn't find one."

Josephson stopped dead in his tracks, dumbfounded by what he'd just heard. He'd had no idea my father had pulled a switch. Josephson wouldn't have allowed such a stunt—it was tantamount to submitting perjured testimony, illegal and grounds for court sanctions and a possible disbarment.

"The jacket that he wore when the officer saw him was home hanging in his closet. And believe me, that was naturally his own idea. I hadn't a clue. It was just a shock to me. It was very deflating to my ego."

My father expected the 1966 gambling arrest to end in victory as well.

Ever since the Safari disappeared in the quake, he'd returned to gambling full-time for his livelihood. The bank moved to foreclose on the houses and he had no other means of support. He tried renting our old house out for a while, but when the renters moved out, he decided to take his best shot, and converted the place into an after-hours joint.

He was continuing Alaska's oldest tradition: prospering from adversity. The earthquake may have devastated much of south central Alaska, but it also brought a floodtide of federal aid, including 3-percent disaster relief loans for many of the property owners whose homes were destroyed. More than a little of the loan money found its way onto the tables at places like my father's, which also were attracting the attention

of the rejuvenated local police and a vice squad run by the Alaska State
Police, who had a lot more energy and muscle than the Territorial
Police they replaced.

According to court records regarding the case, for at least a month
before the raid, the state police officers cased my former childhood
home, recording license plate numbers and sending informers inside.

At six A.M. on January 29, a pair of troopers in mufti took a cab to
the house and knocked on the door. A blond hostess peered at them
through a mirrored peephole set in the middle of the front door, then
let them inside. They ordered drinks, and asked about getting into a
poker game. The waitress directed them to a room where they found
my father at the head of the table, ready to start dealing. One of the
plainclothesmen asked what it would cost to get in the game.

"One hundred dollars with a fifty-dollar minimum," my father said.

The policeman sat down, ordered fifty dollars in chips, and joined
in a game of five-card stud. His companion sat in the other room
counting the house and making mental note of such details as the bartender "mixing drinks." A few minutes later, there was a pounding at
the door. The hostess slid open the peephole.

Several of the officers outside were new to vice, and were unsure of
what it was they were supposed to say. When the woman's face appeared, one tried the friendly approach.

"You know me," he said. "Open the door."

The woman slammed the peephole shut and ran to get my father.
When he appeared at the opening, the officer repeated the same line,
at which point a more experienced policeman stepped forward and said
the magic words: *"We are the police. We have a search warrant."*

My father turned from the door, and a second later someone inside
the house shouted, *"Raid!"*

The troopers and assistant district attorneys positioned outside began
battering at the door. A cop blew a blast on a police whistle.

"Hide the money," my father told the hostess, then started for the
cash register when one of the plainclothesmen blocked his path.

At the whistle the trooper in the card room identified himself and
ordered everyone to remain seated. The raiders arrested my father and
a few others, then began taking the place apart, preparing to confiscate
the contents of the house, as is routine in such cases. Several of the
troopers hoisted the bar; when they did, they found a car battery rigged

for use with magnetized dice—bad news for my father's customers, but even worse news for him. The police brought in a photographer to record the scam, and sent pictures off to the newspapers. The police figured the best way to put a gambler out of business was to show everybody he was a cheat.

The pictures of the rigged table left my father bitter. He claimed he'd bought the bar with the battery already hooked up but never used it—an unlikely story. As long as my father had been running gambling houses, he'd been altering the odds. Evidently, no one seemed to mind.

"The next day, or two days, he was back in business," said one Anchorage gambler. "The same people that had seen the photo of the battery in the paper were playing with him again because he was so entertaining. He was a unique person, people liked him. It didn't matter. They were being entertained. They were laughing about it."

But material in his FBI file suggests that gambling was something of a way station until my father's other plans came together. He wanted to go into real estate.

Right after the quake, he'd applied for a disaster relief loan to construct an apartment building. More than a few fortunes were built following the earthquake by those able to snag some of the federal money. The program worked for the politically connected as well as average families and business owners. And of course, if you were a member of the former, you did a little better than the rest.

My father hadn't owned the Safari, so he couldn't get in on the money tide engulfing ruined business owners in the 4th Avenue slide zone, but the Small Business Administration was more flexible, and agreed to lend him $65,000 for his apartment idea. The loan, however, went on hold when a background check turned up a rape charge.

My father was outraged when told this. The accounting of this episode in his FBI file reflects his anger and humiliation as he stormed into the local FBI office, demanding to know who had told the SBA such a thing.

He explained to one of the agents on duty that the closest he'd come to a rape was the time one of my teenage babysitters was assaulted by her boyfriend and my father was the one to call the police. (I remember the incident. The boyfriend had driven up to the house and my babysitter went to sit with him in his car. The only other thing I remember is my father and a police officer questioning me later about what I'd seen, which wasn't much.)

The FBI agent took notes and told my father he'd be in touch. The next day he called my father back. The agent didn't outright admit that the bureau had made a mistake; instead he offered several suggestions as to how my father might correct the situation.

"It was suggested that he advise SBA officials to re-contact sources in Washington, D.C. concerning him to determine his involvement in the 4/62 incident in Anchorage," the agent's notes say. "Or he could suggest to the SBA officials, since the matter was a local matter, the SBA can review the records of local law enforcement agencies for the complaint and facts of the incident in which he is allegedly involved."

My father never got the loan.

In May 1966, my father went on trial for the gambling arrest at the house on Fireweed Lane. After four days of testimony, he and three other men were convicted. My father was sentenced to three months in jail and a one-thousand-dollar fine. Josephson appealed on the grounds that the search warrant was illegal because it hadn't been served during daylight, as specified by the warrant. He pointed out that the raid occurred at 6:30 A.M., well before that day's 8:28 sunrise. He lost his appeal to a superior court judge who wasn't impressed. "Alaska is unique since in some areas there is little daylight during the winter months and much daylight in the summer months," he said. "It is common knowledge that gambling and sale of illegal liquor rarely occur during daylight hours."

Not long afterward, the FBI decided that my father wasn't tied to the Mob and closed his case. But before doing so, my father volunteered for a final interview. A typed, one-page memo of the meeting begins by stating that my father "admitted being identical with the John Francis Rich arrested by the Alaska State Police . . ."

From that point on, my father took command of the interview, refusing to be intimidated. He explained his knowledge of federal gaming laws, then added that "he was well acquainted with the Federal Anti-gambling statutes and feels that he is not stupid enough to knowingly violate these laws." My father concluded the interview by admitting that he was "a well known gambler and that any equipment or paraphernalia that he needs in his gambling activities can be purchased at numerous stores in Anchorage."

When he made the trip to Michigan, my father was in the middle of taking his case to the Alaska Supreme Court. He was out on a post-conviction bond and couldn't afford any more trouble. As soon as he returned to Anchorage he called Josephson's office and left a message with the secretary. She wrote up a note and stuck it in my parents' divorce file.

"7/28/66—Mr. Rich in. Has just returned from Mich [sic] where he went in response to a call from ex-wife's relatives that child was being badly neglected. Expected to take child with him but was stopped by wife's atty. Is going to move for custody."

Me reunited with my dad, spending a winter's day at the Bird House Bar in 1967

CHAPTER SEVEN

LIFE WITH FATHER

Sometime after my father's visit to Ironwood, my grandmother's health began to fail and she died the following spring. During my last winter in Ironwood, I moved in with my mother's sister Sandra and her family, becoming the daughter Sandra always wanted, and I began to feel more at home.

I hardly ever saw my mother and that may have been for the best. It had become too painful to be around her. Once my aunts took me to a hospital where she was staying. I wasn't allowed to go into her room and was forced to view her through banks of windows. If I stood on my toes, I could see her lying in bed, her black hair contrasting sharply with the white sheets. All of my contacts with her were like this: full of mystery, barriers—real and imagined ones.

During my last visit with her, when I was nine, she was staying in a nursing home—a white Victorian building in downtown Ironwood with a wide porch across the front. I'm not sure who made the plans, but I was to get her and we were to walk to the theater a few blocks away to see a Walt Disney movie.

The lobby of the nursing home smelled all sweet and flowery, like the odors in the funeral parlor where my grandmother had been laid out in an open casket only a few weeks earlier. I passed several old women in wheelchairs, then climbed the stairs to my mother's room. The room, drenched in sunlight, was bare except for a small bed and a chair where my mother sat. She reached for me as I came through the door. I went to her, she hugged me and began to cry.

I pulled away. She kept reaching for me and trying to stroke my hair, her hands trembling each time she touched me. I wanted to get to the movie and I didn't want to stay in that place a minute longer. *If we just went to the movie, maybe everything would be okay, maybe she'd stop weeping.*

We never went to the movie. My mother didn't want to waste our visit inside of a darkened theater. Instead, she took me downstairs for lunch in the dining room, a big, high-ceilinged space with pale yellow enameled walls. All around sat elderly men and women; some of them were polite and sweet as my mother proudly introduced me. *I was her daughter, see? I had come to visit her. Isn't that nice?*

I left that day telling myself that when I turned sixteen—for some reason that was the age that came to mind—I would take her out of such places and care for her myself. My child's reasoning told me that all she needed was someone to love her. For a long time I believed it could be that simple.

Soon after my visit, Aunt Sandra made it clear why I'd been sent to her: It was to say good-bye. "Your father has sent for you," she said a couple of days later. "You're going to live with him in Alaska." Sandra was heartbroken, but we both agreed that my place was with my father.

I hadn't been told before the visit to my mother for fear I would tell her. No one wanted a repeat of what had happened the last time my father had tried to take me. That spring, my mother was on the brink of being permanently institutionalized. An affidavit signed by my father in my parents' divorce file indicates that a few months earlier, in March, she told him over the phone that she had no idea where I was.

I have recently talked to my former wife, FRANCES ANN RICH. She states that she does not know the whereabouts of our child, KIM MAUREEN RICH. On information and belief, KIM MAUREEN RICH is being cared for at the Divine Infants Hospital, Wakefield, Michigan. This child is not with her mother as the decree of divorce contemplated she would be. Defendant desires to have custody of the child awarded to him by modification of the decree, or in the alternative to have a welfare investigation undertaken by the Alaska Department of Health and Welfare, with the cooperation of Michigan authorities.

I had never been placed in any hospital, but that didn't matter. Within a few weeks, the courts awarded my father custody. Joe Josephson remembered how rare it was at that time for a father to seek custody of a child, especially a man with a criminal record.

"It was very sincere on his part," he said. "Sometimes people come into your office and they are in a custody battle in which the child is incidental. The child is just a pawn and they're just angry at each other and they're in a power struggle. I didn't really get that impression with Johnny. My impression was that he really wanted to have custody."

Everybody who knew my father says the same thing: My father *wanted* to be a father. But aside from what would be considered the obvious reasons, no one could really tell me why. I've always known that my father loved me, but what would move a thirty-four-year-old man who'd spent the better part of his life living as a bachelor—coming and going as he pleased and never having to worry about anybody but himself—to want to take on the responsibility of parenthood?

I found the answer in a box of aging records, in a basement storage vault in the State of Connecticut Department of Children and Youth Services. There, in a file marked *John Francis Galenski,* is the only documentation of my father's childhood, spent as a ward of the state. Like my own, his childhood was filled with repeated abandonments and adults who couldn't be depended on.

The file opens with a note from his social worker telling of the difficulty in finding a home to take him when he was first turned over to state authorities at one and a half years old. The first two homes he went to turned him back, complaining that he cried too much. A third family that already had three foster children eventually took him in, and would end up keeping him throughout his early childhood.

There is no description of the home, or of the parents, or even where they lived, except that it was somewhere in Connecticut, probably around Hartford.

A medical report in the file tells of a despairing and physically troubled boy. He suffered from a host of childhood maladies, including rheumatic fever, and until age seven he wet the bed. His social worker describes him as an emotionally needy child who "likes to be a leader and doesn't always play well with other children. He loves affection from anyone."

Other behavioral problems brought the foster family—whose name was blackened out in the records to protect their identity—to the point of wanting to give him up.

"This is about John. I would like to have you get him another home," the foster mother wrote in the first of three lengthy letters to his social worker in autumn 1940. The handwritten letters contain a litany of complaints and insights into my father's character.

"He does not get along at all with the other three children . . . at school, Teacher [sic] tells me the same thing," the foster mother wrote. "He is very selfish and jealous. It is his nature I suppose.

"I rec'd [sic] a letter again yesterday about stealing milk money in School from the Teacher also he tore a little Girls umbrella . . . I can't understand it . . . I do more explaining but just does not do any good. And he is no fool, he knows too much."

In order to avoid a heartrending confrontation, the foster mother asked that my father be allowed to stay until he made his first Holy Communion in October, which he did. She wanted his removal from the home to coincide with the family's anticipated move into a new house. That way, she surmised, it might ease my father's sense of being deserted.

"It's a good time now while I have an excuse of moving," she wrote. "I will tell him that I've got to do it on account of so much work in moving. He would not feel so bad telling him we have got to do this for—a-while [sic] . . . I don't like to say this but its [sic] better then [sic] to have him cry his eyes out . . . it will not break his heart so much as he will be expecting to come home later."

For whatever reason, the foster parents changed their minds and decided to keep my father.

While my father lived in the foster home, his mother came and went from his life. She moved from one Connecticut mill town to another, working as a maid, a factory assembler, and a store clerk. She visited her son once a month, bringing sacks of new clothes she carried with her on the bus.

"She keeps John looking very nice," his foster mother wrote his social worker in 1942. "His clothes are grand."

The foster mother and Helen became close friends, writing and talking frequently. The foster mother once described Helen as a "good girl who has had a hard time of it." On several occasions, Helen even asked the foster mother to adopt John, but never carried through on her request. My father remained a ward of the state until Helen's failed marriage to Ziggie Wolanski.

Young Johnny Rich never really *had* a father; he was probably determined that no kid of his would ever go without one. Nothing meant more to me then, or now, than my father's choosing to have custody of me. His devotion seemed apparent from the moment I arrived at Anchorage International Airport in the early summer of 1967.

The six-hour, nonstop flight from Chicago to Anchorage seemed endless. Since I was traveling alone, the stewardesses had sat me near the galley, where they could keep an eye on me. Throughout the trip, they kept bringing me things—peanuts, coloring books, and a deck of playing cards; anything to keep me in my seat.

During much of the flight I visited with a couple of college-aged men who sat next to me, telling them over and over how I was going to Alaska to live with my father. I told them about Yukon, our old house, and the earthquake, but mostly I talked about my father. I hadn't seen him since his visit to Ironwood the previous year, and I'd been gone from Alaska for three years, but I had some definite ideas about who I thought he was.

"My dad is rich," I said. "He has lots of money and he sent me lots of gifts."

The men just nodded and smiled at this and my other nine-year-old pronouncements. In between our conversations and catnaps, they endured a couple of rounds of Old Maid and Go Fish. Throughout most of the flight I felt a combination of boredom, anticipation, and worry. Would I recognize my father? What was my life going to be like? I was so worked up by the time the plane landed, I would have run for the door had it not been for the people in front of me.

I must have been quite a sight as I scampered down the boarding ramp, my arms full of stuffed animals and dolls. Behind me a stewardess, who walked me off the plane, also carried an armload. I kept straining to see around the line of passengers in front of me, craning my neck from side to side, hoping for a glimpse of my father inside the terminal at the end of the walkway. Just before passing through the door, I finally spotted him. I recognized him instantly.

He was leaning against a wall just a few feet away, a jacket slung over his arm and a toothpick in his mouth. I felt elated as I walked toward him.

"You still my girl?" he asked, and he wrapped one arm around me as I ran up to him. I smiled.

After speaking briefly with the flight attendant, my father grabbed some of my toys, and we went and collected my luggage. From there, we headed to the airport cafeteria for glasses of milk and a shared tuna sandwich. As we sat at the counter, he hardly spoke; instead, he just kept looking at me. I, on the other hand, just kept babbling away; I was nervous, excited, and extremely happy. I felt something that day I hadn't felt in a long time—I felt like I belonged.

That first day back was filled with joy. In the car was my old friend, Yukon, who spent the trip into town nuzzling my head from his station in the backseat. During the drive, I remember how my father laughed aloud when I asked why all the trees had been burned.

"They grow that way," he said of the spindly-looking black spruce that grow plentifully in the swamplands upon which much of Anchorage is built. To celebrate our new start, my father took me clothes-shopping at Caribou Ward's—the local name for Anchorage's Montgomery Ward.

The store was the height of shopping in Anchorage for many years. Built not long after statehood, it anchored the east end of the Northern Lights Shopping Center, a long, enclosed strip mall. The store's biggest attraction was its escalator, the first ever installed in Alaska. It went up only one story, but local kids would come from across town and line up just to ride it. I was four the last time I'd been there and had my photograph taken on Santa's lap. A newspaper photographer was also there and took his own picture, which ran in the paper along with about a half dozen shots of other children. "HEY, MOM" was the caption that appeared beneath my picture. My mother, of course, saved a copy and neatly folded it into my baby book.

My dad and I rode the escalator to the second floor, where the little girls' department was located. From the moment I pulled a pair of pedal pushers off the shelf, it became obvious that my father was out of his element. He couldn't understand why I wouldn't want a pair of pants with legs that extended all the way to the floor.

"But *Daaad,*" I whined.

With that, my father flagged down the nearest saleslady, who I then kept in tow as I rummaged through the department. My father stood to the side, shrugging his shoulders every time I asked his opinion.

"You're the boss," he'd say, and then turn to the sales clerk. "Yeah, sure, sure. That's fine. We'll take it."

By the time I was through, I'd picked out several pairs of pants, including a tangerine orange pair of pedal pushers, several shirts, and a navy blue sweater—my only concession to my father.

"It gets cold here," he said. "You're going to need it."

We climbed back in the car and we went to Paul's Salon for my very first visit to a beauty parlor. No more home haircuts for this kid.

"What would you like us to do, Johnny?" Paul asked my father as he spun me and examined my hair.

"I don't know. Do whatever you think is best," my father said. "I'll be back in an hour."

As soon as he left, Paul sent me to a hairdresser, who went to work snipping, teasing, and spraying, with me agreeing to everything. When my father returned, I looked like a country music singer, with my hair swept up into a bouffant with ringlets cascading down the back.

For dinner that night we began what would become *our* family tradition—dining out. My father didn't cook, even though he knew how to keep house. He was tidy, and was one of the few men I've ever met who regularly scrubbed the bathroom. But aside from toast and TV dinners, I'd never seen him get anywhere near an oven or put together a meal.

"Who's this?" the owner of La Cabaña, one of Anchorage's oldest Mexican restaurants, asked my father as we sat in one of the booths. "This can't possibly be that little, itty-bitty girl I remember."

My father laughed.

"Yeah, it looks like she sprung up, but not much."

And there we sat, just my father and me having dinner, a scene that would be repeated countless times in the years ahead.

After dinner, we went to my father's house. If I'd had any doubts about his status in the world they would have vanished the moment I laid eyes on where he was living. It was simply the biggest house I'd ever seen: a spacious, brand new, two-story home at the base of the Chugach Mountains.

I loved the feel of the nearly empty living room and its banks of windows with their panoramic view of the mountains. The house had all the latest in design, appliances, and home furnishings: recessed lighting, a large wooden deck off the living room, mirrored closet doors, even a master bedroom with its own bathroom and outdoor deck. I spent half of my first night scurrying up and down the stairs, exploring every nook and cranny.

As soon as I settled down and unpacked, my father and I planted ourselves in front of the television in what would become another familiar scene in our family life. Just the two of us, watching television, usually in silence, but always together. Sometimes Yukon would take up the middle.

Thus began my life with my bachelor, gambler father.

At the grocery store, we would hold long debates at the frozen food counter over which TV dinners to buy: steak or turkey? The small, rounded chicken pot pies? Or the larger variety that took a whole forty-five minutes to cook? Whatever we decided on, it'd be two of everything—two turkey pot pies, two meatloaf dinners, two spaghetti and meatballs, two whatevers. As far as I was concerned, if a meal wasn't ready in twenty-five minutes or delivered on a tray, it wasn't a meal.

Sunday afternoons were our "Family Day." Sometimes we'd spend the day at Big Lake. Other Sundays were spent catching a matinee and going to dinner. Our other family activity was to go to the auction.

My father was both extravagant and cheap. While others remember him as someone who was always quick with a loan and who never talked or complained about money, I remember that he seemed to think of nothing else. Once when he was hospitalized for a hernia operation, I bought him what I thought was the perfect get-well card. "You can certainly expect a lot of sympathy from me," it said; "besides, it's cheaper than flowers."

Like any gambler, sometimes he had it and other times he didn't. Early on I learned to dread asking him for money. He'd either angrily snap at me if funds were low or he'd open his wallet and hand me any amount I wanted. Aside from his expensive cars and clothes, nearly all the things he owned were auction-house bargains. On Sunday, we'd hit the Pacific Auction.

For a man who preferred to drive only Cadillacs, it's hard to figure why my father was so attached to the one-story, red, oversized house that was home to Anchorage's biggest and most popular auction. This wasn't a place where original works of art and the contents of millionaire estates were sold off. This was an Everyman's Auction, where surplus military gear and basement leftovers attracted as much bidding as the occasional diamond ring, the casualty of someone's recent divorce.

I think my father liked the process of bidding on something—and beating someone else out of it—as much as he used the auctions as a cheap way to furnish his gambling houses and even our homes. The latter became a never-ending source of frustration for me. If it fit through the doors at the auction, chances were good it'd end up in our house, from cases of bananas ("eat them quick before they rot") and cans of corned beef hash to safes, lamps, and stereos. We were such regulars that my father didn't need one of the white cards with numbers stenciled in black, the first thing newcomers grabbed when they walked in. All my father had to do was raise his hand.

If he could get it cheap, he'd buy it—sometimes I think it didn't matter what it might be.

Like the mynah bird he picked up once. Always wanted an exotic bird, he told me. Besides, it was too good a deal to pass up. But the black bird didn't talk. Instead, it squawked, twenty-four hours a day. Drove us both nuts. My father finally covered the bird's cage with a blanket and crammed it into a closet. Even then you could still hear it. Within a week the mynah was gone.

"I gave it to a friend," my father said sheepishly when I asked what had happened to the bird. "I told him the bird could talk."

Sunday evenings were often spent at a bar called The Pines, where we'd go to catch the children's show of a nightclub hypnotist named "Belonte."

Belonte, whose newspaper advertisements called him the "World's Greatest Hypnotist," was a popular performer in Anchorage in the late

1960s. He had a pencil-thin mustache, wore his light-brown hair combed into a pompadour, and dressed in crimson lamé dinner jackets. His adult show included having the hypnotized participants prance around the stage like roosters—or he'd tell them that they were nude, or that the members of the audience were nude. The children's show was considerably less risqué, but no less silly, with the children told to act like trained seals or pretend their seats were on fire. At the end, one of the boys would be selected, handed a guitar, and told he was Elvis Presley. Then he'd be escorted to center stage, and over the speakers would play a scratchy recording of "All Shook Up."

Without fail, when Belonte asked for children to volunteer for the show, my father would nudge me out of my seat. I agreed, hoping maybe that night Belonte would pick a girl to be Elvis.

It seems I grew up in nightclubs. During that first summer, my father often took me with him while he made his nightclub rounds. Usually I waited in the car, listening to his eight-track tapes. Whenever I'd ask what he was doing, he'd always answer, "Little girls are meant to be seen and not heard."

Occasionally he'd take me inside, and I remember the first time I ever walked into a topless bar, a tiny place called the Sand Box, located in a part of town called Sand Lake. As we walked up to the door, I sensed it was not like the jukebox bars Aunt Sandra could feel comfortable taking the family to in Ironwood. On the door was a sign that read NO MINORS. When I pointed it out to my father, he just chuckled.

"We don't work in a mine," he said, as he pushed open the door.

Inside, he led me to a corner of the bar and ordered me a Coke, while he talked to the bartender. I drank my soda quietly, embarrassed and trying to avoid looking across the room to where a nude woman danced on a small stage.

Probably for reasons like the above, by fall I learned that my father had only been granted a provisional custody by the court. Just before school began, he told me that I'd only be allowed to live with him on the weekends. Until he'd proven himself a stable parent, I would be staying with a family of his choice and one deemed acceptable by the court.

Welcome to the household of Tuck Hurn, Sr.

. . .

There were two things you never did in the presence of John "Tuck" Hurn in his own home: You never tossed a hat onto the bed, and you never, ever took out a broom and started sweeping. A hat on the bed was bad luck; the touch of a broom doomed you to an arrest.

Tuck acquired these gambler's laws somewhere between the potato fields in Tennessee where he learned his trade and the northern shores of Cook Inlet, where he built Anchorage's—and one of Alaska's—biggest underworld empire.

Every professional gambler has his little list of superstitions. Tuck disliked peanuts in the shell, believing them to carry bad luck. This was hard on his wife, Jean, who loved to eat peanuts at baseball games back home in Nashville. Since Tuck usually attended ball games only to see whether his bets would fly, she'd have to leave him and sit on the other side of the stands to crunch a few nuts.

Tuck's gambling houses had equally strict rules: no cheats, no drugs, no violence. No married man ever left flat broke; if a man's money was gone, Tuck shooed him from the table, gave him a sawbuck, and sent him on his way.

Tuck also made his money running a numbers racket that was played mainly by the blacks of Anchorage. The numbers in Alaska was like the numbers everywhere—a player bet as little as a dime or a quarter and wrote a three-digit number on a pad kept by the neighborhood policy man. Once a day, the policy man handed over his slips and his cash to a runner or "bag man," who took them to the headquarters. The numbers were drawn from a set of capsules containing the numbers zero to ten. The order in which they were drawn determined the day's winning number. The number paid off five hundred to one, which meant a dime played would return fifty dollars; a dollar, five hundred dollars.

Tuck had figured out a way to minimize the aggravation from the cops when it came to his gambling houses. He pitched his games mostly at the town's older, established businessmen, which made the joints nearly bulletproof.

It might take three months to work up to a raid of a Tuck Hurn house; plainclothes officers would have to spend months hanging out and becoming familiar with the right people, and once in on the action, had to spend heavily—this wasn't the beer-and-a-whistle sort of bust that my father had gotten caught in.

Tuck's clients came mostly by invitation. He ran a continuous high-stakes poker game at the "Step-and-a-Half Ranch." The "ranch" was one of Tuck's card parlors set up in a boarded-up old farmhouse located in a wooded area east of 5th Avenue, near the Glenn Highway. Despite its dilapidated exterior, the front door opened to reveal a first-class mini-casino outfitted with poker and blackjack tables, craps tables, a bar, and a jukebox. The ranch even had matchbooks made with its name stamped across the cover. Each night, the ruined farmhouse was surrounded by a steady parade of cars, many belonging to card players who regularly participated in games where up to $100,000 a night changed hands.

An old-school criminal who lived by the phrase "Honor among thieves," Tuck had his own set of rules for the law.

One time, Anchorage police chief Earl Hibpshman led a raid on a room of Tuck's located downstairs from a restaurant. He and his boys went in with warrants, arrested everyone, and began to confiscate the furnishings—until they realized someone had tossed all the cash into a safe and locked it.

Chief Hibpshman asked Tuck to open the safe. Tuck refused. As usually happened on gambling raids, the police had brought along a judge for just such a turn of events. The judge wrote out a search warrant and Hibpshman sent for the police locksmith.

The safe cracker arrived and went to work. While they waited, Hibpshman, a few of his subordinates, and Tuck Hurn sat down for a friendly game of pinochle. They ran through a few melds, time wore on, and the safe still wasn't open.

Anchorage was a small town, and even smaller when you started subtracting the people who didn't break the law. Tuck Hurn and Earl Hibpshman had been bumping up against each other for years.

"Why don't you do something legitimate for a living?" the chief asked once.

"I'm a professional gambler," Tuck said. "I'm going to keep gambling."

"Well, Tuck," Hibpshman said, "you know what I do."

"Yeah, I know," Hurn answered. "But you'll never get me for the same mistake twice."

So far that had been the case, but Hibpshman's patience was running out.

"Tuck, will you just open the safe?" Chief Hibpshman finally asked.

Tuck smiled. "Nooooo," he said in his molasses drawl as he peered over the tops of the cards in his hand. "I could . . . but it's against my principles."

It took some time, but the safe was eventually opened.

Born in a backwoods Tennessee town but raised in Nashville, at sixteen, Tuck Hurn headed for New York City, where he put in time as a soda jerk and worked for bookies. He returned to Nashville in the late thirties to run gambling houses and bootleg joints until World War II, when he served as an airplane mechanic.

"His rank went up and down like an elevator," recalled his wife Jean. "One time I'd get a letter, he was a sergeant. The next time, it'd be corporal, private or something because he was always being busted for something, gambling, being late for roll call—you name it."

After the war, Hurn set up shop again in Nashville, running card games. The operation worked well provided that when he was raided, his case went before a judge, who, like some of the beat cops, was paid off with so-called ice money. But federal agents who swept through town in a vice cleanup in the early fifties weren't as agreeable. They chased Tuck out. He'd heard Alaska was a good place for gambling and prostitution. In 1951, he moved to Kenai and started a bordello, only a few miles from a small army post. From there on Tuck Hurn kept getting richer.

Tuck's wife, Jean, had married him in Nashville, but divorced him fifteen years later for cheating on her and for knocking her around. As she puts it, when the war ended he came home and "tried to drink up all the whiskey Seven Crown was making."

While they were apart, she converted to Catholicism and clung to the faith with a convert's passion. She sent their six children to Catholic schools and worked at a church-owned hospital as a nurse. She didn't approve of Tuck's life in Alaska. Gambling was one thing; prostitution was another.

Tuck married again, got divorced, thought about his prospects, and sent for Jean. By this time he was out of prostitution and well established in his Anchorage gambling business.

Tuck needed Jean for more than a few reasons. Some of their older children had moved to Anchorage to be with him. He needed someone to manage the household, which also included twin baby girls by his second wife.

Jean thought it over and accepted Tuck's offer of a three-month trial run. She never went back to Nashville, even though she never remarried Tuck. "One time was enough," she later said.

Tuck is said to have liked my father from the moment he saw him driving his white Cadillac and talking on its car phone. He was also impressed with how my father figured out a way to tack the fee for the prostitutes who did business at the Safari onto his customers' credit cards by calling it "room service."

"He was the first guy to introduce credit cards in the business," said one of Tuck's sons. "Daddy loved John's guts and brashness. He called him a 'good kid,' and he was the only business partner the old man invited over to the house. Your father became his protégé."

It was for that reason that my father asked Tuck if he would board me at his house over the school year.

"What difference will one more make?" Jean responded when Tuck asked if I could live with them for the winter.

The beginning of my fourth grade school year I moved into the Hurns', sharing a room downstairs with their twin girls. Two other older sisters also lived in the home. The other children, three boys, stopped by continually. The house was always full of people.

Despite Hurn's gambling empire, home was home. Around the Hurn house, life was no different than at any of the other spacious split-level homes in the new subdivision in Sand Lake, where Tuck and his family lived. The kids went to school, the moms stayed home; the only difference between the Hurn household and some of the others was that the Hurns were southerners, with polite, southern ways.

At the Hurns', I was taught to address my elders as "sir" and "ma'am" and not to sass them, lest I get a swift swat on the bottom. I learned to like southern cooking—hominy grits for breakfast and chicken fried steak or fried chicken for dinner.

The Hurn household ran on a short leash. The twins and I had to be in bed on school nights by nine P.M. We each had chores to do and we washed the dishes every night after dinner. Once I asked if we could get an automatic dishwasher; Jean just laughed. "Honey, I've already got a dishwasher, in fact I got three of 'em."

Weekends became a time of seesawing emotions. I didn't mind it at the Hurns, but I longed to be with my father and I lived for Friday night when he'd pick me up. But as the winter wore on, it became apparent that my father led a fast life and that it was going to be difficult for me to keep up.

He was constantly in motion and everything was always changing. Nothing was permanent except him, and he was like quicksilver. During my first year back, he ended up moving four times.

When I first arrived, he was living in the large house near the mountains. Without explanation, he moved out of the house by summer's end, then into a succession of three different apartments. Moving quickly became a way of life. In later years, we moved almost every six months, from apartment to house to apartment, with my father haphazardly orchestrating every change of address, and me left packing and unpacking the boxes.

We left furniture behind the way other people leave worn-out clothing. The only items we kept, other than the color television, were a few things from Fireweed Lane and my father's treasured dining room table.

The table's top, nearly four feet in diameter, had a shiny, reflective surface of fake walnut. I discovered the table's true value one day when I tugged on the top. It lifted off, and beneath was the green baize of a padded poker table. He'd had it custom-made and it must have cost a small fortune.

My only insight into how my father made his living came in the stacks of poker chips kept in his closets. His favorite bath towel was imprinted with the image of a craps table. Once I found him washing dollar bills in the kitchen sink of one of the apartments he'd moved to, and then taking the currency in a cloth sack to the laundry room for a spin in one of the dryers.

"I like clean money" was all he would say when I asked what he was doing. (A former undercover police officer who used to raid my father's gambling houses explained that my father was probably washing away the marking powder used by the vice squad to raid his joints.)

But more troubling than the constant moving and the odd things my father did were the hours he kept.

The first time he left me home alone at night occurred one of the first weekends I went to stay with him that fall. He had moved to a small one-bedroom apartment downtown, and it was around midnight when he got up from where we'd been watching television to take a shower. Eventually he emerged from the bathroom dressed, looking ready for a night on the town.

A feeling of unease swept over me when I realized he was going to leave me there by myself. I asked if I could go along.

"I have to go to work," he said, offering no other explanation for what kind of work he might be doing in the middle of the night. He then wrote the name of the nightclub and its phone number on a sheet of paper and put it by the bed. The bar was only a couple of blocks away, he explained.

"Yukon will look after you," he said. "You can call me there if you need anything."

He sat at the foot of the bed, tying his shoes. Behind him the actor Don Ameche was on the TV screen advertising recordings of classical and romantic music. "The Flight of the Bumblebee" was playing in the background. For the remainder of the weeks we lived in that apartment, the ad aired about the same time every night as my father prepared to leave. Every time it came on, I'd feel a huge lump in my throat.

Those first few nights were the beginning of what would become a pattern for years.

Every night my father would leave just before *The Tonight Show* aired. I hated it. Every creak and buzz of the walls and furnace would startle me, and I'd sit in bed listening for the burglars I was sure were lurking somewhere in the house. I was both drawn to and repelled by horror movies. Each one that I saw came back to haunt me late at night. My mind would conjure up images of the Grim Reaper, hacked-up bodies, and werewolves coming through windows, climbing the stairs, or lying beneath my bed.

I became intimate with the late-night TV schedule, always falling asleep with the television on. I learned to hate the exuberant brass introduction to the "Star-Spangled Banner," which signaled the end of my evening's company.

The mall, many years after my father's store had come and gone.
COURTESY CARR-GOTTSTEIN PROPERTIES

CHAPTER EIGHT

SECOND CHANCES

I remember four gifts I bought for my father; two were Christmas presents and the third and fourth—a bottle of Brut, his favorite cologne, and a dress tie—I gave to him for his birthday one year.

He acknowledged each present with a warm thank-you, as when he opened the brightly wrapped box containing the travel alarm clock I'd bought for him my second Christmas back in Anchorage.

It was the small, folding type, set inside a black vinyl case. I'd bought it at a local jewelry store, the same place I had gotten his previous year's present, a jade desktop pen set. I had carefully saved my allowance to buy each, purchasing them on layaway.

I remember the day my father unwrapped his clock, and the look of astonishment that came over his face.

"Did you buy this?" he asked.

I nodded yes.

He held it in his hands, opened and closed it several times, then looked over at me.

"This is really nice," he said. Then he fell silent for a moment. "Thank you."

Now I realize what I was doing. I had picked out gifts that reflected, not who my father was, but the man he longed to be: someone people respected, the kind of man who needed a pen set, a travel clock, a nice tie. He came close to being that kind of man in the spring of 1968 when he met Ruth Beck.

My father always had a lot of girlfriends, women in their early twenties who had come from Seattle or Portland to work in Anchorage's strip clubs. Most looked older than their actual age, or maybe they just looked tired. Many were bleached blondes who wore too much makeup and went by names as phony as their hair color.

Usually I didn't have much of a chance to meet them unless you count the times when my father poked his head into my bedroom to show them his sleeping daughter before they would head off to his room. I resented those early morning show-and-tells with total strangers.

These women were a mixed blessing for me. I was afraid to get attached to any one of them because they might not be around long. Yet the ones who lasted longer than a one-night stand provided a welcomed female presence in the house and acted as intermediaries between my father and me on the subjects I was too embarrassed to broach, such as asking for money to buy my first training bra. They also gave me clues as to who my father was, or as it sometimes turned out, who he wasn't: One girlfriend insisted I wish my father a happy Hanukkah one Christmas, adding to my store of evidence that my father was a Jew.

Some I didn't like; others, like Vicki, I adored.

Vicki was a slender natural blonde, who wore wire-rimmed glasses that made her look like the brainy college coed she once was. Before coming to Alaska she had attended Stanford University, where she was paying her way through school dancing topless. She'd made a name for herself by running for student body president on the "Topless Platform." Her campaign buttons featured a simple black-and-white cartoon of a pair of breasts. Her eye-catching campaign even gained her a write-up in *Playboy*. They still remembered her in the student affairs office when I called Stanford years later, but no one knew whatever became of her.

There was something fresh and new about Vicki. She wasn't like the others. She was into the popular "natural" look of the time, relying on little makeup and usually going braless. Fond of the outdoors, Vicki introduced me to Alaska's natural wonders, taking me to all the tourist attractions my father never seemed very interested in.

I also liked another girlfriend, who went by the stage name "Stormy." Stormy, who also worked as a topless dancer, had platinum-dyed hair which was cropped boy-short, she wore big hoop earrings and weighed all of about one hundred pounds. She was tiny, waifish-looking in appearance, and my father used to kid her about being "flat as a board." Stormy became like a big sister to me during my early teen years. I could confide in her about my school crushes, borrow her jeans, and tell about the time I first smoked marijuana.

But like all the other girlfriends, Vicki and Stormy came and went. None of them ever lasted very long; and none was anything more than "girlfriends"—none acted like a mother. Except Ruth.

Ruth Beck was different—older, probably in her late twenties or early thirties, and prettier than most of the women my father dated. She had fiery red hair and resembled Ann-Margret. Her old friend Carmen Lewis remembers what a beauty Ruth was.

"She was gorgeous. She had real delicate features, like her nose, just so tiny and dainty. Gorgeous smile; red, thick hair, just beautiful. She was fun-loving. Just loved having a good time. She loved to dance. She was a good friend, somebody you could talk to."

Ruth and Carmen worked as cocktail waitresses together at the Club China Town, where my father met Ruth. Like most Alaskans, Ruth, who was from the East Coast, had come north to start over. She was widowed and would sometimes show me photographs of her dead husband, a big, bearded man with gray hair who looked much older than my father. Every picture showed him surrounded by a bunch of kids. Carmen said Ruth had five children from her first marriage, which ended in divorce. The man in the photograph was her second husband, who died not long before she had arrived in Alaska.

Carmen and Ruth were good friends. Carmen, who had spent much of her childhood in Alaska, was waitressing to save money for nursing school. She said Ruth had come to Alaska after having to relinquish care of her children to their father when she could not earn enough to support a family.

My father met Ruth during the spring of 1968, and by that November, they were married. For Carmen, and Ruth's other friends at the bar, this was not good news.

Carmen was intimidated by my father. She knew he was a gambler and had heard he ran prostitutes. She'd heard stories of him trying to talk other waitresses into taking up the life.

"He had such a low opinion of women," she said. "Some woman must have really hurt him. Sometimes just the way he would look at you. You knew you could look at the man, and you could see the brain working back there. And you knew he wasn't thinking of anything real good. He was a type of person where I knew I didn't want him for my enemy, that's for sure.

"But Ruth said she loved him. Everyone who knew her tried to talk her out of marrying him. They all knew what he was involved in. I kind of got the impression that she believed that it would be different with her somehow."

Carmen felt better about the union after talking with my father one night about Ruth.

"He said he'd reached a certain point in his life and he felt a need to settle down and try to share his life," recalled Carmen. "He really loved Ruth. He really wanted things to work out."

Prior to their marriage, when school let out that spring, I moved out of the Hurns' and in with Ruth and my father. Like so many others from my childhood, the Hurns faded from view. I saw everyone again at Hurn Senior's funeral in October 1969.

Life with Ruth and my father was stunningly normal. She did the things mothers do—cooked, cleaned the house, and when school started that fall, she packed me lunches and even sewed me a wardrobe. Stepmothers are rarely welcomed with open arms, but in my case, Ruth was.

Before Ruth, I took care of the house and myself for those weekends I was home with my father. She protected me, as mothers do. When I unknowingly gave my father's collector coins—a quarter with an eagle stamped on both halves and a Kennedy half dollar with the president's face on both sides—to a door-to-door greeting card salesman, Ruth interceded on my behalf.

The coins, known as minted mistakes, were worth hundreds of dollars each, and I had given them away for a $1.75 box of cards. When first questioned by my father about what happened to the coins, I lied, saying I hadn't seen them. Later, when I tearfully admitted the truth to Ruth, she talked to my father and I never heard another word about it. If she hadn't been there, there's no telling how angry he might have been.

Ruth was kind to me in ways that I recognized and appreciated, even then. For our first Christmas together, she spent days making a stuffed doll that she told me was for someone else. I was heartbroken; it was the most beautiful doll I'd ever seen: eighteen inches tall, made of soft pink canvas and dressed in a tomato-red dress with black felt buckle shoes and hair of yellow yarn. After it was finished, Ruth let me play with it occasionally, but she made it clear that she'd be sending the doll off before Christmas to some niece. I reluctantly gave up the doll, but on Christmas morning it was under our tree, where Ruth intended it to be all along.

My first year back in Alaska, my father forgot my birthday. Ruth made sure that didn't happen a second time. On my eleventh birthday she threw a party for me, serving up a homemade cake and giving me a Cinderella wristwatch mounted on a ceramic statue of the Disney version of the character.

Ruth did for me the things my mother once had, and she was able to do what my mother never could: She helped my father attempt one of the most difficult transitions of his life—to get out of gambling. Prior to meeting Ruth, my father had been laying plans to go straight; to try to be the kind of father and family man I needed, and wanted, him to be.

In the fall of 1968, my father opened his own business—The Viking Center and Brother International—a legitimate store that sold vacuum cleaners and sewing machines from a small rented space in Anchorage's first indoor shopping mall.

Located across Northern Lights Boulevard from the Bun Drive-In, The Mall—originally called The Mall at Sears—had opened in February, and was an instant success. Although only one story, the building had more than 232,000 square feet of commercial space, more than half belonging to the Sears store. Anchorage's own Carr-Gottstein Properties, Inc., built The Mall in concert with a Los Angeles mall developer. Carr-Gottstein anchored the west end with the newest of its own grocery stores. Sears sat at the other end. In between were nearly thirty smaller stores, some locally owned, some branches of national chains like Russell Stover Candy, Zales Jewelers, and Kinney Shoes.

To lure shoppers from the old shopping district along 4th and 5th avenues, and to convince store owners to lease space, the developers needed a gimmick. They chose the theme of Main Street USA, outfitting The Mall to resemble a southern California interior decorator's idea of what the main street of a small town in, say, Kansas might have looked like around the turn of the century—wooden park benches, wrought iron streetlamps, and a fake carousel. The latter was actually half a carousel set against a wall, with mirrors arranged to give the appearance of the real thing.

Carr's grocery painted a mural on one of its walls that showed cowboys, a horse-drawn carriage, and a Carr's market—three things that didn't exist around the Anchorage area at the turn of the century. But then Anchorage never did have much of a sense of its own history.

To give the shops the look of stores lining an actual street, many stores installed quaint-looking windows and doors, instead of wide, impersonal openings. Andy's Sweets, Treats 'n Eats, a replica of an old-fashioned candy store, sold penny candy out of big glass jars, and filled its end of The Mall with the scent of fresh caramel popcorn.

By Anchorage standards, The Mall was gigantic. The city already had a couple of enclosed strip malls, but none was like the shopping malls they had Outside.

"Outside" was anywhere in the Lower 48 (which is how Alaskans refer to the forty-eight contiguous states). Even the weather page in the local newspapers referred to the rest of the country as "Outside," listing the temperatures in five cities—Seattle, San Francisco, Los Angeles, Spokane, and Chicago.

Nearly everything I owned, ate, adored, or aspired to came from Outside—and all I really knew about Outside was what I saw on television.

Newcomers to Alaska often describe how they dreamed of coming here since they were children, believing it to be a wondrous wilderness full of wild animals, towering mountains, and endless adventure. For me, Outside was where I longed to be. I wanted to go to places like the Great Plains. I remember the first time I drove across the country in my late teens, and throughout Nebraska and Iowa I kept poking my head out the car window asking, "Is this it?"

Outside represented everything Alaska wasn't. It had network TV shows that aired the night they were supposed to be shown. The only national live television I saw as a child was Apollo 11's landing on the moon on July 20, 1969. It took Alaska's congressional delegation to bring a satellite feed of the event to the state. CBS covered it continuously for more than twenty-four hours, and my dad and I watched part of the programming from a bar at Big Lake. I was amazed; we couldn't get live sports, but we could get live TV from the moon.

Outside the summers got really hot and people went to the beach. Outside had cities like New York, full of tall buildings where you could live in a penthouse apartment so many stories up you had to take an elevator to get to it. Outside had suburbs, a concept I heard a lot about on television and which fascinated me for years. Someday I was going to visit a *real* suburb.

I was no different from most kids raised in Alaska, or for that matter, stuck on a farm somewhere in the American Midwest. If you weren't in the media centers of the U.S., you felt like you were nowhere. But it was even worse in Alaska because it *was* nowhere. Television and movies only made reference to the place when somebody was being sent away—some demoted GI, or some flunky professional who was being transferred to Alaska: meaning *the End of the Earth*.

Even though a decade had passed since statehood, Anchorage was still the backwater. The town had grown to include three high schools, but it still had only two television stations, two movie theaters, four radio stations, and still only two roads in and out of town.

Alaska's isolation also served to insulate it from the political upheaval shaking apart the rest of the United States. It may have been the Summer of Love on college campuses across the nation, but in Alaska, student protests, much less mass draft-card and bra burnings, were virtually unheard of.

Local teens did what they could to emulate their counterparts in the rest of the country. They had the Bun to hang out at and Northern Lights Boulevard to cruise. Like the adults, they developed their own social hierarchy, carving up the town into a variety of cliques: greasers, soshes, basies, and those who fell somewhere in between.

"Greasers" were the car goons and piston heads and lived in Sand Lake or the back stretches of the Seward Highway. "Soshes"—junior achiever types—came from the west end of town; "basies" were the military brats.

"We felt trapped here," said Malcolm Brown, a friend who attended West High School in the late 1960s. In the school cafeteria, Brown and his buddies took solace in The Animals' hit song, "We Gotta Get Out of This Place." It spoke to them and they played it like the national anthem.

"We had a jukebox in the lunchroom and we played it endlessly," Brown said. "Music was our link to Outside. I thought there was more to life than Anchorage. I thought if it was okay here, it must be real good someplace else."

In 1968, I was too young to belong to any teen group. But it didn't take me long to develop a sense that I was living in a space colony rather than the forty-ninth state. To this day, there are people who think Alaska is a foreign country. Some can't even find it on a map. Part of the problem is map makers who, because of space restrictions, usually place Alaska in a corner, somewhere out in the Pacific, next to Hawaii, or off the coast of the state of Washington.

Everyone I knew who traveled Outside, myself included, invariably had to endure questions like: "Do you live in an igloo?" "Do you have cars?" "Is it dark all the time?"

No. Yes. No. We didn't have Disneyland, either. Or *American Bandstand*; or Hollywood. In 1968, though, we finally had an honest-to-goodness shopping mall, even if it looked like something from a toy train set when compared to the multilevel wonders Outside. And what's more, my dad had a store there.

Selling vacuums and sewing machines started as a sideline for my father. The previous winter, he had begun supplementing his gambling income by selling Morris, Pfaff, and Bernina sewing machines door-to-door. He worked for a local hustler who specialized in bait-and-switch scams and operated out of a series of storefronts. He'd no sooner open up than there would be a going-out-of-business sale, offering big discounts on equipment with inflated price tags.

"The guy was a real promoter," said Mike Fullerton, who before entering and retiring from the Anchorage Police Department got his start in Anchorage working alongside my father for the same boss. "The guy would open a shop, have a grand-opening sale and then six months later have a gigantic, everything-must-go closing sale. He'd then move down the street, change the name and have another grand-opening sale."

Fullerton and my father offered home demonstrations of machines that their boss hyped in TV commercials. A prospect would call and ask for a demonstration; my father and Fullerton would trot out the cheesy model, then say they just happened to have a better quality machine in the car, a $400 value for $225 because they'd just repossessed it and didn't want to haul it back to the shop. Customers' greed often won out over common sense. My father sold a lot of "repossessed" machines. When Fullerton tired of his boss's shady ways, he opened his own shop, and my father switched allegiances.

"Johnny could make pretty good money selling those things," said Fullerton. "I think in between his gambling and his other activities, when he'd run dry, he'd come work for us for a while and build up his nest egg and go from there."

When my father finally opened his own store, he sold a few Kirby vacuum cleaners, the Swedish-made Husqvarna sewing machines, and Brother sewing machines and typewriters.

He told me with pride about how Husqvarna started nearly three hundred years ago supplying muskets to the Swedish army. Besides the white enamel-coated sewing machines, the firm also made chainsaws and motorcycles.

The sewing machines were expensive—a thousand dollars for the top-of-the-line model—and I wasn't to touch them unless my father was supervising. But I could watch him give demonstrations all day. He'd run fabric under the needle like an expert tailor, producing colorful bands of scallops, satin stitches, arrowheads, and buttonholes. The pricier models came with cams that varied the stitch, allowing the user a choice of up to fifty different stitching styles.

"A Husqvarna Viking sewing machine is all the sewing machine you could ever want," my father would tell prospective customers. "It's built to last a lifetime."

He called the Husqvarna "the Cadillac of sewing machines."

With Ruth at his side, my father devoted himself to the store, putting in long hours day and night. I worked there after school, straightening up and watching the showroom if my father was in the back making a repair or out running an errand.

I was the happiest I'd been in years that fall and my father seemed happy as well. Unknown to me, however, there were legal and financial problems from the moment he opened his store.

In July, the state supreme court refused to hear his appeal of the 1966 gambling conviction. He hadn't paid the fee to have a transcript of his trial prepared. In August, he had to start serving his three-month sentence as part of a work/release program.

Until the end of November, he left work each night at seven P.M. and checked into a halfway house downtown. I thought he was just working late, and not getting home until after I was in bed. I never realized he hadn't been coming home at all until I read his court file years later.

In the middle of his sentence, my father's troubles mounted. The district attorney charged him with perjury for allegedly lying when seeking state aid in paying for his appeal. In a legitimate legal gambit known as the *forma pauperis,* or "pauper's oath," he described his financial woes for the court: the repossession of the Fireweed Lane house, his lack of savings, and his difficulty making the $112 monthly payments on his new Chevrolet Monte Carlo.

The D.A. thought my father had money he wasn't mentioning. He noticed the same thing that caught the eye of the social worker reviewing my mother's mental health case back in 1964: my father's penchant for expensive new cars and car telephones.

"While Mr. Rich says he has nothing, he manages to drive a new car which is equipped with a telephone in it—has full-time employment," said a very frustrated Doug Baily, Anchorage district attorney at the time, in one of my father's many court hearings on the matter.

The case, which ran through November, put my father through the wringer of circular logic. At his court hearing he couldn't be arraigned on the charge—the first step in any criminal proceeding—because he couldn't afford an attorney. The court couldn't appoint him a lawyer unless he took the pauper's oath—the very thing he was accused of violating. My father and Joe Josephson, his attorney of five years, parted company over this case, my father accusing Josephson of telling him to take the pauper's oath, causing all his troubles, and Josephson angry that my father hadn't paid his bill. The car, my father explained at one hearing, was necessary to his line of work, which at the time was barely bringing in enough income to meet his expenses.

"Do you have any money, sir?" asked the judge at one hearing.

"Sir, this is exactly what this charge is about," my father answered. "I petitioned the court to appear *forma pauperis*. I stated that I did not have the money for an attorney and I wanted an attorney for another case of which I am now doing time and am on a work release."

The court adjourned without taking any action. A few days later, the court reconvened, but again my father couldn't be arraigned because he didn't have an attorney. The judge finally appointed a lawyer to examine my father's records to see if he could take the pauper's oath so that an attorney could be appointed for him, thus permitting his arraignment on the perjury charge.

"I don't know, I'm so pitifully behind now, I'm twenty-one thousand dollars in the hole at last count," my father testified. "I have problems with several suits pending against me right now which are all filed in court. No sooner do I make an arrangement to give one collector money than the rest swoop down on me and I can't seem to arrive at a solution with my creditors."

The only things he owned outright were some furniture, his clothes, jewelry, and a one-hundred-dollar television. He said four different lawyers had turned down his case because he was broke.

"You may step down, sir," the judge said after my father testified. "It's perfectly obvious to me that Mr. Rich complies with the rule concerning indigency. The only thing that he has which might be negotiable is the TV set, which he thinks might be worth a hundred dollars. I can take judicial notice of the fact that he can't get an attorney to represent him for a beat-up TV set or for a hundred dollars if he could sell it."

Over the D.A.'s objections, the judge appointed my father an attorney. A few weeks later, the case was dismissed.

While my father was engaged in his courtroom battles, I had my own struggles. Fifth grade was not going well. That fall I'd enrolled at Denali Elementary School, my second school since returning to Alaska and my third since first grade. I knew all too well what it meant to be the New

Kid in class—loneliness, ostracism, and a gnawing yearning for acceptance. Other kids always view New Kids with suspicion, and Denali was about the toughest school in town.

If Anchorage had what could be called an inner-city school, Denali was it. Located near the heart of downtown, on the eastern edge of the Park Strip, the school served an area that stretched from the housing projects of Fairview to the handsome bungalows and cottages of the west end of downtown.

Many of Denali's students were minorities, children from single-parent families, and children whose parents were drug addicts or alcoholics. The school also housed the Anchorage School District's special education program—for children with learning and physical disabilities—in its east wing. It was a hard place to try to fit in, and I didn't make things any easier.

In many ways, I was not much different from my dad. I was mouthy, I acted tough and defensive. Lonely and scared, I developed an attitude problem and this was reflected on the social skills grading section of my report cards. I pulled in N's, as my father once said, as if they were "going out of style."

I hated the N's, which stood for "Needs Improvement." The rating system included "Outstanding" and "Satisfactory," but I never got a single O or S. I didn't "Use time wisely," I didn't "Get along well with others," nor did I "Accept constructive criticism." I don't think teachers liked me, and I can't say I blame them. I also made myself an easy target for the likes of Martha Upicksoun.

Martha, who was my age, was half Inupiat Eskimo and half white, and she was the tallest girl in school. She was one of the "constants"— as longtime students at the school referred to themselves. I was a "temporary," and therefore fair game. Martha was the unofficial queen of Denali Elementary and I was afraid of her from the moment I saw her sitting in my class. Martha hung out with boys. Like me, she acted confident. She too wasn't afraid of telling people off. But then, also like me, circumstances had taught her to be aggressive.

Her parents had moved to Anchorage from the interior Alaska village of Tanana in the early sixties. Martha did well at Denali until about fifth grade when white kids, even those who had been her friends, began hurling Native slurs at her during kickball games on her street.

"It was only a couple of isolated incidents, but it hurt," Martha would tell me years later.

Angry, she vented her rage at the most obvious, and safest target: the so-called temporaries, we kids who were new to the school. Not only did I seem the kind of person who was asking for it, it seemed to Martha that I could take it.

One day after school Martha and a pack of henchmen greeted me as I walked out the back door. Neither Martha nor I can remember what I had done to incur Martha's wrath on *that* particular occasion, but we agree I had probably shot my mouth off.

Martha and her group dragged me to the middle of the ice rink where no one could see over its wooden walls. While a couple of kids held my arms, Martha repeatedly punched me in the stomach. It's the only time I've ever been hit in the gut, and I still remember the wrenching pain. More than the physical pain, I felt overwhelming humiliation. Martha stopped only after a man walking by on the sidewalk noticed the ruckus and broke things up.

I was the only kid Martha had ever hit, she would later tell me. Not surprisingly, it wasn't long after that episode that she and I became the best of friends. Maybe because we finally recognized what we had in common. We are still friends to this day. Martha, a graduate of Yale, is also a journalist. She was right back then; I could take it. And what lessons I learned that day on Denali's playground would go far to toughen me and prepare me for rougher times at home.

Not long after my father had won his day in court, he received a call from a state trooper named Jim Vaden, who had some questions about the vacuums my father was selling.

Jim Vaden was among the toughest state troopers in Alaska. He'd joined the force at twenty-two, right after the earthquake. Being a cop was in his blood. His great-grandfather was an outlaw turned Texas Ranger.

After a year of writing tickets on every traffic stop he pulled—even his trainer called him a "hard-nosed son of a bitch"—the muscular, handsome rookie was transferred to Ketchikan, at the southern tip of the southeast Panhandle, where he volunteered for undesirable assignments such as patrolling the town of Craig, known to his cohorts as "Little Chicago."

Craig was tiny, with only 250 year-round residents and two bars. But during the summer, those bars were filled to fighting capacity with drunken, brawling fishermen. One year, a gang of rowdies threw the town marshal off the dock; ever since, when fishing season started in late spring, the state police commander in Ketchikan would send a couple of troopers to keep things cool in Craig. When Vaden volunteered for the duty, the commander decided to break with tradition and send only one trooper. When Vaden arrived, the mayor asked, "Where's the other trooper?"

"How many towns have you got?" Vaden answered. His first night in Craig he made thirteen arrests.

After Craig, Vaden went to Haines, the terminus of the state ferry line and the start of the shortest overland route into Alaska. Haines wasn't happy to have Vaden around. He liked to stay busy with chores such as painting a grid on the northbound highway so that from an airplane he could better gauge the speed of truckers pushing the limit. The word on Vaden in Haines was that he'd arrest his own mother for jaywalking. In fact, years later, when his father, a big-game hunting guide, was indicted with sixty-three misdemeanor counts of game violations, Vaden refused to make any calls on his behalf even though at the time he was deputy director of the troopers, the second-highest-ranking official in the division.

Haines may not have appreciated such enthusiasm, but the state troopers did, and early in his career, Vaden began to climb the promotion ladder, rung after speedy rung.

The first time I met Vaden was in 1984, when he was deputy director of the department. At the time, I contacted Vaden to see what he could tell me about my father's background. He invited me to meet with him at his office.

He greeted me at the door with a strong handshake and a warm smile. There was something comforting about his mannerisms and the way he spoke; something beyond polite professionalism. I didn't know at the time that Vaden had been the chief investigator of my father's murder.

He was kind and generous with his time and provided me with as much information as he could. For that reason, I would call him back again and again over the next several years as I unraveled my father's life story. It was Vaden who gave me my father's FBI rap sheet. I'll never forget what he said the day I called and asked for it.

"Jim," I said, "now, don't hold anything back. I want to know what's there, be it robbery, rape, or even murder."

Vaden let out a chuckle.

"I think you're going to be disappointed," he said. "Your father's reputation was always much bigger and worse than he actually was."

If anyone would know this, it was Jim Vaden.

Vaden first met my father when he was working as a special investigator for the state attorney general, who saw a need to open a special investigations office to look into Anchorage's growing incidence of white-collar crime. The city's white-collar crime statistics tracked its population growth as if on rails. Most cases involved consumer fraud by bait-and-switch outfits like the one my father had worked for. The attorney general set Vaden on the case, but there were so many operations that Vaden had to limit himself to cases involving $30,000 or more. One involved a door-to-door sales scheme pitching 16mm home movie kits. The operators had bilked Alaskans out of more than $1 million, said Vaden, before they were shut down.

In the spring of 1969, Vaden fielded a call from the Anchorage dealer with the franchise for Kirby vacuum cleaners, who was angry that my father was undercutting his prices, selling a $350 Kirby for $150. The dealer claimed the machines were hot; how Melodrama, postmodernism, and Japanese cinema! else could my father afford to sell them so cheaply?

Vaden knew my father by reputation, which put him on the "B" list in trooperspeak. That meant he was one of the dozen or so shady operators in Anchorage considered career criminals. Their crimes weren't heinous, but aggravating: disorderly conduct, gambling, porn, pimping or prostitution, fencing stolen goods, running after-hours clubs.

"I don't think Johnny was a bad guy," Vaden once told me. "I have never heard anybody say that John was a danger to police officers. If you caught Johnny doing something wrong, he'd say, 'I did something wrong,' and go to his attorney and fight it in court. It wasn't like you were going to break down the door to his after-hours club and be met with a barrage of gunfire."

But a fraud complaint was a fraud complaint, and there was also the allegation of receiving stolen property. Even if the other dealer hadn't complained, Vaden would have paid my father a visit sooner or later, just to make sure everything was aboveboard.

He stopped by the Viking store and introduced himself. There were four Kirbys on display near the front window. As Vaden spoke, he walked to the vacuums.

"Who's your supplier for these machines, John?" Vaden asked.

"What in the hell are you talking about?" my father snapped.

Vaden explained that he'd heard the machines had been stolen. "I need to see some proof from you, some shipping documents, or some invoices, to prove otherwise," he said.

"Who complained?" my father asked, clearly agitated.

"I can't tell you that, John," Vaden said as he turned back to the vacuums. "Now look, this can be taken care of simply if you just show me the paperwork."

"It's none of your damn business!" my father shouted. "You got no business being here. I'm running a legitimate business and you cops won't leave me alone."

"John, listen," Vaden said. "I need to know where you're getting these vacuums. Who's your supplier?"

"I don't have to tell you a damn thing," my father shot back. "I'm trying to run a clean operation. What the hell is going on here? The normal Kirby dealer is ripping everybody off. Why aren't you guys over there rousting his joint?"

Vaden pressed on. "John, if you'd just show me your paperwork on these machines, I'll be out of your hair."

"I'm not doing anything wrong," my father said. "You got questions? Get a search warrant."

"Fine. If that's the way it's going to be," Vaden said, and he turned and left.

Now, more than ever, Vaden was convinced that the vacuum cleaners were hot. Besides my father's hostility, he'd noted that none of the

Kirbys in the window had serial numbers. He had to move quickly before my father ditched the goods.

Vaden returned to his office and contacted the National Crime Information Center asking for reports of stolen Kirby vacuum cleaners. We need serial numbers, NCIC said. Vaden then called Kirby corporate headquarters. No, there had been no vacuum cleaner hijackings, but there had been reports of counterfeit Kirbys, as well as complaints about reconditioned machines being sold as new. The company representative explained how Vaden could check the legitimacy of my father's machines by using ultraviolet light to look for serial numbers inscribed beneath the on/off switch.

Vaden got off the phone and began work on the papers needed to get a search warrant. The court closed at four-thirty; he arrived with minutes to spare and got a judge to issue a warrant.

Vaden was waiting at the Viking store the next morning at nine A.M., thirty minutes before the store opened. Besides the warrant, he had a hand-held black light. My father wasn't there, so Vaden went into the restaurant next door for a cup of coffee. He watched from the window of the phony German rathskeller facade as my father walked up and began to unlock the door to his store.

Vaden put down his coffee and walked outside. He stood behind my father, listening to the lock click.

"Good morning, John. I think we've got a little unfinished business here," Vaden said, handing my father the warrant.

My father didn't say a word. He read the warrant and began gathering up the vacuums and moving them into the back shop, where Vaden began pulling the switch covers. It took him half an hour to go over the ten machines in the store. The entire time, my father stood over him, alternately sulking and shouting. Vaden ignored him, working quickly and neatly, reassembling each machine before moving on to the next. When he was finished, he took a machine as evidence, promising to return it in a few days if everything was jake.

By the next day, Vaden had most of his answers. First, he called NCIC and Kirby with the list of serial numbers he'd copied off the machines. Kirby confirmed that the machines were clean. They'd been shipped from the company's factory to an authorized dealer in California. Vaden called the dealer, asking a clerk if there had been any thefts from his warehouse. The clerk put him off until Vaden explained the reason for his call, then fetched the company owner.

The owner told Vaden he'd sold the vacuums to my father. When Vaden asked about the cut-rate selling price, the owner explained that Kirby gave him a big discount if he bought large shipments. To move all the machines, he'd created his own little distribution network, a gray market of sorts, which included my father. It wasn't illegal, but it did violate his contract with Kirby.

"I'd appreciate it if you wouldn't pass this information on to Kirby," the owner told Vaden.

But it was too late. Vaden's inquiry had spurred one at Kirby. Eventually my father's Kirby connection was put out of business. Even sooner, though, The Viking Center and Brother International shut down.

I don't know exactly why my father's store closed. All I knew was that one day shortly before it closed, he came at me with a fury I'd witnessed only one other time.

My father had a brutal temper, and I knew this the day I saw him beat my mother. In the year I had been back in Alaska, I saw him lose his temper many times. When my father could not cope, when he was frustrated or perhaps hurt, he flew into violent fits of rage. His anger grew in momentum until it reached a point of no return. His face would turn beet red, and his voice would rise several octaves as he'd slowly work himself up into a full tantrum. The change in his tone of voice was my cue: Things had gone too far; I'd done something wrong and crossed the line. He'd slam his fist down on the table; angrily crumple a piece of paper in his hand; throw some small object across the room.

He once yanked a doll from my hands and while I stood there trembling, he tried to break it in two. It was my new Barbie doll, but no matter how he jerked the doll with his fists, it wouldn't break. It was the new Twist-and-Turn Barbie designed to bend at the waist. His face turned redder and redder as the doll refused to cooperate. Finally in frustration, he popped off the doll's head, turned, and marched into the next room. Earlier that same day, during one of his fits, he'd thrown a box of my toys down the garbage chute.

My father was impatient, and he had unrealistic expectations of what a little girl was capable of doing. He would become furious with me when I couldn't complete what he considered simple tasks, such as to make a pot of coffee or start his car for him. He was so unpredictable that anytime he asked me to do anything, I did so as if my life depended upon it. I was terrified of making mistakes. I once threw up into a plate of food, because he frightened me so badly when we went out to dinner one night.

On another occasion, while Carmen's younger sister was over at the house, we were in the kitchen making sandwiches and horsing around. I accidentally dropped a bottle of catsup, and it shattered. Years later, Barbara Smart still vividly recalled that day.

"I've never seen anybody shake so badly," she told me. "You were scared as if you were going to get killed. You were physically shaking. We cleaned it up and you were trying to hide the pieces of glass so that nobody would know."

I was so upset that Barbara told me not to worry, she'd take the rap. She didn't tell her sister Carmen the truth until years later.

"I would never have survived as his daughter," Carmen said while recounting this episode. "I wasn't nearly as mouthy as you were. But I think you had to be in order to survive."

The good news about my father's temper was that it was like an afternoon cloudburst, it came and went quickly. After the scene with the Barbie doll I simply waited a few minutes for him to cool down. I then picked my Barbie up off the floor and went downstairs to the Dumpster and pulled out my toys. He never said another word about either incident. Aside from breaking objects, yelling and screaming, my father had never laid a hand on me except for infrequent spankings. At least not until that afternoon when we were alone together in the store.

I'd asked to be paid my weekly allowance. He told me he couldn't pay me, but I kept asking why not. Finally he started yelling, and came at me from across the room and began slamming his hand across my head—in full view of everybody walking by outside in The Mall. Like that day inside the hockey rink, I felt more humiliated than hurt.

After several seconds, I wiggled away and ran off to the women's bathroom around the corner. There I hid in one of the toilet stalls, trying to contain my sobs and refusing to come out, despite the gentle coaxing of one woman who had witnessed the entire scene and kept asking if there was anything she could do.

"I'm fine," I said, trying to contain the flow of tears running down my face. "*Really,* I'm fine."

But I wasn't. For a long time I was afraid to go near my father. I was shocked and terrified by what had happened. For days I slinked around the house, barely speaking to him. It would take me even longer to understand that my father's anger that day didn't stem from his inability to pay his daughter's allowance. He was on the verge of losing not only his store but, more important, he had lost Ruth as well. Johnny Rich had struck out once again.

One of my father's competitors told me years later how the rumor on the street was that my father was shut down for using prostitutes to run the business. Another said he'd heard my father was cheating his suppliers. I was offended by the first response since I knew it wasn't true; the only two women who'd ever been in that store were Ruth and me. The latter reason might have had some truth to it. But to this day, Jim Vaden blames himself.

He believes that by ending my father's supply line of vacuums, he halted my father's biggest source of income. Vaden said there would never have been any reason to contact Kirby headquarters if he'd been able to talk to my father's dealer first. Maybe the operation wasn't exactly on the level, but it wasn't criminal and Vaden would have dropped the matter.

"Your dad's source of vacuums probably would have continued. But you know the code of the criminal element, 'Thou shall not squeal.' "

I knew what Vaden was talking about because my father once told me about snitches.

"Stool pigeons are the lowest life form on earth," he said. "You never hit a snitch to get even. You wait until they're in a crowd somewhere, like a restaurant or bar, then you walk in, point them out and announce loudly, '*So-and-so is a snitch.*' "

In March, Ruth and my father filed for divorce, and by May it was finalized. He and Ruth had been together a year and married a little more than six months. Ruth was the only one who really said anything to me about their breakup, telling me only that she and my father just didn't get along. I never witnessed anything between Ruth and my father to give any clue as to what had happened.

Carmen believes it had something to do with my father's temper. She'd once walked into our house while he had Ruth cornered, and was screaming at her. Ruth just stood there, speechless and paralyzed with fear.

"She was very meek, eyes-downcast-on-the-floor type of thing. Just broke my heart. Just really made me mad. I've always been a real fighter—I can't stand to see people being bullied," Carmen said. "I know she was afraid of him and that probably was a big issue. He was very controlling and domineering. Ruth was such a fun-loving person, free as a bird. Happy-go-lucky. I don't think she could handle the constraints.

"I know he tried. It's a shame it didn't last. She could have been a good mom to you."

I never saw Ruth again. I've heard she lived in Alaska a few more years before returning to the East Coast to live closer to her children.

Two of Johnny's entertainment enterprises as advertised in the newspaper in the late 1960s

CHAPTER NINE

FATS DOMINO AND THE 736 CLUB

In my baby book, my mother noted that as a toddler, my favorite things were listening to rock 'n' roll on the radio and dancing. My mother had taught me to dance; my father taught me to love music.

Some parents pushed classical music at their children; my father's passion was popular music, and he exposed me to the likes of the Beatles, the Rolling Stones, Elvis Presley, and black artists like Ike and Tina Turner and Ray Charles. When the movie *Woodstock* came out he took me to see it, and I was probably the only kid under seventeen in the place.

My father had eclectic tastes. Sometimes he'd go through a phase and buy everything he could by Johnny Rivers or Neil Diamond. I knew all about the Hollywood nightclub the Whisky A Go-Go, because Johnny Rivers recorded an album there and my father had it. He listened to hippie groups like the Mamas and the Papas, as well as folk groups like the Kingston Trio. His apartments and his cars were temples of technology, and as a hobby he sometimes installed sound systems for his friends in their homes and businesses, usually nightclubs. As soon as eight-track tape decks came out, he had one at home and one in his car. When reel-to-reel tape recorders were introduced into the home market, he picked up not one but two, so he could record from one to the other. His first two tapes were of Ray Charles and Steppenwolf. To go along with his new sound system, he got a pair of state-of-the-art speakers, which he played at full volume, usually around five A.M. when he'd come home from the nightclubs. Before I was born, in the late 1950s, he was even busted once in San Francisco for playing his music too loud. All I could do during those early morning boom sessions was to walk out of my room and yell at him to turn it down.

So it seems a natural that my father would eventually try to make a living in the music business as a concert promoter. His first show was scheduled in July 1970, and he was bringing one of his favorites to town: Fats Domino.

The concert was my father's second attempt at a career in some aspect of the music business. After the demise of his sewing machine shop, he briefly took over the management of the North Starlight Lounge, changing its name to "Le Pussycat" and turning it into a go-go club. He was merely cashing in on the latest entertainment rage.

Since the mid-sixties, Anchorage nightlife had been ruled by white vinyl boots and fringed bikini tops and bottoms that shimmied when shaken. Anchorage had not only gone go-go, it had gone topless, with such acts as the Buckeroo Club's Big Bertha (advertised as the "Big-Big-Big 275-pound bombshell!") and the Trophy Room's Tiger A-Go-Go Girls. Other clubs featured hack rock bands fronted by scantily clad women performing dance routines to the music. Even the staid old Idle Hour Supper Club, a favorite of local pols and military officers, offered Jimmy Zee's Swim & Watusi Revue.

With these clubs showing the way, my father opened Le Pussycat, booking the Jades and J'Adorables, a four-man, three-girl act from Vegas, as the bar's first band. He advertised them and the club in a medium-size ad in the December 1, 1969, *Anchorage Times*. The ad, a copy of which now rests on my desk, blared "NEW OPENING TONITE, LE PUSSYCAT, FORMERLY THE NORTH STARLIGHT LOUNGE, PRESENTING DIRECT FROM LAS VEGAS' NEW INTERNATIONAL HOTEL, THE FABULOUS JADES AND J'ADORABLES, FLOOR SHOWS AT 10, 12 & 2 A.M., NEW MANAGEMENT, NEW ENTERTAINMENT, NEW POLICY (choice cocktails, fast service)."

The ad reminds me of what it felt like to be eleven years old and sitting in a darkened nightclub, surrounded by flashing colored lights and a room full of partying people. My favorite song was Otis Redding's "Try a Little Tenderness." It was my dad's favorite song too, and I remember him telling me how Redding had died in a plane crash. I recall the way my father still dressed the same in the late 1960s as he had a decade earlier and I miss the way we used to dance together to the club's records when the band took its breaks.

Naming the bar Le Pussycat was my father's idea. In radio advertisements, he used the music from Tom Jones's single "What's New, Pussycat?", over which an announcer's voice would talk, introducing whatever acts were appearing at the club.

My father was a big fan of the enormously popular and handsome Welsh singer, who took songs previously recorded by black artists and introduced them to a white, mainstream audience. My father and I religiously watched Jones's weekly television variety show. Even I thought there was something thrilling about the way Jones would take scarves and handkerchiefs tossed to him by women in the audience, wipe his chest, then fling them back at his hysterical fans.

Outside, Le Pussycat wasn't much to look at, just another square, flat-roofed building painted white, but inside it was spacious—with seating for three hundred—and elegant, by Anchorage standards.

There was a big square bar at the center of the room, with a mural of a dragon behind it. Off to one side was a pool table and cigarette machine; to the other, an elevated stage and dance floor.

I thought it was incredibly glamorous. Sometimes I'd sit backstage while the band members put on their stage makeup. Once the show began, I'd sit at one of the tables near the front of the stage, drinking 7 UPs or Shirley Temples, completely entranced by the Jades and J'Adorables. The dancers changed costumes for each song, but their outfits tended to look alike—bikini panties, oversized pasties, and fishnet stockings. Sometimes they'd tote toy rifles or don Indian headdresses. At the finale, they went totally topless. Between songs, the guitar player would ask questions like "How many virgins are there in the house? Please raise your hands. . . . Thank you, please meet us at the stage door after the set."

This always drew a laugh from the crowd—and from me, although I had no idea what he was talking about. I thought maybe it had something to do with astrology. Since I knew I was a Pisces, I didn't raise my hand.

Two more rock bands followed the Jades and J'Adorables, including an all-girl group from the Philippines named the St. Paul Sisters. But once again, Le Pussycat, or at least my father's involvement in it, didn't last, and my father launched his newest venture as a concert promoter.

My father loved Fats Domino, the only performer to outsell every fifties star except Elvis Presley. He worked for months preparing for the concert, first subscribing to *Billboard* magazine, then eventually booking Fats for two shows a night, July 29 through 31, 1970, at the three-thousand-seat Sports Arena, an old military Quonset hut.

Once he'd hired the Sports Arena, he booked the most expensive suites at the Westward Hotel for Fats and his band. His buddies bugged him to spend more heavily to promote the show, but my father was convinced that in an out-of-the-way place like Anchorage, a big act like Fats Domino would sell out by word of mouth. It wasn't an entirely unreasonable argument. Fats was on the comeback trail, and recently had a hit on the radio—a cover of the Beatles' "Lady Madonna."

And it was true that no matter who played Anchorage, Anchorage came to the show. The city was just big enough to be worth the while of major and not-so-major entertainers—as well as a convenient stopover for tours hopping between Japan and Europe. Anchorage certainly was starved enough for entertainment to sell out practically every performance—Bill Cosby, Odetta, Louis Armstrong, Carlos Montoya, even Leonard Bernstein and the New York Philharmonic Orchestra had played Anchorage, all of them enjoying what came to be known as the Alaska Standing Ovation. If an entertainment event occurred within Alaska's borders, people stood up and clapped until their palms were raw.

So my father felt it was smart not to waste more than a thousand dollars promoting a giant like Fats Domino, even though the Fat Man's heyday was past. He did buy ads in the newspapers, but his promotional effort was mostly the thin cardboard posters that he and I stuck up several weeks before the show in the windows of businesses around town. I even got to meet Fats and have lunch with him and my father. Afterward, my father gave me a gift from Fats: a small ring with a row of little pearls in the center between two rows of similarly sized jade balls. Then he showed me the gift Fats had given him—a watch with a paper-thin gold band and a square face outlined in small diamonds. The crystal on the watch was thicker than the watch itself. The watch was one of Fats'; he'd bought the ring for me.

But from the moment I arrived at the Sports Arena on opening night, I sensed something was wrong. The hall was silent and empty except for a few technicians scurrying around the stage. As the eight P.M. showtime neared, I took my reserved seat in the front row, just a few feet from the makeshift stage erected on the arena's floor.

People began trickling in; six or seven sat near me, another six or seven were at the back of the hall. I fidgeted in my chair, trying to see who was coming in and wondering what was going on. Where was the rest of the audience? Why weren't there people pouring into the arena? The clock ticked past eight, but no more people arrived. The stage, with its rented upright piano down front and empty bandstand chairs, looked lonesome and cold.

At eight-thirty the band finally appeared. The lights dimmed, and a single spotlight shone on the piano stool. A man walked out to the microphone stand near the piano and introduced Fats Domino, who appeared dressed in a green sequined suit with matching shoes. He sat at the piano and struck the opening chords of "Blueberry Hill."

The band joined in, playing as if they were in front of a full house, when in fact there were about forty people in the whole place. Fats smiled and pounded the keys through song after song. Some of the people in the sad little crowd began dancing in the aisles, and everyone was clapping along. Midway through the set, Fats kicked the piano stool away and stood in a crouch, bumping the upright with his considerable belly. The old piano stuttered across the stage, leaning backward at each jolt but recovering its balance thanks to Fats' firm hold on the keys. The audience roared. I felt as if I were watching the first rock 'n' roll show ever.

Then suddenly Fats threw his weight one final time, and the piano toppled over with a crash. We all gasped, then squealed with delight as Fats leaned over his fallen instrument and kept right on playing.

He and his band played a solid two hours, and if any performer ever deserved the Alaska Standing Ovation, it was Fats Domino, who got as much of one as the small audience could muster.

As soon as the band left the stage, and the hall emptied, a gloomy silence descended. I had to hang around waiting for my father, wishing

I could have left with everybody else. I sat in the foyer, near the rest-rooms. The small crowd didn't create much of a demand for beer or soda pop, so the attendants were able to shut down early. Nearly all the lights had been turned off by the time I plunked myself down on one of two folding tables set up by the front door. The security men and a few stagehands walked silently about.

I sat on the table for twenty minutes or so when the door to a room to my right opened up and the band manager stood in the doorway. He and my father had been in the room going over the receipts. As he opened the door, I could see my father sitting at a gray metal desk, looking beat. The band manager was leaving.

"John, I can't give Fats this," he said to my father. "I can't send him home with only a thousand dollars."

"It's all I got," my father answered wearily.

It was a little better the next two nights, with maybe two hundred people a performance coming in the door.

"Johnny kept thinking, 'The next night, the next night—they're going to come in the door,' " said Fred Adkerson, who prior to going into bail bonding had written an entertainment column for the *Anchorage Times*.

Years later Adkerson ran into Fats in Las Vegas and had a cup of coffee with him. Fats said that he had never played a house as empty as the Sports Arena. Things looked so bad that first night that Fats asked my father before he was to go on stage, "Are you sure we weren't supposed to open up tomorrow night?"

Adkerson is convinced the show failed because my father refused to spend more on advertising. That fits. Johnny always liked to save a buck.

"It had to be the biggest embarrassment and most humiliating ex-perience in John's life. I know it would be mine," Adkerson said.

No one had to tell me how awful the experience was for my father. I felt it the moment I saw him sitting at the desk opening night. To make matters worse, after the disaster my father had to defend himself against fraud charges brought by a travel agent who had taken a post-dated check for the band's plane tickets.

My father's lawyer, a public defender, was able to get the case dis-missed by showing that my father hadn't intended to defraud anyone; the judge agreed that the postdated check constituted a promissory note, and that in accepting it, the travel agent had assumed some of the risk of putting on the show.

My father might have regretted the outcome of his venture into music promotion, but he always maintained that it wasn't his fault or Fats Domino's, but Anchorage's, as he related to Herb Soll, his public defender.

"How could you do something like this?" Soll asked my father the first time he came into his office. "Fats Domino is passé. This guy's a has-been. Who would book Fats Domino and expect anyone to go and see him?"

"Oh no. Fats is a very smart fellow," my father answered. "There's a certain nostalgia for his music that has him filling houses on campuses and different places around the country. I checked this out very carefully. He's no longer at the top of the charts, but his name is enough to draw sufficient crowds all over the place. He's a steady player in the better hotels in Vegas and once in a while he has these breaks in his schedule where he goes off and does a concert and fills the house every time. Anchorage just isn't in tune. The surveys and charts I looked at reveal he's still quite alive. Whenever he does a concert, he sells out. It'd be just my luck that this would happen."

Soll spent several hours getting all the details of the concert, demanding that my father tell him everything.

"I didn't really know your dad until the case, that's why I had to get the whole story out," Soll told me. "Johnny indicated that he was a showman, a promoter. That it was part of him and he saw an opportunity to make a legitimate dollar. He was very good at explaining things and answering questions. That's why I remember it more than other cases.

"He was so candid that he would tell you things that would kind of say that he'd been a shady character as far as his associations. He was just so honest about what he had done. He was a very friendly, congenial person. Very open. He was all of that. I liked him."

Besides straight answers, my father gave Soll something else—an appreciation for Fats Domino. Soll had never paid much attention to popular music when he was in college, so Fats never meant anything to him. Within months of handling my father's case, Soll had collected every Fats Domino record he could get his hands on after my father convinced him he should listen to his music.

"I've been a great fan of Fats Domino and have all his records at home. I adore him. I started listening to him seriously after this case and it changed my attitude completely. I'm a Fats Domino man," Soll said.

Not long after my father's concert, radio stations were recasting fifties rockers as legends, not has-beens. Three years later the movie *American Graffiti* came out, with a pre-Beatles soundtrack. I'd think, *If only my father had waited.*

My father was down, but not for long. A year later, he worked with another promoter to bring Rick Nelson to town, just before he gave up concert promotion all together.

In the fall of 1971, we moved for the last time, settling into the only house I'd ever lived in with my father for longer than a six-month stretch. But it was hardly the home I'd envisioned.

That Thanksgiving, we moved to a large, three-bedroom house in the 700 block of 12th Avenue, located in the heart of Fairview.

Next door, an electrical substation squatted behind a tall chain link fence topped by barbed wire. Beyond that, an empty lot led to the easternmost of the Twin Tesoros on Gambell. Directly across the street was Alexander's Body Shop, run by Alvin "Big Al" Alexander, a tall, muscular black man who drove a bright green Corvette with the name of his shop painted in big gold-and-white letters on the doors. Everything Big Al owned or wore was green and gold—the shop van, the shop sign, even his mechanic's jump suit—everything except his silver Bentley. A troop of buxom women could usually be found teetering around the garage in spike heels and vibrantly colored skintight pants.

A block behind our house was the Nevada Tavern, one of the town's roughest bars. A big part of the Nevada's clientele was the neighborhood pimps and their girls, who also hung out at Mark's Drive In, on the other side of Al's Body Shop.

Our house seemed to have been built in parts; the lower half was made of log, the upper half had plywood siding; all of it was slathered with muddy brown paint, making it look like an overgrown shack. I hated the house for how ugly it was, but I hated it more for what it meant in my life. After his string of business failures, my father went back to what he knew best—running after-hours joints—and he turned our home into a gambling parlor called "The 736 Club."

Not long after we moved in my father called me to the front door.

"Look here," he said as he pulled up the green shag carpet covering the floor of the enclosed front porch.

By ourselves, my father and I nearly filled the tiny space. There was only one small window on a side wall to let in any light. Even in summer, the entry was always dim, damp, and cold, lit only by a single bulb beside the interior door.

My father wanted to show me his new security system—a lump under the shag carpet that turned out to be a foot of board nailed to the floor parallel to the outside door. As he jerked the carpet aside, he pointed to the piece of wood, then reached for the crowbar he'd leaned against the entry wall and began to fit it in between the wooden slat and the door. Next, he showed me how to place the forked end of the crowbar under the door handle, bracing the notched end against the strip of wood.

"This makes it virtually impossible to break down the door," he said. "If anyone applies pressure from the outside, the crowbar forces that pressure up against the door frame. To take out the door, they'd have to take out the entire wall."

Now why would anyone want to do that? I remember thinking at the time. I assumed that the point was to protect me from robbers, and it made me feel safer.

Soon my father began building an addition onto the back which eventually became the billiards room, and he then set about decorating our house like a cheap barroom lounge.

Inside, the first thing you saw was a wall covered in leopard-print flannel, with a telephone on a box shelf in the middle. In what had been the dining room, just off the foyer, my father hauled in a couple of worn couches separated by a pair of end tables holding a pair of big ceramic lamps made to look like goddesses holding grapes. His poker/ dining table and a craps table filled what had been the living room. On the walls he hung a couple of posters. One was of a naked blonde beneath the heading *A Woman's Erogenous Zones,* with descriptions and arrows pointing to various parts of her anatomy. Another contained a list of recommendations on how to handle a nuclear attack, the last suggestion being to "bend over and kiss your ass good-bye." A curtain of red and gold plastic beads separated the rooms.

We slept upstairs; a thick black drape kept customers from venturing into our quarters. My bedroom felt as if it once had been part of an attic; my double bed nearly filled the small room with its slanted, dark purple walls. There was a spare bedroom across a short hall and my father's room across from it.

Every morning at around five A.M., a crowd poured into the house, fresh from the last bootleg joint or legitimate nightclub. All kinds showed up, from cocktail waitresses and nightclub band members to celebrities visiting Alaska. My father's friend Al Bennett, who worked at the club as a card dealer, swears he saw Jack Lemmon in the joint one early morning.

I didn't see Jack, and at the time I couldn't have cared less if Mick Jagger was in the place. I wanted everybody out. It was like living in a bar. Every morning, the stereo would go on, and I'd lie in bed trying to ignore the cloud of cigarette smoke that rose through the house, along with the chatter of voices and the clink of glasses, punctuated by people cheering and pounding the padded sides of the craps table. There was no escaping the noise or smell. To secure the back of the house, which ended at an alley, my father had boarded up the windows, including the one in my room. All I could do to fight the fumes was spray air freshener. I'd sleep fitfully until my alarm clock went off at seven, then I'd get up and head downstairs to face a whole new set of challenges.

The place was like a nightclub a half hour before closing time. People were everywhere—on the couches, around the craps table, in the kitchen. Sometimes I'd have to stand in line to get in the bathroom, behind hookers and madams, the occasional heroin junkie and middle-aged drunks.

I'd have to move through a crowd of strangers in the kitchen just to grab some breakfast. Then I'd quietly go back upstairs, finish getting dressed, come downstairs again, find my father, kiss him good-bye, and jump in a cab to take me to school.

·   ·   ·

That fall I had entered seventh grade at Wendler Junior High School, but when we moved, I was no longer within Wendler's attendance boundaries. I put my foot down and told my father the same thing I told Wendler's principal—I wasn't changing schools anymore. By the end of my sixth-grade year, I'd entered and left two more new schools, bringing the total to six since entering public school.

I took taxis to school since my father couldn't often leave the club when it was in full swing. He insisted I ask the dispatcher to send his old friend Chic Phillips, and we always took the same route, a fifteen-minute drive through three neighborhoods, past the city dump, a couple of gravel pits, and a birch forest. But I might as well have been traveling from one universe to another. Wendler's student body was a mix of middle- and upper-middle-class whites and a smattering of minorities, and the neighborhoods across from the school represented the breadth of the student population. There was College Village, where many of the city's doctors lived on streets named Stanford and Princeton; Roger's Park, a solid middle-class neighborhood filled with modest cottages and towering birch trees; and Anchor Park, with smaller homes filled by large families with long histories in Anchorage.

Wendler didn't have the problems associated with the poor neighborhoods surrounding Clark Junior High in Mountain View, or the reputation for toughness that Central had, located near downtown. It also lacked the snobby reputation of Romig, next to West High, where young teens from Anchorage's wealthier families attended school.

With its kelly green trim, white paint, and green-and-white ram's head painted on the exterior gymnasium wall, Wendler was immaculate. The white linoleum floors shone with fresh wax every morning. Graffiti didn't survive long on the walls at Wendler, any more than frayed jeans and backtalk. The halls echoed with conformity and regimentation.

I entered Wendler emotionally and almost physically exhausted; worn down by my father's unpredictable nature and his unconventional life-style. I continued to care for myself, getting myself up in the morning, taking care of the house, tending to my wardrobe needs, worrying about what I was going to eat, and when. But I'd grown weary of it all: the constant moving, the come-and-go girlfriends, the relentless anxiety of being left home alone at night.

But that fall marked a turning point in my life. Once I entered Wendler and began socializing and comparing my life to others, I discovered just how different my life was, and my relationship with my father would never be the same.

I entered Wendler a homely-looking, mostly friendless preteen. I wore no makeup, my clothes were outdated, and I kept my frizzy brown hair pinned away from my face. That all changed by the end of my first year. I'd discovered teen boutiques, frosted eyeshadows, and Love's Lemon-Scented cologne. Every night I slept in hair curlers the size of orange juice cans that left my hair in big, bouncy curls that fell about my shoulders. But more important, by mid-year, I had finally made friends—lots of them—and they were the sole reason I refused to leave Wendler.

I didn't fit in immediately, but sometime during the fall semester, I found myself passing notes in the hall, talking all night on the telephone, and being invited to parties. At the time I thought it had something to do with a somewhat popular boy at school who developed a crush on me. Mostly, I think I might have gotten easier to get along with.

Most of my friends lived in City View, the neighborhood we lived in before moving to Fairview. Some had known each other since first grade—in my experience, an amazing display of continuity. When my friend Cindy Williams showed me where in first grade she had scratched I HATE MARY on the side of her wooden dresser (a reference to her best friend across the street, Mary Gray), I was envious that any two people could know each other that long.

After school, my friends and I gathered in each other's bedrooms listening to albums by the likes of Carole King, Elton John, and Crosby, Stills, Nash and Young. We invited each other to slumber parties where we stayed up all night talking about boys and playing "pass-out," a game in which we took turns taking deep breaths and squeezing each other around the waist until we fainted.

On Friday night we'd hang out at the Fireweed Theater, a huge place with a giant red-carpeted lobby framed in plate glass windows. From inside the theater I could look across Fireweed Lane and see my old house, stripped of the birch trees that had once shielded it from the road.

At school, I decorated my locker with magazine photos of teen idols Davey Jones and Bobby Sherman. I went to school dances and basketball games. My favorite subjects were art and poetry. I acted in plays; I learned to square-dance, to pole-vault, and to play volleyball. I even tried out for cheerleading. After school, I hung out at the nearby ice cream store, drinking chocolate milk shakes and staring at a dark-haired Italian-looking counterman named Tony, on whom I had a desperate crush.

I lived two lives—the life I knew at Wendler and my life at home— and I struggled to keep them separate to the point of lying to my friends' parents. I told them my father sold vacuums. I lied partly because I wasn't sure what to call whatever it was my father did. He and I had never talked about it and it wasn't an option covered in class during Career Day. He wasn't like my friends' parents who were home-makers, artists, lawyers, doctors, judges, airline pilots, and even cops.

The first time I heard my father describe what he did for a living was when he had come to pick me up at a girlfriend's house. I was in the other room when he arrived and he stood in the kitchen talking with my friend's mother. She asked how the vacuum business was going.

"I haven't been in the vacuum business for years," my father said. "I'm a professional gambler."

I deeply resented him then for his honesty. He embarrassed me, and what's more, he threatened to shatter the delicate facade I'd erected of the home life I wanted my friends—and more important their parents—to believe I lived. Ironically, despite my efforts to hide what went on at my house, my closest friends couldn't have cared less. They were always complaining about how "boring" their parents were and how exciting my dad seemed. Typically, in turn, I wanted nothing more than to have a regular "mom and dad" kind of household. The kind of place where cops didn't beat the door down in the middle of the night.

In hopes of avoiding police raids, my father set up the parlor as a private club, like the Elks Club or Moose Lodge, complete with officers and a board of directors. To gamble at our house you had to be a member, or a member's guest. There was no membership fee, but members were asked to sign a contract stating that among other things the signatory was eighteen or older and not "a member of any censorship group or law enforcement agency, nor working for any such group or agency, directly or indirectly."

According to the contract, members of the club were supposed to "subscribe to the view that free American adults have the right to choose for themselves what they do in a private club which excludes minors"; and that they were joining the club to "satisfy [their] own interest concerning the world in which we live, including matters pertaining to gambling; games of chance, skill, sports and the promotion of entertainment and sporting events."

The contract also asked members to declare "that taste is a personal matter, of no concern to government, and that adults should be free to exercise their own judgment with regard to matters concerning the management of their membership's activities, just as they are free to exercise their own judgment in matters pertaining to politics, economics and religion."

That was my dad: Johnny Rich, First Amendment Warrior. But the cops came anyway, and I was home during two of their visits.

"All right, get up!" a man's voice, deep and commanding, boomed at me from the doorway at the foot of my bed. "Get dressed, let's go. You're coming with me."

A split second earlier I'd been jolted from a dead sleep by the sound of my door being kicked open. First there was a loud thwack followed by a warbling noise as the hollow-cored door vibrated. I popped my head up and my heart was racing as I tried to focus on the figure that stood in my doorway shining the beam from a flashlight into my face.

"What for?" I asked, half asleep and irritated at the intrusion.

He waved the flashlight around the room, illuminating the bright purple walls, my giant stuffed turtle, a big stuffed dog, and the coffee table next to my bed, which was covered by my collection of dozens of miniature stuffed animals—bears, tigers, mice, dinosaurs, rabbits. Finally, he lowered the light.

"Who are you?" he asked.

"Kim Rich," I said.

"How old are you?"

"Thirteen."

The policeman sighed and dropped the flashlight to his side.

"Okay, you stay here," he said, then he shut the door and left.

A few minutes later the scene repeated itself. This time I told the Flashlight that his partner had said I could stay.

The first time the police showed up was around Thanksgiving 1971. The second time occurred in May of 1972, when I was near the end of my eighth-grade school year. When they came the second time, I was awakened by the growling of Bernard, a big, floppy-eared Doberman pinscher who was the newest edition to our family.

The night of that second raid Bernard pushed my door open and stood at the top of the stairs emitting a continuous growl full of menace. I heard yelling downstairs.

"Hey, come call this dog or we'll shoot him!" a man shouted. I walked to where Bernard stood and looked down at the uniforms.

"Oh, brother. C'mon, Bernard," I said, tugging on his collar and pulling him back into my room.

The raids had a ritualistic pattern. Each time the police would storm through the house, arresting everyone and charging my father with maintaining a gambling establishment. During the raids, the police would haul away not only the gaming tables and gambling gear, but the couches, chairs, tables, and lamps—tearing the wallpaper, dumping ashtrays, and emptying the refrigerator of my father's beer and my soda pop.

One of the Anchorage police officers who led the raids was Ted Carlson, a lean Oklahoman who knew my father from the days when Ted had run a bar in town called the Palomino, before joining APD's vice squad. Carlson—who signed the complaints that led to the raids—made sure the arresting officers grabbed my father's print of "A Friend in Need," one in a series of paintings by C. M. Coolidge depicting dogs playing poker. This always amused my father.

"That's what I call hard evidence for a gambling rap," I overheard him tell his new attorney Jim Johnston one day as the three of us stood on the loading dock of a police warehouse. We had gone there to claim the stuff grabbed in the second raid. I was amazed at what I saw— ashtrays filled with cigarette butts and ashes, half-empty bottles of soda pop, packages of cigarettes, piles of gambling chips—all stuffed into plastic bags, marked with black felt pen. There was even one bag that contained $124.

"I got the cash. I could have had anything else, but I couldn't have the picture of the dogs," Johnston recalled with a laugh.

Johnston, a Harvard graduate with a law degree from Stanford, first met my father when my father sought him out to handle his divorce from Ruth. Like my father's lawyer before him, Johnston did what he had to do in order to put food on the table in a town where criminal defense and domestic law were about the only ways a young attorney could earn a living.

The red-haired and ruddy-faced Johnston learned early on that my father was no ordinary client.

"He had a reputation for crooked games. But I think any gambler involved in the after-hours-joint level does," Johnston said.

Johnston also soon discovered that my father relied heavily on the courts—and not muscle—to resolve his conflicts.

"To me, implied violence, or at least the threat of violence, would be an acceptable means of resolving a problem in the underworld. In the dealings I had with Johnny, that wasn't anywhere on the list of options. Not even at the bottom. He brought me a check once that a preacher had given him in a poker game. He was offended that a preacher would be playing poker, and furthermore, one who would bounce a check. It was the sort of thing where others might consider resorting to blackmail. But not John, he goes to his lawyer and wants to sue him in small claims court."

Johnston doesn't recall what became of the case, or if a lawsuit was ever even filed. What Johnston clearly remembers, though, is my father's take-charge attitude when it came to all of his legal affairs. This was no more apparent than the day Johnston happened to be in court during the one-thirty arraignment proceedings and found my father sitting among the other defendants.

"I walked into the courtroom and there was John in the box. I was shocked. He looked kind of bedraggled, as if he'd been arrested and he'd just been hauled off from wherever he was. I went over to him.

" 'Is there anything I can do? What's going on?' " Johnston asked.

" 'Don't worry about it. They can't make it stick. It was a postdated check. I'll just get the PD [Public Defender] and they'll get it thrown out,' " my father said.

The check my father was referring to was the check he'd written in the Fats Domino debacle.

"I was amazed at the time how analytical he was about it," says Johnston. "He knew the law. He was absolutely right. That would have been an *A* answer in law school. There he was, being charged with a felony and yet being so cool about it. I was impressed."

When it came to other legal matters, my father took a similar approach. One of the first gambling cases when Johnston represented my father involved a gambling house he operated in Spenard, a suburb of sorts that's part of Anchorage. The house was raided in October of 1970. A few poker players had arrived for a game when one of them overheard on the police scanner the police listing off the license plate numbers of their cars parked outside. Everybody left before the police arrived, including my father. The police went in anyway and raided the place even though no one was there. They eventually tracked down my father and charged him with operating an illegal gambling house. Once again, when it came time to go to court, my father told Johnston not to be concerned.

"I was told not to worry about it because they couldn't prove he lived there, because it was rented in somebody else's name," Johnston said. "I kept saying, 'Hey listen, John, you know all they got to do is get this guy in whose name the utilities are in and drag him into court.'

"Well, they didn't get him into court. They got a subpoena and it was never served. The case was in court, ready to go, and was dismissed just before the jury was brought in. They couldn't serve the papers and they couldn't prove that the guy was abating service so they just dismissed the case. Your father had it figured out. I mean he had it called."

No sooner had the case been dismissed than my father told Johnston to get a written order over to the court asking the judge to release the property the police had taken.

"The last time he had been in that situation his lawyer had the paperwork prepared to hand to the judge when the case was dismissed. Well, I didn't have it, but I sure got it over to the judge in a big hurry. We went down to the warehouse and got the stuff out," Johnston said. "He knew the legal system—what it could do for him and how to manipulate it. He needed to have a lawyer fronting him. But in doing the technical work, he knew how the system worked."

My father's casual attitude about the busts carried over into our home. For him, the raids were a cost of doing business; petitioning the court for the return of confiscated furniture was a minor but inescapable aggravation, like filing for a building permit or paying a parking ticket. He didn't think he was doing anything wrong. But I hated the mess the police left; I hated them barging into my bedroom; I resented them for threatening to shoot my dog; and I hated the way I felt ashamed whenever my father's name appeared in the newspaper.

But the police turned out to be the least of my father's problems. Shortly after the second raid, an old debt came back to haunt him.

The knock came at the door one night as I was standing at the refrigerator looking for a snack. It was after ten; my father was upstairs in his room, where we'd been watching the late news on television. The knock startled me—something about it wasn't quite right, but without hesitating, I closed the refrigerator and walked to the front of the house.

As I turned the knob, someone tugged on the door from the other side and pulled it open. I realized why there was something wrong. No one ever knocked on the inside door. Visitors used the doorbell, because the exterior door of the porch was usually secured with . . . the crowbar!

Oh my God! I thought, remembering how I'd let Yukon in a few minutes before. *I forgot the crowbar!*

As the door opened, a bearded man with greasy dark hair that hung to his shoulders poked his head inside.

"Johnny home?" he asked in a menacing tone.

I sensed a terrible danger.

"He's upstairs," I said. "I'll go get him."

I rushed to get my father. When we returned downstairs, the bearded guy and another man were standing in the front hallway. They were dressed in jeans, flannel shirts, and heavy boots. My father tried to draw them aside to talk, but the one with shoulder-length blond hair pointed at me, then at one of the living room chairs.

"You—sit down right there," he said. I did as he said, noticing that he had a rifle tucked under his left arm. My father had hung another dark curtain between the living room and the front hallway. The man stood, right shoulder protruding through it, occasionally glancing over at me. I should have been frightened, but instead I was mad. My father got on the telephone and began yelling at somebody.

"What the hell is this all about?" he shouted into the receiver, his voice as high-pitched and angry as I'd ever heard it. "Get your god-damn punks out of here! I want these sons of bitches out of my house now!"

My father continued to yell into the telephone. After a few minutes, the gunman told me to go upstairs. I did so, thinking as I walked up the stairs that I would escape from the house and go get help. A friend of my father's lived only a few blocks away. He'd know what to do.

When I got to the top of the stairs, I walked into the spare bedroom. The window on the far wall overlooked the carport roof; I could jump, cross the roof, climb down into the alley, and run to my father's friend's house.

That thought lasted until I was halfway through the window.

I had my right leg on the sill, ready to climb out, when something caught my eye. In the glow cast by the corner streetlight I could see the shadow of someone walking back and forth in the front yard. I watched the shadow until I could make it out—it was of a man carrying a rifle. I froze, watching first the shadow and then its owner as he paced past.

When he'd moved away again I backed away from the window. As I did, the front door slammed. I raced to my father's bedroom, which had a window overlooking the front yard, in time to see the three men leading him toward the empty lot behind the Tesoro station. I ran to the phone, hands shaking, and dialed my father's friend's number. As soon as I heard his voice I began screaming.

"They got my father!" I wailed. "They got my father! They got guns! You gotta come help us! You gotta come!"

Before anyone could answer I threw down the phone and ran back to the window to see where the men had gone. Then I heard a sound like a loud firecracker. I ran back to the phone, but no one was there. I knew it was a gunshot. But I didn't panic; I just kept thinking, *My father's okay. My father's okay.*

I sat on the corner of my dad's bed trying to figure out what to do next, when after only a few minutes I heard my father's voice in the front hall, and his friend's too as they entered the house together. They'd bumped into each other in the driveway. I ran down to greet my father.

"Everything's fine," he said, as if he'd just gone out for a pack of Luckies.

Years later, the friend told me what had happened. The men had been hired by another local underworld figure to collect a debt my father owed from the Fats Domino concert. The thugs may have meant only to frighten my father into paying up, but as they led him to a car parked behind the gas station, he bolted for Gambell Street and its stream of traffic, figuring if they were planning on killing him, they'd have to do so in front of plenty of eyewitnesses. His would-be abductors fired one shot, missed, and fled.

When I asked my father that night what was going on, he just smirked. "It's none of your business," he said.

My mother's funeral card

CHAPTER TEN

RUNNING AWAY

The trouble between my father and me had actually started the summer of 1970, when I was twelve. I'd announced that I wanted to enroll in a week-long Christian Bible camp.

I'd learned of the camp from a flier hanging on a bulletin board at a teen center set up in the lunchroom of Wendler, where I went every day that summer vacation to hang out, play pool, and listen to the jukebox.

At the center I did a few art projects and got drunk for the first time. Some friends and I got our hands on a bottle of Jack Daniel's and spent a couple of hours in a nearby alley taking turns slugging down the booze until our heads were spinning and we were puking our guts out. It wasn't long after this preteen rite of passage that I noticed the flier for the Christian camp. My father despised organized religion and once told a friend that he felt it was the "biggest scam of all."

"You're paying for it with your own money," my father snapped at me the day I asked him for the twenty-five-dollar registration fee.

"Fine," I told him, and I did, by saving up some babysitting money and a few paychecks from my first job at the Pink Elephant Car Wash.

It was probably for reasons like this that my father continued to call me by my nickname, "The Little Monster," which originated from the fits I'd throw as a small child when I didn't get my way. As a preteen, I not only continued this practice, I often did what I wanted to anyway, regardless of what my father said.

A schoolbus chartered by the camp picked me up at our house early one Saturday morning. I was half asleep as I clambered aboard, struggling to hang on to my bedroll, knapsack, and a couple of stuffed animals. I took a seat in the back and silently stared out the window during the drive to the camp, nestled deep in a birch forest about an hour north of town.

From the moment I arrived, I was in a state of shock. I'd never been camping before; I hated using an outhouse; I was nearly eaten alive by the mosquitoes; and I was miserably homesick.

I and about a dozen other girls slept on canvas cots in a musty-smelling old army tent. Each night I shivered myself to sleep in temperatures that dipped to 40 degrees. Every morning I awoke to a cold shower taken in a makeshift locker room constructed out of sheets of plywood erected on concrete slabs. Afterward, I'd head to the main dining hall for a breakfast of cold sausage and doughy hotcakes served on flimsy paper plates. While we ate, one of the camp counselors recited the morning's Bible verse.

I spent my days paddling in a canoe around a small nearby lake or sitting in the crafts room gluing sequins and weaving yarn onto everything imaginable. Occasionally we'd be taken on guided hikes through the woods. Every night we'd be herded back into the dining room for dinner, more Bible verses, and a sermon by the camp preacher.

The camp was run by Pentecostals who practiced nightly the laying on of hands and speaking in tongues. The evening service usually ended with everyone standing and waving their arms in the air and shouting "Praise the Lord!" Later, we'd all slip off to our tents, where we girls would take turns accompanying each other to the outhouse. With all the talk of the Devil and demons, we weren't taking any chances as to what might be lurking in the surrounding woods.

One night, when I came down with a head-splitting earache, the camp minister spent half an hour with his hand cupped over my ear yelling, "Satan, I command thee to leave this child in the name of Jesus Christ Our Lord!"

On another night, we all stood in the parking lot in the glow of a harvest gold sunset, crying and clutching each other as a pair of boys fell to the ground and declared themselves "saved" as the preacher stood over them yelling "Hallelujah!" I overheard one of the counselors say that the sunset was God's blessing us for saving the two lost souls.

The camp had a powerful impact on me and I returned home a true believer.

I walked off the bus in front of my house, my arms brimming with a stack of religious pamphlets, two new Bibles, and a head full of Bible stories. The bus no sooner pulled away than I walked into the house and began telling my father that if he didn't find the Lord, he was doomed to hell.

"That's a bunch of crap!" he yelled, grabbing the Bibles and pamphlets from my hands and heaving them out the door. I went chasing after the Bibles, frantically trying to catch each one before it landed in the driveway, the pamphlets fluttering around my head like butterflies.

The Bible camp episode was only the beginning of what became my unconventional teenage rebellion against an even more unconventional father.

As I entered my teens, we began fighting constantly—not unusual in most parent-teen relationships, but in our case the roles were reversed. All our fights followed the same pattern: I'd rail at him for his gambling, late nights, and the friends of his I didn't like. Because there was nothing about his life I liked, I was determined to be the opposite of him.

"Why do you have to be such a moralistic bitch?" he shouted at me during one fight. "Why do you have to hang out with straight people?"

"Because they're not like you," I yelled back.

And my father was *not* like other fathers I knew. The most vivid example occurred near the end of my sixth-grade school year when I came home and found him smoking marijuana. I was stunned. I'd just been through a segment in class on drug abuse and I was convinced, as the lesson had taught, that only depraved deviants smoked pot. I'd seen marijuana once before when my father had taken me to a house where he was doing "some business," which usually meant he'd hole up in some backroom talking over his latest deal. He'd left me in the living room with a couple of hippies who were passing a joint back and forth. They offered it to me; I declined, petrified of what they might do next. They just laughed and walked out of the room. I was furious with my father for placing me in such imminent danger.

That afternoon when I came home and saw that the door to his bedroom was ajar, I peeked in. He couldn't see me, but I could see him passing a joint to another man in the room. He had his stereo on full-blast and hadn't heard me come in. I was too shocked to say anything. The teacher had said that you were to report drug sightings to school authorities, or the police. Now, what was I supposed to do? This was my *dad*.

It wasn't, however, as if he didn't *try* to be a good parent. During my first seventh-grade semester, Yukon ran away or was stolen. All we knew was that he never came home after being let out one day. I must have cried myself to sleep for a month. Finally, my father drove me to the dog pound to find a new pet.

I became discouraged when, after several trips down the aisle that separated the pens of yapping pups, I didn't find a suitable replacement for Yukon. Then my father called me over to where he was kneeling in front of one pen.

"What about this one?" he asked.

I peered into the kennel, and there, in the corner, cowered a black-and-white border collie. We were told he'd been picked up without a collar eating out of garbage cans a few miles north of town. My father had the attendant open the pen and we had to drag the dog out just to take a better look at him. Except for the color difference, he had long fur, just like Yukon. We liked him instantly. No sooner had we gotten him in the car than I decided to also call him Yukon.

That same fall when one of the girls from my circle of friends refused to invite me to her birthday/slumber party, it was my father who saved the day by suggesting I go anyway.

"Think of it as a peace offering," he told me of his plan to have me buy a birthday present and deliver it the night of the party. "I'm sure they'll ask you to stay."

He then had me bring along my pajamas and pillow, "just in case." He waited in the car while I walked up to the door. Moments later, I came bounding back to get my things. He was right.

For me, these memories represent a gentler side of my father, who was sometimes more patient and a better parent than I ever gave him credit. Regardless of whether we were getting along or not, every other day or so he'd still put his arm around me and ask, "You still my girl? You know I love you."

It wasn't enough, however, to keep our life together from unraveling. So, at age fourteen, I left him.

One morning, instead of having the cabdriver take me to school, I directed him to drive me downtown to the Anchorage office of the state Division of Family and Youth Services.

I know where I got the nerve, but I'm not sure where I'd gotten the idea. I think it might have had something to do with Susan Ball.

At Wendler, most kids used their counselors to help them figure out class schedules and choose electives. My counselor became my best friend. Susan was in her twenties, a soft-spoken, attractive woman who wore her straight brown hair in a pageboy. Every chance I got I was in her office, talking about everything going on at home and inside me. She became older sister and mother figure rolled into one, listening to my hopes and my fears, but mostly to stories about my father.

Inside the DFYS building, I gave my name to a receptionist and took a seat on a cold plastic chair in the dreary green, fluorescent-lit waiting room. Scattered at my feet and all around the room were beat-up blocks, dolls, pull toys—nothing a teenager could use to untie the knots in her stomach.

Frances Milner, the division supervisor, stepped into the waiting area and gestured for me to follow her into her office. When I sat down and began talking I kept returning to a single thought.

"I don't want my dad to get into trouble," I said. "I don't want bad things to happen to him."

He must have wondered what had happened. I no longer bought my father gifts that reminded him of the man he wanted to be. Instead, I seemed to despise him for who he was and reminded him constantly of who he was not. Up until that point, the sum of my father's life was made up of a series of small victories and many larger defeats. For years, he hadn't been able to turn his life around financially or personally. Then I turned on him.

As conflicted as I was about going to the child welfare authorities, I didn't know what else to do. Aside from the gambling at our house, my father had been losing his temper more frequently. A change had come over him. What had for years been mostly an affectation of speech and gesture, intended to intimidate and maybe blow off steam, had grown into the impulsive manner of a tyrant.

For years after my father's death, I was haunted by two questions: Why did he hit my mother? Why did he hit me?

How do I tell anyone about the love between my father and me and then tell them about the bruises? How do I explain what it meant when I curled into a little ball every time his voice began to rise? Why is it to this day when someone yells at me I cower and hear his voice, not theirs? Which offenses from our childhoods are forgivable and which ones are not?

I can still feel the depth and ferocity of his anger, an anger that seemed to get worse as I grew older.

Once, as he was leaving the house, I asked where he was going. He slammed me against the hall closet door and held me there with his forearm across my chest as he screamed, *"Do I have to put up with the third degree every time I leave the house?"*

He came home one afternoon when I didn't expect him. I had invited a couple of boys I knew as friends to come over and listen to my new Black Sabbath album. He chased the boys out of the house and began screaming at me and pounding me with his fists while I tucked my head into my chest and drew my knees toward my abdomen.

But the worst episode occurred shortly before I left home, and it's the only time his reasons were apparent to me, even then. I'd lied to him, and what's more, he was beginning to suspect that I was using drugs.

Despite the middle-class makeup of Wendler's student body, my junior high was like every other American secondary school in the early seventies. Most drugs—speed, marijuana, and psychedelics like mescaline and LSD—came in via ninth-grade dealers who had connections at East High, just down the road. I smoked pot, took psychedelics and occasionally speed. Unlike some of my more adventuresome friends, I'd only once smoked pot before going to class and never ever did psychedelics while in school. I couldn't imagine squaring off with the principal in his office while high, as some of my friends had done. My friends and I weren't ruffians; we were never arrested and we didn't sell drugs. We just did them. I didn't even smoke cigarettes because I'd learned to hate the smell of them. Despite my father's smoking marijuana, I knew he'd kill me had he known I was taking drugs.

For a while I went to a psychedelic dance hall called Shaky Acres, where bands with names like Bomax and Freddy Fleet and Fast Feet played in a darkened gymnasiumlike room that pulsed with flashing colored lights. Upstairs was a smaller room with ultraviolet lamps to set off the Day-Glo scrawls painted across its walls and ceiling. My friends and I were just old enough to catch the tail end of the sixties, which as a social phenomenon, at least in Alaska, extended into the early seventies.

One of our rare father-daughter talks had to do with Shaky Acres. He expressed reservations about my going there.

"I know all about the place," he said one day while we were riding together in his car. "There's a lot of drugs, and I don't want to see you get involved in them."

"Oh no, I know better," I told him, lying through my teeth. "I'd never do anything like that."

That summer, I fell in with some older kids from a trailer park south of town. Some friends and I hung out there. I lied about what went on, telling my father I knew a girl who lived with her parents in the trailer. Her name was Rhonda and she *did* live there—but with her husband; they were both around twenty. After school started, my father began to suspect what was going on and he confronted me.

The fight began in the dining room when I asked permission to go to Rhonda's. He asked to meet her parents. We began arguing about it and he accused me of lying to him. As we yelled at each other, his voice began to rise and I knew I had to get out of there. I ran for the door, but halfway out, he grabbed me by the hair and dragged me back inside. As I struggled, he began slapping me and we stumbled into the kitchen. I fell on the floor, curled into a ball, as he began kicking me, the heel of his shoe striking the side of my head, again and again and again.

The next day when I got up for school, I looked in the mirror and saw a deep, purple bruise covering my left ear and extending across my lower left cheek. I vainly tried to comb my hair to cover it. My father had to drive me to school that day because he needed to sign some enrollment papers. He was standing to my left when he brushed my hair aside and looked at my ear.

"I'm sorry," he said softly. "I'm sorry."

The next day I left home.

I told Mrs. Milner about this episode and she reassured me that everything was going to be all right. Everything I said was transposed onto a Petition of Alleged Dependency read into the court record during a hearing a week later. That night, I was placed in a foster home.

> Sept. 22, 1973. Said Child alleged to be dependent or child in need of supervision AS 47.10.010 142. Kim Rich sought help from school authorities and parents of her school friends when she felt she could no longer remain in her father's home. Mr. Rich engages in activities that keep him away from home late at night. Kim states she is literally a prisoner in the home but alone with two dogs. Kim alleges that she is afraid of her father's violent temper as in past when he has struck her. DFYS respectfully requests 30 days custody. The mother of said child is deceased.

My mother had died the previous March.

I first learned that she was seriously ill in the fall of 1970. My Aunt Sandra wrote to my father with the news that my mother had to have a cancerous lump removed from her neck. I read and reread the letter after he handed it to me, feeling curious and frightened.

I didn't think much about my mother. I remember my father mentioning her only once. We were in his car and I was riding in the backseat and a friend of his was in the front passenger seat. I knew he had a letter from my mother because I overheard him say, "She only writes when she wants money."

Even then I thought his remark was callous; at the same time I wondered, as children of all divorced parents do, whether they'd ever get back together. But I didn't miss her. I can't really say why.

I knew my mother had been hospitalized, but until I got a copy of her medical records some seventeen years after her death, I knew little else. I find her records compelling and difficult reading.

"Frances remained out of the hospital for approximately ten years, returning on 1–7–65," begins the one-page summary of my mother's institutionalization at Newberry State Hospital, where her family had her recommitted.

Like many such facilities, the hospital dated to Victorian days; its red brick walls, peaked roof, and barred windows were the very picture of what most people meant when they said "insane asylum." Set on 560 acres of woods and farmland, Newberry Hospital eventually occupied twenty buildings. Originally there was a blacksmith's shop, along with a working farm and creamery, but by the time my mother arrived for her second stay, the smithy was gone, along with the farm, the creamery, and much of the acreage.

My mother's return to Newberry occurred when mental institutions strove mainly to keep patients from hurting themselves or one another, usually by means of physical or chemical restraints. In other words, she was warehoused, but on an intermittent basis. Whenever she seemed to be herself again, the hospital discharged her to her family's care.

When she was admitted in January 1965, she was coherent, showing symptoms of depression and anxiety, and suffering from memory problems, a probable side effect of her prior shock treatments. She was discharged ten weeks later, and stayed out until October. The following May she was released. In September 1967 she was returned, this time "talking readily but somewhat confused. She was bitter about relations and appeared depressed. Frances ate and slept well but showed little change during the first month of her return."

Aside from weekends and sometimes holidays when a kindly orderly took her home to stay with his family, my mother never again left Newberry, and her family, who infrequently left the city limits for any reason, rarely went to visit.

Lena says she didn't have a grasp of reality, so visiting also didn't make much sense. But like many suffering from mental illness, my mother had good days, and that must have been the case when one relative went to visit and left wondering why she was there at all. When I inquired further, the relative refused to talk about it, afraid that what she would say might upset the rest of the family, or me.

My mother's family was no worse than most other families in the same situation. They didn't know what to do. They were afraid of my mother. She had become a monster to them. She'd swear at them and throw objects. For a long time the family was even blamed for mental illness. Blaming my mother's family now for being neglectful or thoughtless, or simply choosing to remain ignorant is pointless. They might even have done the best they could. All I can do now is look at my mother's records and wonder how things might have been different in another hospital, at another time. Or maybe nothing would have been different.

Under the heading "Behavior," my mother's personal characteristics were described as either "Appropriate" or "Inappropriate." Under the former, she was described as "maintains self in daily activities of living; fairly well oriented; expresses self clearly and distinctly; socializes fairly well; reads and writes." Under the latter, she was accused of having "poor taste in dressing and personal hygiene; lacks motivation or insight; refuses assignments; preoccupied with physical complaints; memory poor at times."

After a month in the hospital, my mother's records say that the doctors put her on a regular dose of intravenous Navane, an antipsychotic drug commonly used to treat schizophrenia. Her behavior improved for a while and she was given "ground privileges." However, these were suspended when she "struck another patient across the ear with a book for no apparent reason. Three days later she refused her medications and became very hostile and combative. Throughout this [sic] balance of this year she continued to resist taking medications and frequently complained of physical problems.

"On January 9th of 1968, she was assigned to a cooking class but ten days later she was dropped because she was upsetting others. She continued to be argumentative over the need or reason for her hospitalization and to resist taking her medications. She had numerous physical complaints and often expressed herself in an obscene and vulgar manner. In December of 1968, she was considered to have shown little change and to have no work assignment."

In April 1969, she complained of stomach pains; an examination found jaundice, prompting doctors to put her in isolation for fear that she might have hepatitis. But the jaundice subsided and she was allowed to return to her room. Her fretting about health problems continued: "She complained constantly about multiple aches and pains and needed to be forced to bath [sic] and go to the dining room. She did no work and was unable to take care of her cigarettes or spending money."

On May 31, 1970, attendants noticed a lump below her right ear. The medical staff treated it with antibiotics but the swelling persisted. After an examination in the hospital clinic, doctors sent her to Pontiac State Hospital, where tests found a malignancy. She had cancer of the larynx. The doctors cut out the tumor and treated her with radioactive cobalt. She refused to undergo further surgery, and returned to Newberry, her face swollen from the surgery and radiation.

But her spirits evidently improved in the next few months, and she became more cooperative. She was returned to her room, where she spent the winter without attracting much notice.

In January 1971, my father sent a brief letter to Newberry, writing: "I am the ex-husband of Frances Ann Chiaravalli [sic] (Rich). I am concerned over the state of her health," he wrote. "Please advise me of her state of health and possibility of release. Myself and her 12-year-old daughter both love her and miss her very much."

Less than a year later, the cancer was back—this time in her liver—and despite her objections, she was sent back to Pontiac, where she began a steady decline. Now considered terminal, she had cancer throughout her body. Her attitude was still belligerent, but she seemed also touched with an awareness of and sadness at her impending death.

My mother's final months are documented in a series of three- and four-line paragraphs filling seven pages of her hospital records, spanning a period of time from when her cancer first appeared in May of 1970 until her death, nearly two years later.

> . . . 37 year old female convalescing from recent surgery on her neck, to return to Pontiac State Hospital soon for re-evaluation of recurrent symptoms. Quite depressed and felt maybe she would respond among other younger patients. Patient is getting very difficult to handle, refuses personal hygiene, requires 2 employees to bathe. . . .
> 9–3–71: Doing well, alert, cooperative. No complaints. May return to original ward. . . .
> 2–4–72: Patient returned to Pontiac. Patient refused treatment. On liver scan metastasis was present. Patient to be treated symptomatically. . . .
> 2–11–72: Steady deterioration, some dyspnea. Oxygen PRN given makes patient more comfortable. Almost complete nursing care. . . .
> 2–14–72: Conditions deteriorating. Metastatic tumor of liver, dyspnea possibly due to tumor of trachea and lungs. Diarrhea. . . .

2–14–72: Dyspnea accentuate to the point that tracheotomy was necessary. Family notified. . . .

2–15–72: Doing well, alert, comfortable, afebrile. Tracheotomy working well, dry. . . .

2–22–72 MENTAL STATUS EXAMINATION: It should be emphasized that this patient is now considered to be terminally ill with proven carcinoma of the neck with extensive local and distant metastasis. This carcinoma has been treated both surgically and by irradiation but still has recurred to a sufficient degree to require insertion of tracheotomy tube during this past week. Currently the patient is bedfast as a result of terminal illness. Her bladder and bowel habits are tidy. Appetite is poor and she is not able to do any significant amount of ambulation. Historically, her sleep habits have been irregular and her behavior frequently uncooperative, negativistic and overtalkative. Mood wise, the patient historically has been somewhat belligerent and inappropriate. It is obviously appropriate that she is now fearful, sad and concerned regarding her illness. Generally her orientation has been only marginal and she has only been in partial contact with reality. She has been considered to be delusional at times and has had a poor memory. Her physical health obviously at the present is poor and deteriorating.

In mid-February 1972, two weeks before I turned fourteen, one of my aunts called my father to deliver the news that my mother was near death. I was told she had one week to live.

"I'm working with your aunts to try to send you back there," my father told me. "I can't afford to go and we're trying to figure out who can meet you in Chicago to make the connection to Ironwood. Your mother's last dying wish is to see you."

So I waited for news of when I'd be leaving.

Two weeks later I was on the phone with a friend when my father told me to hang up. He had been crying.

"Your mother died this morning," he said slowly. "They say she lived longer than expected, by almost a week."

He told me that it was probably better that I didn't get to see her; she weighed only eighty pounds when she died. Then he mumbled something about problems in finding a relative to meet the connecting flight in Chicago. He said she'd been told I was coming to see her and he thought she lasted longer because she was waiting for me to arrive.

I nodded and sat silently, waiting for him to leave the room. As soon as he did I picked up the receiver and dialed my friend's phone number.

"My father just told me my mother died," I said, and I refused to say anything more. I didn't cry, and I wouldn't for a long time.

On March 7, the doctors placed a final note in my mother's file, they called it a "Death Note: *Patient expired today at 4:25* A.M. *Mucus obstructed the tracheotomy tube. Cause of Death: Respiratory Obstruction; Metastatic Carcinoma of Pharynx and Neck; Metastatic Carcinoma in Liver. Relatives notified. Funeral arrangements will be done."*

She died one week before her thirty-eighth birthday.

"Yes, sir."

That was all I said during my first visit to the second-floor hearing room of the Alaska State Courthouse, but that was all it took to get me awarded to the care of the State of Alaska on October 20, 1972—at least until another hearing could be held the next month. At the first hearing—eventually there were five—my father wasn't around. Other adults, including the court master who ran the proceedings, did all the talking.

I had a little more to say at subsequent hearings. Once I asked for a lawyer, but took care to avert my eyes from my father's. He was sitting on the opposite side of the table.

I wanted an attorney because I was afraid that anything I said would be used against him in court. The assistant attorney general representing the state wouldn't promise not to use my testimony against my father, and my social worker suggested that I ask for my own lawyer.

The master ruled that a public defender would be appointed to advise me and extended my status as a ward of the court until a later hearing that would determine how long I'd remain in the state's care.

Once again, my father got his attorney, this time Jim Johnston, to fight for custody. Johnston remembers how hard it was for my father, nearing middle age, to make the changes that I demanded.

"Unless you have some remarkable characteristics, you don't change," Johnston said. "You'd have to change everything. Your friends, your way of looking at people and being with people. Your father would have had to undo the patterns of his adult life. He almost certainly would have had to go somewhere else where he wasn't known

and start from scratch, with no skills. People do that on occasion, but
that's quite a . . . I guess the point about age is that you get tired. He
tried, and he did the best he could."

At first I enjoyed being a ward of the state. I was taken on a shopping
spree for new clothes, but living with foster families got very old, very
quickly.

My first foster family was a young couple with a small baby. He
taught school; she stayed home. They kept insisting I attend their services at their church. I asked my social worker for another placement.

The second was with a family of five who lived in a split-level in
Roger's Park with their two natural daughters, both teenagers, and one
other foster child. Things went badly from the start. I shared a bedroom
with the daughters and we bickered constantly. Besides, I found it difficult adjusting to the routines of regular family life. I disliked it every
time I was made to set the table.

After a couple of months, I asked to return home, but before that
could happen, the court ordered my father and me to undergo family
counseling.

Twice a week, we met with a therapist, a gentle-looking man about
my father's age. Most of my sessions were alone with the counselor. I
felt safe in his office, free to talk about how I wanted to be an artist or
actress or dancer. During sessions with my father, I gradually began to
challenge him on the way he'd raised me. My father gamely endured
my personal attacks. It was not his style to bring his problems to total
strangers. But he never got angry and instead tried calmly to explain
himself. He defended his way of life and that of his friends, prompting
the therapist to ask whether it would be all right with him if I decided
to become a prostitute when I grew up.

"No," he said nonchalantly. "But I had hoped she'd go to blackjack
dealer's school in Nevada."

I was floored. He had no idea what I wanted to do with my life.
He'd never listened to me at all. I'd never expressed any interest in
gambling or in his after-hours clubs. I couldn't believe it. Once when
I told him I wanted to drop out of school when I turned sixteen, he
told me that would be a mistake, that he wished he had more of an
education, and that the only way to get ahead in the world was to go

to college. Now, here he was talking about my getting a job in a Las Vegas casino.

Despite such momentary setbacks, by November I was ready to move back in with my father. He'd done as I asked, removing the gambling from the house. One afternoon, I had my foster mother drive me over to pick up some things. It was a relief to walk inside and find the poker, craps, and billiards tables gone. The house, shabby as it was, looked like a place where ordinary people lived. I decided to walk around and see what the rest of the rooms looked like.

My good mood vanished when I walked upstairs. In the spare bedroom, I found a narrow, padded table beside a studio light and a camera mounted on a tripod. The setup looked weird, scary, sexual, and certainly illegal. I ran out of the house.

"What's wrong?" my foster mother asked.

"Nothing," I said.

"Are you sure?"

"Yeah, I'm just mad at my father."

My foster mother dropped me off at school as lunch period was ending. I ran into my friend Cathy Hart near one of the back doors, in the crowd milling in the halls for a few seconds before settling down in a classroom.

"I need to talk to you," I said, barely able to hear myself over the din of hallway chatter and lockers slamming.

"I can't now," Cathy said. "I gotta get to class, how about later?"

"No, I . . . I need to talk to you *now!*" I said.

"I can't," Cathy explained. "I'm always late for this class and if . . ."

"I NEED TO TALK TO YOU NOW!" I shouted.

My yell—and no doubt the look on my face—stopped her cold.

"What's wrong?"

"My father. Ah, he, he . . . "

Before I could get the words out, I burst into tears. Everything seemed to be exploding inside me. I turned to the fire box on the wall beside me and slammed my fist through the glass door. The noise in the hall stopped for a second, then surged as a crowd gathered around me in a blur.

.   .   .

At our next counseling session, I asked my father what was going on. He explained that he had turned the 736 Club into a nude photo studio, where customers paid to take pictures of naked women.

Later that week the state filed a new petition to extend temporary custody of me through the middle of the next June. Most of the petition echoed the original version, but with an extra note at the end: "Mr. Rich and Kim continue to counsel at the Center for Children and Parents. Although some progress has been made they appear to be at least temporarily deadlocked. Kim doesn't feel she can return to her father's home until his questionable business and home are in separate locations."

PART 3

ENDGAME

Cindy's Health Spa and Massage, after my father took it over in 1973
COURTESY *ANCHORAGE DAILY NEWS*

CHAPTER ELEVEN

CINDY'S

On weekday mornings Jury Assembly Room B–52 in the basement of the Alaska State Courthouse is filled with dozens of sleepy people each holding a plastic cup of coffee in one hand and a jury summons in the other. But by the afternoon, everyone has been farmed out to the courtrooms upstairs, and B–52 is quiet, its blue and gold vinyl chairs empty.

Not long ago I sat in one of those chairs, alone in the room with a court clerk, both of us only a few feet from a television set atop a cart. I was there to see my father, who had been dead for nearly twenty years.

In early April 1973, several months after my father's foray into his "nude photo studio" business, he was subpoenaed as a witness for the prosecution in a murder trial in Anchorage. At the time, I had no idea of his involvement in the case. The trial involved a man named Clarence Wesley Ladd, who was accused of killing a small-time pimp and heroin dealer named Ferris Rezk, Jr., over a business deal that had gone sour.

Since statehood, all criminal and civil trials had been recorded on audiotape. But with the advance of video technology, during Ladd's trial, the court system was considering videotaping the proceedings as well. The video program was eventually scrapped, but not before Ladd's trial and a handful of other civil and criminal matters were taped, and those tapes boxed and forgotten. When I learned that the tapes existed, a court clerk found them collecting dust in a corner of a courthouse storage vault.

The Ladd trial, a month long and the lengthiest Alaska criminal trial of its day, filled sixty-six of the large, black, three-quarter-inch, one-hour cassette tapes. Every witness, every piece of evidence, every remark, even the faces of dozens of spectators who showed up daily, was recorded. My father's testimony appears on tapes 57 and 58.

Having covered courts for the *Anchorage Daily News* for several years I was accustomed to court proceedings, familiar with the judicial system, and had often reviewed portions of trials on audiotape. But nothing I'd been through prepared me for the moment the image of my father appeared on the television screen.

I was stunned. I clapped my hands to my mouth as if to muffle a gasp, but nothing came out. I felt a surge of conflicting emotions; I wanted to simultaneously laugh and cry. The opening minutes of the tape triggered a rush of memories and feelings, of things important and things forgotten—the way he'd grimace, the funny little noises he made when deep in thought, the silly goatee he'd grown that year in his attempt at the "mod" look, how much my hands resembled his.

As he approached the witness stand and spoke, I knew his voice instantly, but I had not remembered what it sounded like, nor had I realized how much my own is like his.

"State your full name for the record," the in-court clerk asked.
"John Francis Rich, Junior," my father answered.
"Your address?" she asked.
"736 East 12th," he said.
"And your occupation?"
"I own a massage parlor."

That's why he was there.

The name of the parlor was "Cindy's," and of all the tearing down and rebuilding that have occurred in Anchorage over the years, I'm amazed that the awkward-looking, flat-roofed building that once housed Anchorage's most infamous massage parlor is still left standing. It was the last business my father would get involved in; the last angle Johnny Rich would work.

The building hasn't been a massage parlor in a long time. A succession of small businesses has come and gone from the five-room structure that, like so many other of the buildings that housed my father's enterprises, was once somebody's home, with a kitchen, bedrooms, and a living room. I remember it as a cramped, dark place, not unlike his after-hours gambling parlors, with a living room, or in this case, a "customer waiting room," furnished with the same variety of auction-house bargains—a cheesy green couch, a couple of red glass lamps, a laminated coffee table, some production-line oil paintings, and a beat-up stereo console. The room was always dimly lit by red or blue light bulbs.

My father took over the lease on Cindy's in December 1972. He always said that the business had a good location. He was right. In those days, Cindy's was located off West 29th Street, a two-lane road that ran east to west, two blocks parallel to Northern Lights Boulevard and its busy commercial district.

I remember going to Cindy's, where I'd sometimes sit with my father in the "living quarters": a large den and kitchen area where we'd watch TV and eat our favorite dessert, vanilla ice cream with chocolate syrup. The nightly bowl of ice cream and syrup had been a ritual as long as I'd lived with him, and that wasn't about to change no matter where we were. While at Cindy's, I tried not to think about what went on in the other rooms. I don't know if customers were there when I was present or not. A thick, dark curtain, not unlike the one that separated our living area from my father's gambling den, hung between the kitchen and the rest of the parlor. Once I stepped into the "Purple Room," so called because of the tinted light bulbs that cast a bruised glow. I found the same type of table that had repelled me so when I found it in our house. The room's ceiling was covered with mirrored tiles. I closed the door and went back to the kitchen for more ice cream.

The name "Cindy's" might have come from the woman who owned it before my father took over the business—Patricia "Cindy" Bennett—although I've heard that it was already named Cindy's when she and her live-in boyfriend/business partner Ferris Rezk took it over sometime around 1971. They turned it into a profitable enterprise selling sex disguised as "massages." Cindy's is the reason Rezk was murdered; it is also the reason my father was killed.

Two men dead. I wish they'd tear that building down.

That September of 1972, when I first went to state authorities asking to be taken from my father's home, just a few blocks away three people whom I would never meet, but whose lives would soon collide with mine—Ladd, Rezk, and Bennett—walked into the offices of a downtown law firm to finalize a bill of sale.

Ladd, who went by his middle name, Wesley, was buying Cindy's massage parlor from Bennett and Rezk. The parlor was Cindy's main stock in trade; Ferris had other interests: a used car lot, a loan-sharking operation, and—according to police—a thriving heroin distribution network.

Ladd had only seen Cindy's once, the same night he put down four thousand dollars cash as a deposit to buy the parlor, which had been one of the first entrants into what was then Anchorage's fastest-growing vice game.

Nobody pretended that Cindy's and its twenty or so competitors were selling legitimate massage services; they were whorehouses, plain and simple. But as in tenderloins all around America, on side streets off Northern Lights Boulevard, the sale of sex in the early seventies had acquired a veneer of respectability, thanks to business names like Bali-Ha'i, La [sic] Chateau, and Misiko's Health Studio.

Historically a transient town with lots of lonely soldiers and airmen, Anchorage was no stranger to flesh peddling. But for decades its prostitutes had worked the streets and bars and hotels, rather than setting up shop in fixed locations. The massage parlor gambit changed that pattern practically overnight.

By getting into the massage parlor business when he did, Ladd, like a lot of others, considered himself getting in on the ground floor of Alaska's next, and its largest, boom ever—the oil boom.

Four years earlier, in February 1968, a thousand miles north of Anchorage, an oil crew found a layer of oil-saturated sand near Prudhoe Bay on the Beaufort Sea, in a region known as the North Slope. The well they named Prudhoe Bay No. 1 pumped nearly 1,200 barrels a day, but the crew's sponsors at Atlantic Richfield and Humble Oil and Refining Co. were skeptical. A 1966 expedition in the area had seemed promising, but wound up losing $4.5 million. Oil companies had been working the Beaufort Sea for years, but no one had come up with anything as good as Prudhoe Bay No. 1, later dubbed the Discovery Well.

On March 13, a second well seven miles southeast convinced even the grimmest skeptics that Alaska held one of the last great deposits of oil and natural gas.

Alaska wasn't new to oilmen. Since World War II the navy had explored a 37,000-square-mile strategic petroleum reserve also located along Alaska's North Slope, but never developed it. South of Anchorage, wells along Cook Inlet were producing 195,000 barrels a day—an impressive figure, but one dwarfed by the second well showed to be under the ground at Prudhoe Bay. That strike was so big and so rich the companies kept it secret for three months before announcing that it had tapped an oil reserve of as much as ten billion barrels of recoverable oil.

Fairbanks became an overnight staging area for the assault on the North Slope. The Fairbanks airport, noted *U.S. News & World Report,* looked as if it were in a war zone, its tarmac strewn with tracked vehicles, trucks, fuel tanks, drilling rigs, stacks of pipe, and prefabricated buildings. At the edge of town, crews were starting the job of scraping a 429-mile road to Prudhoe Bay, and setting the stage for the pipeline that would carry the oil overland down to Valdez, the fishing town that would serve as the pipeline's southern terminus. Everyone was talking about getting a chunk of tundra and turning it into a house in Hawaii.

A year and a half after the oil find, on September 10, 1969, the State of Alaska sold off 450,858 acres of the North Slope in Anchorage during a seven-hour auction. The auction was held downtown at the Sydney Laurence Auditorium and covered live on television. The sale attracted representatives of the world's largest and richest oil companies—Amerada Hess, Getty, Mobil, Phillips Petroleum, Standard Oil of California, Union Oil of California, ARCO, Texaco, Shell, and others. Some collaborated on bids; others went independent.

Many of the oil executives arrived on sixteen company jets that attracted a lot of attention at the airport. Never before had so many private jets come into Anchorage, and never before had the hotels been so booked.

Also attending the sale were more than a dozen top financiers from some of the nation's largest brokerage and investment firms, who came to town to get acquainted with Alaska's potential in the municipal bond market.

"Boy, I'll tell you," said one television announcer, "I don't believe I've ever seen as many pinstriped suits in town as I have in the last few days."

While hundreds filled the tiny concert hall, dozens more lined up outside waiting to get in. Nearly a hundred members of the national and international press were on hand for the sale, including reporters from Europe and Japan and film crews from NBC, ABC, CBS, and the BBC. NBC even sent newsman David Brinkley to anchor the event.

Never before in Alaska's ten-year history as a state had so many people paid so much attention to something that had become so common as oil and gas lease sales. The state had held twenty-two sales before Prudhoe Bay. None of the previous sales, however, covered an area as large or was as rich in oil and gas reserves. For days proceeding the auction, the local newspapers gave the pending lease sale almost exclusive front-page coverage. Only the death of North Vietnamese President Ho Chi Minh rivaled it in news inches. The rest of the world was watching and reacting as well. On Wall Street, the stocks of oil companies expected to participate made substantial gains, creating a flurry of trading activity.

Two days before the sale, ARCO announced it had ordered the construction of the largest commercial oil tankers ever built. The ships, the first scheduled to be completed by the end of 1972, would be used to haul North Slope crude oil to West Coast refineries. It was the largest single order ever placed in an American shipyard.

The more than two dozen representatives in attendance from Bank of America, the state's banking agent, had crafted a *Mission: Impossible*–style plan that involved chartering a DC–8 jet to whisk away the winning bid checks to New York City. The scheme was to get the checks to the bank before the doors opened for business the next morning.

The objective was to collect as much interest as possible—interest that could run higher than $10,000 a day.

"When you're talking about this much money, timing is everything," one banking official understated during a brief, on-camera interview.

The sale brought in the highest total bonuses ever offered in U.S. history—$900 million. Twenty percent of the money was paid to the state immediately. No sooner had the checks left the ground under armed escort than speculation ran rampant about how to spend it. Some wanted to do away with all income and property taxes (Alaska state income tax was eventually scrapped). Others envisioned the state investing in huge fish-processing factories (the idea was nixed). An Oklahoma company proposed building a futuristic city across Knik Arm from Anchorage. Billed as the "Houston of Alaska," it would be like the bottled city of Kandor in Superman comics—covered by a dome, with moving sidewalks and escalators connecting glass-and-steel skyscrapers. There would be no cars; instead an aerial tramway would connect "Seward's Success," as the new city would be called, to Anchorage. It never materialized.

Work hadn't started on the trans-Alaska oil pipeline by the time Ladd invested his money in Cindy's, but he and everyone else believed that once construction began Anchorage would become Party Central for thousands of lonely workers with time on their hands, cash in their pockets, and sex on their minds. A place like Cindy's would be a license to print money.

The forty-six-year-old, twice divorced, renegade Michigander had grown up in and out of reform schools. Although he received a GED equivalency diploma, Ladd was only formally educated until the fourth grade, when his father yanked him out of school to help on the family farm. As a young man, he'd been jailed for a variety of petty crimes, and a more serious felony burglary conviction, before moving to Cordova, Alaska, in 1965. In Cordova, he straightened up and worked as a commercial fisherman, carpenter, cannery operator, and sometime fur trapper.

Ladd moved to Anchorage in 1972 after seven years in Cordova, freshly divorced and with a grubstake of several thousand dollars that he intended to use to get into a new line of business. His red hair and drawn expression became well known in the shadowlands of Anchorage's entertainment circuit, where the massage parlor game attracted his attention.

The parlors were sweaty little money machines—minimal overhead, maximum return on investment. You rented a storefront, divided it up into cubicles, installed some cheap cots. The classier places had whirlpool baths and mirrored ceilings, but most customers didn't care about such niceties. Some customers dropped thousands of dollars a night at joints like Cindy's.

The prices were similar all over town: sauna or steam bath, $5; straight massage, $10; a "local" (masturbation), $20; "French Massage" (fellatio), $40; and of course, "Sex," $50. Also available, one hour with a masseuse/prostitute for whatever reason, $100. Many masseuses worked for an hourly wage, earning around $300 a week.

Ladd was a regular at the Kit Kat Club, a topless bar out on the Old Seward Highway that advertised itself as having the region's only glass stage and "psychedelic" lighting. Small, rundown, and gritty, the Kit Kat operated in the usual way, flying in dancers from Portland and Seattle whose firm young bodies drew a full house every night. In the old Anchorage tradition, the men were eager to buy the girls drinks and jewelry and furs. Ladd was no different; sometimes he spent $100 a night at the Kit Kat.

Places like the Kit Kat also functioned as recruiting centers for the parlors, which employed around seventy girls. Besides dancers, the parlors also hired prostitutes, who saw in the houses a chance to get off the street. The massage parlors offered a predictable schedule, a manager to screen the freaks, and a regular income—as much as $2,000 a month for the big money earners.

The parlors had another advantage. Borough law didn't address such operations, and city law didn't adjust for this latest wrinkle in the sex trade until 1972, when Anchorage mandated that parlors be licensed and that masseuses be "of good moral character," with no record of "pimping, pandering, prostitution, solicitation, lewd or lascivious acts with a child, larceny, robbery, assault with a deadly weapon or other similar crimes." The new law also barred massage parlors from operating between nine P.M. and eight A.M.—until then, their busiest hours—

in residential neighborhoods. Masseuses couldn't solicit or perform "an act of prostitution, cunnilingus or fellatio."

Even so, outside the city limits—but within minutes of downtown— a massage parlor was as legal as a laundromat. By the end of 1972 all but three had relocated to Spenard, a classic American red-light district, as wild and undomesticated as its namesake.

In 1916, Joe Spenard ran the City Express taxi service, which consisted of a bright yellow Model-T Ford plastered with lost-and-found notices, tide tables, and snippets of his personal philosophy. He always wore a yellow duster and top hat, and usually smoked a fat cigar.

Joe homesteaded the tract of woods he cleared around the lake he named for himself, turning it into a resort. The town that grew up around the lake lived up to such shady beginnings; its streets were lined with strip joints, pawnshops, liquor stores, exotic restaurants, and (as of 1972) massage parlors, their facades blinking and neon-trimmed. In the newspapers the owners advertised "Lovely Girls," "Have Masseuses Will Travel," "Thee Body Shop Massage, come on in and get your batteries checked and charged," and "Sensu Massage with Superb Girls."

In the seventies, the borough of Anchorage, which included Spenard and all other areas outside the city limits, contracted for police patrols by the city force, and saw no need to pass its own law against prostitution, since the state and city already banned it. The borough was also slow in tightening up its nudity laws, allowing a proliferation of topless and bottomless bars. Inside the city limits, only the top could come off.

In trying to protect innocent women from baseless charges brought out of malice, the state supreme court had also made it tough to convict someone of prostitution. To do so, the court ruled, an arresting officer needed a witness to corroborate his complaint that an offer of prostitution had been made. Third-party witnesses were scarce in the tiny cubbyholes of Spenard's massage parlors.

The thriving nature of the business and the complicated set of circumstances that worked against the authorities—along with the rumored average weekly receipts of up to $5,000—must have made the $10,000 price for Cindy's seem like a bargain to Ladd. The year before he'd looked into starting a parlor of his own in partnership with a girlfriend who was in the life. They'd bought a house in South Anchorage but before they opened realized they couldn't get a license.

Ladd lost $1,500 on that deal, and shortly afterward went shopping for a car. He stopped at Rezk's lot and wound up recounting the tale of his abortive investment.

Rezk suggested that Ladd check out Cindy's, and that night they visited the parlor. After a quick walk-through and discussion of the business, Ladd handed over the down payment in cash and agreed to pay the $6,000 balance in equal installments of $3,000 each over the course of the next two months. Rezk wrote out a receipt and the two agreed to have Rezk's attorney draw up a formal contract that they could sign later.

The six-page contract Cindy Bennett and Ladd drew up a few days later in the presence of a lawyer and notary public included a thorough listing of all the parlor's furniture according to what room it was located in, either the three massage rooms—the "Red Room," "Green Room," and "Purple Room"—or one of two living rooms, one set aside in the back, next to the kitchen, as a lounge for the girls, the other, inside the front door, where the customers waited. The list included everything from massage tables and couches to knickknacks and towels. The contract set the final payment due on November 26.

On November 27, a snow plow operator in South Anchorage called the police about a 1968 blue Plymouth with a body in the backseat. The car was parked on a quiet street near Angelus Memorial Park cemetery, a few blocks from the Kit Kat Club. Rezk's brown sweater was pulled up over his head and shoulders. A fleece-lined jacket covered him. Someone had fired a single .38-caliber bullet into the back of his head.

The next day, the Alaska State Troopers arrested Ladd and charged him with first-degree murder.

My father told me about his plans for Cindy's while we were driving around one day in early December. I was still living in a foster home and occasionally we'd get together for dinner or go to a movie. He edged into the topic by talking about the difficulties of opening a small business. He said the fire insurance companies were gouging him because of the type of business he ran. Another parlor had been fire-bombed recently, so the insurers felt justified in hiking his premiums, on the assumption that his place was likelier than another kind of business to have a Molotov cocktail tossed through the window.

Then he went off on a tangent, complaining about how shoe companies could sell footwear labeled as made of leather in the U.S. when in fact, he claimed, the shoes were made in Brazil out of pressed cardboard. As usual, I wondered what he was talking about. I don't think he ever came right out and said, "I'm now in the massage parlor business."

He'd tried to open one in the house on 12th Avenue after I'd moved out, or so I learned from his testimony in Ladd's murder trial, but he couldn't get a permit since the house was inside the city limits. Hence his photo studio idea. But he didn't give up on his hopes of owning a parlor. So he cast farther afield. He was about to open a place in Spenard when he heard Cindy's was up for lease.

On December 15—two weeks after Rezk's murder and Ladd's arrest—my father leased Cindy's, agreeing to pay the building's owners four hundred dollars a month. He changed the name to the "New Cindy's Health Spa & Massage."

At that point, I didn't care what kind of business my father was in, as long as it didn't take place in my home. The state dropped its bid to retain custody of me since my father had taken the gambling and photo studio out of the house. But some of his friends were superstitious about Cindy's.

"The place has bad vibes," one told my dad. "One man's already died here, John. You don't want the place."

It wasn't advice my father was willing to listen to. He was five months shy of forty and for the first time in many years, on firm financial ground. After one business failure upon another, he had hit bottom the previous April, filing for bankruptcy protection in U.S. District Court in Anchorage. His bankruptcy file bears witness to the "financial hole," as he called it, he'd been in for years.

The documents list sixty-four creditors, holding $55,422 in outstanding, unsecured debts, not including $1,700 owed to the Internal Revenue Service.

My father hadn't been paying his bills since about 1968. He owed for rent, he owed for fuel, he owed for freight delivery charges. We'd been skipping along from house to house half a step ahead of the bill collectors. His creditors included everyone from ex-landlords seeking hundreds of dollars in unpaid rent to Fats Domino's concert fee of

$4,500 (the debt owed Domino is listed between Denali Fuel [$350] and Emery Air Freight [$37]). A number of collection agencies are listed, each representing a handful of clients.

Eleven creditors have the words "suit pending" or "judgment" printed beside them. My father had been in and out of court so often that he'd frequently show up for judgment debtor hearings without the aid of his attorney. He knew what he needed to do and couldn't see spending any more money than necessary on legal matters he could handle himself. Knowing the power of judges to seize assets, my father tried to have as few of them as possible, and what he did own was frequently kept in other people's names.

My father might have been able to continue ignoring his mounting pile of debts had it not been for the IRS, which was intent on collecting its money. Knowing that the government agents who kept calling weren't going to give up, he decided to settle his tax debt by selling the one true asset he had—his three-and-a-half-carat diamond ring. It was a difficult decision for my father to make, but in the end he felt he had no choice. He needed the cash. But as with so many of my father's run-ins with government institutions and the justice system, the matter wouldn't be that easily resolved.

Just prior to filing for bankruptcy he lost a judgment in a civil suit brought by one of the collection agencies that had been after him for months. When my father didn't—or couldn't—pay the judgment, the agency owner decided to get his money by going after my father's most visible and valued possession: the diamond ring.

One afternoon when I wasn't at home, two state troopers, wielding a court order, arrived at our house. Not only did they snatch my father's ring right off his finger, they confiscated his Rolex watch, a gold ring with the letters *JR,* and his 1964 Chevy El Camino pickup, in addition to some other items. Under the auspices of the court, the collection agency planned to sell off the items in an execution sale to pay off my father's court judgment.

Not only were my father's plans ruined, he was embarrassed, said his attorney Jim Johnston. His only hope of getting the ring and the other items back was to file for bankruptcy. He probably would have done so eventually anyway, but the seizure, coupled by pressure from the IRS, forced him to move quickly. By immediately filing for protection from his creditors, he could get the bankruptcy judge to stop the sale of the rings and the other items. They would then be included in his bankruptcy list of assets to be auctioned off. The first to be paid of his creditors, as always, would be the IRS.

"The IRS was not going to go away," said Johnston. "Regardless, he was going to lose the property. Why not divert the process to settle the one debt that nagged him the most?"

The scheme almost worked. The bankruptcy court judge did order the ring and the other items pulled under his court's jurisdiction. But after that my father's plans fell apart. The court, as is customary, appointed a trustee to handle the sale of my father's assets. In turn, the trustee sold the ring and my father's other jewelry at a private, unadvertised sale for a fraction of their value. (My father wanted them to be sold in an auction, which likely would have brought in more money.)

Both rings sold for $950. My father claimed the diamond ring alone was worth at least $6,000. An appraisal by the buyer found it to be worth $2,500.

After the trustee's fees were paid, there was little money left to satisfy the IRS. My father was livid. He spent months unsuccessfully trying to get the court to rescind the sale. He said he had a buyer willing to pay at least as much as he owed the IRS. But the buyer—the trustee's own lawyer—claimed he had the ring reset with other diamonds and wouldn't be willing to part with it for less than $5,000.

Not only did his plans fail, my father felt cheated and betrayed by the court, which refused to see things his way. Despite his own past experiences at trying to manipulate and beat the system, my father expected the court officials to be fair and honest.

"It was frustrating to your father because here are these upright lawyers and court officials who were as crooked as anything he ever did," said Johnston, who believes that the sale of the jewelry amounted to little more than a sweetheart deal between the trustee and his friends. In those days, there was little oversight of trustees' activities, he said.

The final settlement of my father's bankruptcy case didn't go nearly as quickly as the sale of his beloved ring. After eight months of legal wrangling (including negotiating a settlement with the IRS), on December 13—two days before he signed the lease on Cindy's—my father's bankruptcy petition was discharged. Not only did the event put an end to the ring episode, it erased all the debts that had trailed him for years. My father was finally able to start over.

Attorney Edgar Boyko standing by the model used to bolster his "mysterious mob hit man" defense of his client Wesley Ladd. Alleged Organization gunman sits near upper-right-hand corner of model. COURTESY *ANCHORAGE DAILY NEWS*

CHAPTER TWELVE

THE ORGANIZATION

For several years, the Alaska State Trooper Academy in Sitka, in southeast Alaska, used the murder of the twenty-eight-year-old Rezk as a teaching tool, taking the case apart and examining the evidence more than a thousand times to teach cadets how to investigate a murder—one with plenty of eyewitnesses, an identifiable crime scene, abundant hard evidence, and all the motive any prosecutor ever needed. The exercise gave the cadets lots of material to work with, and more important, it offered ample opportunity to see how the justice system might sometimes go awry.

From the outset, when defense attorney Edgar Paul Boyko called a key witness's mother a prostitute, Wesley Ladd's trial was a seamy circus. The cast included gum-chomping topless dancers, monosyllabic pimps, Las Vegas drug dealers, conspiratorial ex-cons, and of course, Wesley Ladd—a slow-talking ex-fisherman who claimed the murderer had been a mob hitman.

"The evidence will show that Rezk was executed by a person or persons presently unknown, but identifiable," exclaimed Boyko. "The evidence will show he wasn't killed over three-thousand dollars, but something much bigger."

Only a handful of onlookers showed up the first day of trial on March 13, but once the news coverage began, you couldn't buy a place to stand in Judge James A. Hanson's courtroom. He secured the room with an extra armed guard to watch over the crowd of little old ladies in cat's-eye glasses sitting next to underworld types in cheap leather jackets. The trial was the best show in town.

Assistant District Attorney William Mackey said Ladd murdered Rezk because he didn't have the three-thousand dollars for his second and final payment on Cindy's, and Rezk was going to throw him out. Cindy Bennett and a friend of Ladd's, Jack Anderson, were in the room at the time of the killing, but didn't actually see Ladd fire the gun. The shooting occurred moments after Ladd had let Rezk and Bennett in the front door when the couple came to collect Ladd's final payment.

As the trio—with Bennett leading, Rezk in the middle, and Ladd bringing up the rear—walked through the doorway separating the customer waiting room from the kitchen, a shot was fired. Anderson, who was sitting on a couch in the girls' lounge, had his view blocked by Bennett. But as Bennett turned, both she and Anderson saw Ladd standing over Rezk's body with the murder weapon, a "smoking gun"— Ladd's own gun—in his hand. As he stood over Rezk, Mackey contended, Ladd was already constructing his defense. Looking Cindy in the eye, with a straight face, he shouted, "We are the Organization and you don't threaten the Organization, and that's why Ferris is dead." At gunpoint, he made her sign a predated bill of sale for Cindy's before forcing her and Anderson to help him dispose of the body. Ladd told Bennett to keep quiet, otherwise "the Organization's hitman" would kill her, too.

The defense theory was as simple as it was outrageous. Ladd claimed a mysterious hitman had committed the murder, and the gun ended up in Ladd's hands when he struggled with the killer, who slipped away. He said Anderson and Cindy were lying because they feared they'd become targets themselves. Ladd told the jury the hitman had been hired to silence an unruly Rezk, who was resisting attempts to organize the area's massage parlors. The real killer, he said, was a large, dark-haired man named Larry.

From the moment the all-woman jury was selected, tensions flared between the hawk-nosed, no-nonsense prosecutor Mackey and the flamboyant Boyko, a short, graying, bearded man who still spoke with a hint of his native Austrian accent.

In the courtroom, Mackey was a no-style, droning attorney, seemingly convinced that D.A.'s without imagination make good prosecutors. With his military-trim haircut, horn-rimmed glasses, and plain gray suits, he looked like he could have been a state trooper if he hadn't gone to law school. Mackey was an efficient prosecutor with a good reputation, but had the misfortune of practicing in a town with an unsophisticated judiciary and police investigators who were still learning on the job. Prosecutors are trained to be understated and factual, allowing themselves to be hemmed in by the facts and evidence. Boyko knew no such restraint or moderation.

A former state attorney general who sometimes went by the nickname "The Snow Tiger," Boyko had been on the front pages of Alaska's newspapers ever since he arrived in the early 1950s. Known for winning impossible cases, Boyko also had an office in San Diego, and if he wasn't in the newspaper, everybody figured he was in California.

His courtroom style was as much a part of him as the three-piece suits he wore, long after they had gone out of fashion, even in Anchorage. Outside the courtroom, Boyko is guided in his professional and private life by astrology—which he uses to pick juries—and his own canny intelligence. He is a master of clouding simple crimes in vast conspiracy theories. Boyko feeds on a jury's suspicion about the "system," and from the day the trial opens until the day the jury acquits his client he establishes a secret communication with the jury, suggesting that things are being kept from them by the judge and prosecutor. At one point during the Ladd trial, Mackey accused an assistant in Boyko's office of helping Ladd fashion his "Mob hitman" defense, but he could never prove it.

To this day, Boyko still recalls Ladd's active imagination. After being released on bail, for example, Ladd was hauled back into court after it was discovered he was planning to escape. Ladd and a crony had plotted to hijack an airplane, fly it to Georgia, pick up millions of dollars in counterfeit money, then fly to West Germany where the other guy said someone would buy the cash. Ladd was arrested the day he was to leave.

The money scheme was a piece with Ladd's "Larry" defense. First he said he hadn't been there, then he said nothing happened, next he claimed the shooting occurred during a poker game in which he shot Rezk to keep him from killing Anderson. But the version that got the most attention in court was a five-page, handwritten script Ladd had given to a fellow jail inmate who was to memorize it and present it as true testimony at the trial. The man, Buddy Nichols Abner, testified, but instead told how Ladd had tried to get him to lie. The script called for Abner to say he'd met Bennett in September 1972 and was a regular customer at Cindy's. He was to say he'd been present when Rezk was killed, and that he saw a "short, bald man standing over the body with a short-barrelled pistol." Mackey pointed out that the description fingered Jack Anderson as the shooter. Abner was to say he bought "sex and drugs" from Bennett, who according to the script had told Abner that Rezk had a "good supply" of drugs from Nevada. Accompanying the script was a Ladd-drawn diagram of the interior at Cindy's. Boyko waltzed between these conflicting accounts by offering the same explanation as Ladd: His client lied so many times to keep from having to reveal the identity of the real killer, who worked for mobsters threatening to move into Anchorage.

Boyko didn't like Ladd, but he liked high-profile cases. "I thought Ladd had very low self-esteem and a great need for power and recognition," Boyko told me many years later while sitting in his downtown Anchorage office.

Initially, Boyko quoted Ladd a hefty fee, thinking that might discourage Ladd from hiring him. It didn't. No sooner had Boyko begun work on the case than it became apparent that Ladd didn't have any money. The public defender's office was called in and the PD contracted with Boyko, since he was already familiar with the case.

"I felt that he probably killed Ferris Rezk," Boyko said. "The stories were to some degree viable. He gave me three totally conflicting stories and until the moment when I rose to make my opening statement, I had not decided which one to play."

"So why defend a guilty man?" I asked.

"He still needs a defense . . . and the guiltier he is, the more he needs me," Boyko answered. He then offered an explanation of one of the basic tenets of the American criminal justice system: It's up to the jury to sift through both the defense and the prosecution theories to arrive at the truth. The system works, Boyko said, at least "seventy percent of the time."

Boyko's Mob hitman defense might have sounded like a desperate, crazy ploy, had the prosecution not subpoenaed the one witness who personified exactly what it was he'd been talking about: Johnny Rich.

My father never told me about testifying at Ladd's trial, nor did I see the newspaper accounts of his day in court. My father was called to testify about a conversation he'd had with Ladd two nights before Rezk was murdered, in which Ladd supposedly asked my father to loan him the money for his final payment on Cindy's. Police learned of the conversation through a wiretap on Bennett's phone when my father related it to her soon after Ladd was arrested.

My father contended that Bennett had called him for his help and advice, asking if he knew anything about Ladd's "Organization." The prosecution waited until the end of the trial to force my father to testify, calling him in as a rebuttal witness, even though they'd had the conversation on tape for months. They knew his credibility would be a problem. They were right.

On the stand, my father was relaxed. Where other witnesses fidgeted or had to be reminded to speak up, my father sat straight, occasionally leaning to one side and stroking his chin. His voice was audible at all times. Except for the occasional smirk and once slightly raising his voice, he spoke in a measured, calm tone. He was respectful and polite, addressing the attorneys as "sir."

But from the moment he began his testimony I was struck with how much my father looked and acted every bit the underworld kingpin Boyko would convince the jury he was. For me, the experience of watching his taped testimony was deeply troubling. There was something disturbing about his phrasing: his use of the word "joints" to describe his businesses; the way he called an unsavory underworld figure a "young kid idiot"; and his conceding that he paid a "five-hundred-dollar finder's fee" to a male friend of Bennett's who helped my father secure the lease on Cindy's.

As I continued to watch the tapes, I began to doubt whether he was telling the truth about the conversation with Ladd. He lied about other matters while on the stand, some inconsequential, others important. He looked and sounded like a man who had studied film clips of the Kefauver Committee hearings, not so much for what to say, but how to say it. While he never refused to answer a question on the grounds that it might incriminate him, the "I don't knows" and the artful dodging of sensitive questions had a familiar ring to them. His intelligent, yet elusive manner was reminiscent of the big-city racketeers who were compelled to testify in 1950 before the Senate Special Committee to Investigate Organized Crime in Interstate Commerce (chaired by Tennessee Senator Estes Kefauver), which offered many Americans the first glimpse into the inner workings of organized crime.

As the tape rolled by, I wondered if my father had ever seen the film clips. And then there was the way he almost seemed to gloat over the fact that he'd beaten Ladd out of Cindy's.

"Mr. Ladd asked me if he could borrow three thousand dollars," my father testified. He then recounted in elaborate detail how Ladd had approached him late on a Friday night, at the Kit Kat Club, and asked to borrow the money. My father relayed how he grilled Ladd on what Ladd needed the money for and what kind of collateral Ladd could offer.

"I remember asking him what he needed three thousand dollars for," my father said. "He said he had a final payment due to pay off the purchase price of Cindy's . . . he asked me if I had three thousand dollars. I said, 'Yes' . . . He couldn't see why I wouldn't loan it to him. I said I wouldn't have it long if I just loaned it to everybody that come along and asked me for three thousand dollars. That was about the extent of the conversation."

Prompted by a question from Mackey, my father then told how he even offered Ladd some free legal and financial advice that night.

"Well, I told him that I didn't think he had any problems at all. He said that he had to have the money there within the next few days or the man was gonna take the place back. I said, 'Oh no, if he's got a note, the first thing he'd have to do is sue you' . . . I told him then that it would take six to eight months before they'd be able to get it into court . . . I told him if he couldn't raise the three thousand dollars to pay off the note in six to eight months, he didn't want the joint anyway."

His direct testimony took less than twenty minutes, but Boyko kept him on the stand for nearly four hours of cross-examination, asking him about everything from his business interests and his cars to when he was last in Las Vegas, all the while insinuating that my father had ties to organized crime. Throughout Boyko's questioning, my father remained elusive.

"Tell us again, Mr. Rich. What was the date of that conversation?" Boyko asked in one of his opening questions.

"It was Friday night," my father said. "Pretty late at night."

"Friday what?" Boyko asked.

"Friday before the Saturday," my father responded with a smile. Some in the courtroom laughed lightly.

Boyko wanted to convince the jury that my father was lying and that Bennett had staged their phone call for the benefit of the authorities. Asked why my father never went to the police with what he knew, my father said he'd spoken with an assistant in Mackey's office months before the trial and the assistant had told him what the police and prosecution had long thought—that he wouldn't make a good witness.

"Did you think you wouldn't make a good witness?" Boyko asked.

"I don't know," my father answered.

Boyko then queried my father about why Cindy Bennett had called to talk about Ladd.

"I don't know," my father answered.

"Do you have any idea, Mr. Rich, why Cindy Bennett would ask you, a total stranger, if you knew anything about any 'Organization'?" asked Boyko.

"No. I assumed she'd been through a fantastic experience and she was trying to find out what was going on herself," my father said.

"Can you think of anything that would lead her to believe that you, a total stranger, would know anything about any Organization?"

"I don't know . . . It wasn't particularly strange to me, no," my father said. "I have people asking me questions all the time. I've been here almost twenty years in Alaska. I'm consistently asked by people questions of who knows who and who knows what."

It was the kind of answer Boyko might have hoped for. Initially, he fought to keep my father off the stand; he knew he was winning, and didn't need the jury hearing anything that might damage his case.

Boyko had managed to discredit both Bennett and Anderson, pointing out how Anderson had first told the police a story that protected Ladd. It was only after he was threatened with a charge of accomplice to murder that he changed stories. Bennett had reported Rezk missing and didn't come forward until police found his body. She had lied to police because she believed Ladd's stories about the Organization, she told the jury. But Boyko punched a huge hole in her credibility. When first questioned by police, Bennett had told them Ladd had killed Rezk, but that she thought there might have been another man in the room in addition to Anderson. On the stand, she recanted this, saying she was confused at the time of the shooting, and might have only imagined the presence of a fourth man.

Throughout the case, Boyko insisted that Ladd wasn't on trial—the Mob was, and only Edgar Boyko had the courage to confront organized crime's presence in Alaska. He demanded that Judge Hanson force the state troopers and the city police to release all bar and massage parlor crime reports for the past eighteen months. Boyko went so far as to say that Mackey and the entire state government, including Gov. Bill Egan, were covering up the Mob's arrival in Anchorage out of embarrassment at not being able to stop the invasion.

"I will not allow Wesley Ladd to be railroaded to save the political hide of the Egan administration," Boyko hollered at one point when the jury was not in the courtroom.

The claims so outraged Mackey that the trial disintegrated into petty disputes between him and Boyko, and both were cited for contempt of court. And even when Hanson wouldn't allow a piece of evidence, Boyko made sure that a taste of it reached the media beast.

Ladd's defense was tailor-made for the times. In the early 1970s, Mob paranoia was at its peak in Anchorage. Rezk was the second denizen of Anchorage's demimonde to be killed in four months. Mysterious firebombings and arsons had occurred, aimed at the operators of shady businesses, criminals, and police informers. Word on the street was that Mafia chieftains from Outside had sent scouts to check out Alaska. The Mob hoped, the story went, to reap untold wealth once construction began on the trans-Alaska pipeline. The media loved this story, and gave the Mob angle more play than the murder itself. Hanson had to issue a gag order to keep Boyko from talking to the press after a disc jockey related Boyko's Mob theory over the air.

To illustrate his theory, Boyko hauled into the courtroom a three-dimensional miniature replicating the interior of Cindy's massage parlor, complete with couches, kitchen appliances, and pictures on the wall. The model was peopled with ten-inch figurines. There was Cindy in a red dress that she filled out rather well; Wesley Ladd stood in the kitchen in a neat blue suit. The victim was face down on the floor; behind him, in a brown suit, was the "fourth" man, looking very sub-human, seated with a gun in his hands. The "hitman" wore brown because Boyko had learned that a study revealed that people don't trust men in brown suits. Boyko's elaborate model, produced by a professional artist and considered a progressive trial maneuver, totally outclassed the prosecution's simple line drawings on large sheets of paper. In addition to the model, he introduced a professionally produced videotape that showed the murder weapon didn't "smoke" when fired, as Anderson said it had.

Once introduced as evidence, the model sat at the center of the courtroom, where the jury could ponder it each day, checking its angles, mulling over the possibilities, wondering what went on in the massage rooms not shown, wondering what kind of woman would work at such a place, what kind of man would own such a business?

Such a man might know the answer to one of Boyko's favorite questions, asked of nearly every prosecution witness, including my father.

"Have you ever heard of the Midnight Ranch in Nevada?" Boyko asked midway through his cross-examination.

"No, I have not," my father said.

"Ever heard of a man named Bob Gordon, an Organization man from the Midnight Ranch who attempted to organize massage parlors last November and furnish girls for them for ten percent?"

"Never heard of any such man," my father said.

And my father hadn't. If anyone knew the inner workings of Anchorage's underworld, he did. He might have been able to explain this to the jury in a way they would understand had he not had his own problems. Testifying at Ladd's trial created a dilemma for my father—it went against everything he believed. Even if he'd wanted to testify against Ladd, he wouldn't have dared walk in that courtroom without being subpoenaed. And as usual, his life was complicated, making it hard to give straight answers. He kept his Cadillac registered to his old girlfriend Stormy. As he'd done before to shield assets, he put the car in her name and then had her sign a power of attorney that allowed him to act as her legal and financial representative. That way he could control whatever of his property he had placed in her name. Now he had to explain this to a jury of bank tellers and housewives who had sat through four weeks of lurid testimony from the likes of exotic dancer and former Ladd girlfriend "Angel Dust," and ex-cons who talked about rubbing people out by hammering pencils into their ears.

By comparison, my father didn't look so bad. But he'd worked the angles so long he'd built a life full of secrets, half-truths, and contradictions, and Boyko asked him to account for each and every one of them. I couldn't help but think how my father had spent his entire life painting himself into the corner he found himself in that day in court.

When Boyko started questioning my father about his income and businesses, my father ducked the question.

"What is your annual income, Mr. Rich?" Boyko asked.

"Right now I don't know," my father answered.

"How much income did you pay taxes on?" Boyko asked.

"I don't remember. I don't know," he answered.

"Was it under thirty thousand dollars?"

"Yes," he said.

"Was it under twenty thousand dollars?"

"Yes," he said.

"Was it under ten thousand dollars?" asked Boyko.

"I don't know."

How could my father earn less than ten thousand dollars when he leased a nine-room house? Boyko asked. He pointed out that my father also owned a Cadillac and an El Camino, had two businesses, two bank accounts, and wore expensive-looking clothes.

"You dress pretty well, don't you, Mr. Rich?"

"No, not normally," my father said.

"Just for court?" Boyko asked.

"Yes, just for court," my father answered.

Boyko not only forced my father to reveal that his car was registered to Stormy, but that she was listed along with a bartender and a man who ran porno bookstores as officers in the 736 Corporation, the entity my father created to run the 736 Club, which in its most recent form had been the nude photo studio. The sparring would have been hilarious had it been part of a courtroom parody.

"It's got some kind of number that escapes me and you'll have to forgive me. I'm not too familiar with the nightlife, but uh, uh, 376? Does that ring a bell?" Boyko asked.

"Our club is basically a private club," my father answered.

"A private club for camera buffs? Is that what you're telling us?" Boyko asked.

"It's a private club for whatever purpose its members vote it to be," he said.

"Well, other than taking pictures of nude models, what have those private members voted to do down there in the past?" Boyko asked.

"Well, right now we voted to close it down 'cause it wasn't making any money," my father said.

"Well, what was the club formed to do?" Boyko asked.

"Well, the club . . . the original basic sponsorship of the club was to sponsor events which raise money for the club," my father reasoned.

"What kind of events?" asked Boyko.

"Oh, boat races at Big Lake," answered my father.

When Boyko asked to see the membership list, my father said the Anchorage Police Department had it.

"Why in heaven's name would the City of Anchorage Police Department be interested in Big Lake boat races, Mr. Rich? Why did they take your membership list?" asked Boyko.

"To investigate our members," my father answered.

"Oh, is there something to investigate about your members that you know of?" Boyko asked.

"Well, I believe they found a poker game going at one time," my father answered.

"More than once?" Boyko asked.

"Yes. Several times."

If Boyko, or anyone, had bothered to stop by the house on 12th Avenue, they would have found that my father was telling the truth. The gambling was long gone. About the only games at the 736 Club that spring were the late-night checkers matches between Al Bennett and me.

Bennett (no relation to Cindy Bennett) and his girlfriend, Shannon, whose last name I never knew, were my new roommates. Because my father couldn't trust the girls at Cindy's, he usually slept there so that he could keep an eye on the cash register. But I didn't mind his absences because of Al and Shannon's company. For the first time in my residence at the house, it seemed like a home.

Al was slightly built, with a narrow, hooked nose, thinning black hair, and pencil-thin mustache; Shannon was blond and perky, a regular girl next door.

It was something like a family, with Al filling in as a substitute father. Al helped me with my homework, counseled me on how to deal with boys, and made sure I got to bed at a decent hour. He liked to cook dinner and he expected me to be home at mealtime, a schedule I didn't mind keeping. Shannon, who danced at one of the topless bars, was like my big sister. Al's occupation was a matter of mystery. Sometimes he did odd jobs for my father; other times he helped sell artwork by his father, an oil painter who specialized in touristy Alaska scenery.

Al also made sure I got up from my afterschool nap to go to work at the Tesoro station—a job I'd picked up early that spring.

Boyko saved his best shots for questions on the massage parlor business and my father's role as the owner of New Cindy's. For nearly an hour he asked my father about how the girls were hired, where they came from, and whether or not they were supplied by Outside crime syndicates. My father told him most girls had worked as topless dancers; the parlors were independently owned and operated. He was candid in explaining the genesis of the "Greater Anchorage Health Spa Association," formed by eight local massage parlor operators on what my father called an "emergency basis" to combat negative publicity from the trial. In his testimony, Ladd cited the association as further proof that the Mob was trying to organize the parlors.

Like the defunct 736 Club, the association was my father's attempt to seek legitimacy—find a way to work with the cops and city lawmakers—for an otherwise illegal and unsavory trade. He envisioned stricter licensing, health inspections, tax accountability, getting drug traffickers out of the business, and generally finding a way to ward off the inevitable clamor to rid the city of the parlors altogether. The jury might even have believed him had he not lied about something so obvious as the true nature of the business of massage parlors.

"It's an association of massage parlors, isn't it?" Boyko asked.

"That's what it is, sir," my father answered.

"And the massage parlor is primarily engaged in prostitution, isn't it?" asked Boyko.

"No, it is not," he said.

"None of your massage parlors engage in prostitution that you know of?" Boyko asked.

"Not that I know of," my father answered.

"And that's as true as the rest of your testimony?" asked Boyko.

"Yes."

Boyko concluded by asking how my father came to own New Cindy's. My father insisted he'd leased an empty building. He made it clear that Ladd had been taken by Rezk, who had never even bothered to transfer the lease on the building to Ladd's name. He explained that he was not making five hundred dollars a night, as Boyko claimed. Throughout, Ladd sat motionless, occasionally scribbling notes on a yellow legal pad and pushing them under Boyko's nose.

As the tape rolled by, I began seeing my father, not as a daughter, but as others saw him. And as Wesley Ladd saw him. My father appeared to be everything Ladd had hoped to be when he moved to Anchorage: powerful, connected, and rich.

"To the best of my knowledge Ladd bought nothing," my father said, telling how he even had his lawyer make sure that the premises were unencumbered before he took out a lease.

"Well, what did he give this note for that he was supposed to be owing a payment on?" Boyko asked.

"He gave a note on the air of the sky as far as I'm concerned," my father answered.

"Now, if there was and if Wesley Ladd did buy something over there that you now have, you sure don't want him coming back claiming it, do you?" Boyko asked.

"I don't see how it'd be possible," my father said.

"Well, particularly not if he goes to the penitentiary for killing Mr.

Rezk. He wouldn't be able to come back and haunt you, would he?" asked Boyko.

"Why should he haunt me?"

"You don't want Mr. Ladd coming around saying, 'Hey, I bought this, I want the place back,' " asked Boyko.

"How can he?"

After fifteen hours of deliberations the jury returned Saturday, April 7, with a finding that Wesley Ladd was not guilty of murdering Ferris Rezk. Asked to explain the verdict, a juror told a reporter, "Part of it was knowing there's something much bigger involved."

I wish my father hadn't been so damned cocky.

Gary Zieger with the truck allegedly used in the murder of "Zee Zee" Mason
COURTESY *ANCHORAGE DAILY NEWS*

Wesley Ladd in policy custody after being charged with my father's murder
COURTESY *ANCHORAGE DAILY NEWS*

CHAPTER THIRTEEN

THE GATHERING

The trial was over with. John Rich didn't bring the most damaging evidence against me. It was bugging me a little bit about the fact that I had been ripped off for $10,000 and that nobody would even want to listen to my story. I mean, I tried to tell the truth at the beginning. . . . And the fact that I had been just more or less taken for that $10,000, and then instead of finding out if I was guilty or innocent . . . the police authorized Cindy to recover the property, which she did. She took all the furniture, which wasn't much, but still it was paid for, it was really mine. And this did bite me. I mean, it was on my mind not really about losing the place, but about John Rich living on easy street while I am sitting down there in Cordova digging clams, making my bucks the hard way, because I knew in my heart that I had not beat nobody out of nothing.
—From Wesley Ladd's confession, taken by Trooper Jim Vaden, February 1, 1974

Acquitted but penniless and bitter, Wesley Ladd returned to Cordova. Telling friends he wanted to get as far away from people as possible, he stayed in a cabin on remote Mummy Island—a mile-long outcropping about seven miles across the water from Cordova.

On the island, Ladd spent a few weeks harvesting clams, hauling them to Cordova in a small skiff to sell to restaurants. On one such trip he stopped at the Cordova House hotel and restaurant for coffee and a sandwich. The owner introduced the new waitress—plain, pudgy Virginia Kay Pinnick, eighteen.

Pinnick may not have been a looker, but she had a sweet disposition. She was new to Cordova, having recently moved there after a family friend helped get her the job at the restaurant. She and Ladd spoke only briefly, but long enough for her to mention that her mother, Caye Mason, was Boyko's bookkeeper. Ladd wasn't sure he remembered meeting her.

Pinnick's and Mason's was a troubled relationship. The mother, according to court records, had always been unstable. A native of Iowa and twice divorced, she'd come to Alaska in the early sixties with her first husband, working as a baker, a seamstress, and a bookkeeper as she moved her four children from one small mining town to another.

For a while she ran a store in Sutton, once the supply center for a coal-mining area named Jonesville sixty-one miles north of Anchorage. Then they lived in Chitina, another dying mine town.

Mason had owned the Chitina Hotel & Bar, but lost it when she fell behind on her bills and the sellers moved to foreclose. She countersued, but lost when a judge ruled the entire sales contract illegal because it violated state liquor laws by not placing Mason's name on the bar's liquor license. Mason appealed to the state supreme court and moved to Eagle River—a bedroom community of Anchorage nestled in the Chugach Mountains, about fourteen miles north of town—to wait out the legal battle.

Mason's idiosyncrasies included a continuing story that she was dying of a rare form of cancer. Virginia had been hearing the tale most of her life. For two years Mason ran around with her head shaved and wearing wigs, claiming she'd lost her hair to radiation treatments. Now and again she'd leave the kids, explaining that she had to go out of town for medical care. No one knows where she actually went. Like everyone else who knew Mason, Virginia believed her mother's story, doing whatever her mother wanted her to do, always living with the fear that her mother might die any day.

About ten days after meeting Pinnick, Ladd was traveling back through Cordova to catch a flight to Anchorage. He bumped into Pinnick at the bar, and before long was offering her a free plane ticket to accompany him. They left that afternoon.

Once in town, Ladd, Pinnick, and Mason began hanging around together. Mason and Ladd really hit it off, Pinnick would later tell police investigators. Both were in their forties, they had many acquaintances in common, and both liked to dance. Mason was intrigued by Ladd, Pinnick would later say. Her mother had heard about Ladd around Boyko's office and believed him to be a major underworld crime figure. Pinnick was never as clear with authorities as to what her attraction to Ladd had been. Shortly after the trio had been brought together, Ladd began sleeping with both women.

Between assignations, Ladd visited one of his old haunts—Papa Joe's, a small, raunchy strip bar also known as "PJ's," which sits on a wide spot along Spenard Road called Dead Man's Curve.

One afternoon Ladd went in looking for a bartender who owned a pickup truck. Ladd's idea was to borrow the truck and use it to haul halibut as part of a new money-making scheme to buy the fish in Cordova, then sell it in Fairbanks. The bartender explained that he'd sold his truck, but pointed to a young man with blond hair who had just walked in.

"There's a guy with a truck," the barman said.

The truck owner was Gary Allen Zieger.

The former East High School student, who was born and raised in Anchorage, was just nineteen when he was charged in one of the most vicious and shocking killings in Anchorage's history: the slaying of Zingre Lynee "ZeZe" Mason (no relation to Caye Mason), a pretty, twenty-year-old ground hostess for Japan Airlines.

The 1970 graduate of Dimond High School was last seen on August 22, 1972. Six days later a group of small children playing in a large gravel pit in South Anchorage found Mason's half-clothed body in a clump of bushes. She had been savagely beaten about her head and stabbed repeatedly with a double-edged knife. State trooper investigators found drag marks and bloodstains leading to her body from a set of four tire tracks nearby. They determined that her attacker had murdered her someplace else and then dumped her body in the pit.

Five days after her body had been discovered, the troopers arrested Zieger. Witnesses had seen Mason hitchhiking the day she disappeared, including watching her climb into a truck matching the description of Zieger's white 1970 four-wheel-drive Chevrolet. Later that day, a trucker hauling gravel from the site spied a truck fitting the same description in a far corner of the gravel pit. After the troopers seized Zieger's vehicle, they found that the tread on his tires matched the tire marks found near Mason's body, and they also found what they believed to be small amounts of human blood on the passenger side in the cab of the truck.

In January, Zieger went on trial. Numerous pieces of evidence pointed to him as the killer. But the loss of critical blood samples and conflicting testimony led to his acquittal on February 1.

Zieger's trial was the first of two major cases Assistant District Attorney William Mackey lost that year; the next would be Ladd's.

I remember ZeZe's murder. The killing received widespread publicity, so much so that the judge presiding over Zieger's case declared that an impartial jury could not be found in Anchorage and moved the trial to Kodiak. Unlike the Rezk killing, which occurred in a realm that felt far removed from my own, ZeZe's murder hit home.

Mason was the second young Anchorage woman to die under similar circumstances within an eight-month period. Celia Beth Van Zanten, eighteen, a student at Anchorage Community College. She was found murdered on Christmas Day in the McHugh Creek Campground, fifteen miles south of Anchorage, after she left her home in Turnagain to walk to the store.

The deaths of Van Zanten and Mason sent a shudder through Anchorage, and police investigated each with vigor. Not until the Mason killing, however, did they have a suspect they believed was responsible for both. While some investigators later ruled out Zieger as Van Zanten's killer, it didn't stop his reputation among law enforcement from growing. Police began trying to link Zieger to numerous other unsolved killings throughout Alaska. Around the squad room, he became known as a sociopathic killer, someone who was considered extremely dangerous and who had no regard for human life.

For girls my age at the time, Zieger's notoriety meant we shouldn't hitchhike, or we too might end up tossed into a gravel pit or found nude and frozen on the icy banks of a nearby creek. The deaths made my friends and me feel vulnerable in a way we had not felt before. We had heard the stories of college girls who met similar fates Outside, but until Van Zanten's and ZeZe's deaths, we did not think something like that could happen in Alaska.

Zieger and Ladd had met in jail and remade their acquaintance the day they ran into each other at PJ's over drinks. Ladd described his fish-hauling idea. Zieger agreed to meet him in Cordova a few days later.

But when Zieger arrived, they learned the price of halibut had dropped in Fairbanks, and they canceled their plans and decided to return to Anchorage. Since Cordova isn't connected to the rest of Alaska by road, Ladd, Zieger, and Pinnick took their two cars and boarded the state ferry to Valdez.

The ferry reached Valdez at about five A.M. The trio hung around for three hours, eating and resting. At around eight, as they were starting the 304-mile trip to Anchorage, the Cordova police chief alerted state troopers that a man matching Zieger's description was suspected of burglarizing an explosives warehouse the night before.

Before leaving Cordova, Ladd, Pinnick, and Zieger had stopped at a bar where Pinnick introduced Zieger to a man who worked for a drilling company that occasionally did blasting work. Zieger asked if he could buy some dynamite. The two men left the bar together.

Near noon the next day, on the road with Ladd and Pinnick, Zieger stopped for gas. A trooper pulled him over and searched his truck. He found not only two cases of dynamite but eleven pounds of marijuana. Zieger was arrested and taken to Anchorage, where he was jailed on a fifty-thousand-dollar bond. He was charged with burglary, grand larceny, and possession of narcotics with intent to sell.

Ladd and Pinnick continued on to Anchorage.

Back in Eagle River, Ladd, Pinnick, and Mason set up house. Ladd shared a bed with Mason at night. While she was away at work, he carried on an affair with Pinnick.

Still scheming to make money, Ladd turned to marijuana, figuring he could buy wholesale in the city and sell it on the street in Cordova. He began calling around town for suppliers. He found one in Guy

Benny Eugene Ramey. Ramey, nineteen, a dealer and heroin addict who went by Benny, was a friend of Ladd's who also hung out at PJ's.

Ramey fancied himself a motorcycle mechanic, but mostly he stole to pay for his drugs. Ladd had met Ramey when buying a hot rifle from him the year before. He described his marijuana plans, Ramey voiced interest, and soon the two of them and Pinnick began making drug runs back and forth to Cordova. When she could get away from work, Mason would go along. At the Anchorage end, the whole group stayed at her house in Eagle River where Ramey and one of Mason's sons shared a cabin on the property.

The one-room cabin, just a few feet away from the main house, was a crude affair. Although electrified, it had no toilet or running water. A pair of bunks arranged in an L stood to the right of the doorway, with one bunk abutting a small, roughed-in closet. Beyond the closet was a porcelain double kitchen sink set into a wooden countertop above which was a plywood medicine cabinet fitted with cheap, mismatched hardware. Beige linoleum, the kind popular in older public facilities and on military bases, covered the floor. The walls and ceiling were a mix of white and silver—white from the expanses of Sheetrock and silver from the vapor barrier on lengths of fiberglass insulation. To the left of the sink hung a Coca-Cola restaurant clock. Boxes of belongings and construction materials were scattered throughout, making the place look like a boys' clubhouse.

When not in Cordova, Ladd, Ramey, and Pinnick stayed around the house. Ladd was drinking pretty heavily and using amphetamines; he swallowed the booze to wash down as many as forty tablets of speed a day. Ramey had his heroin.

In mid-July they began to talk of taking over Cindy's massage parlor.

At first it was just vague chatter, but as time passed the chatter turned serious. Earlier, Mason and Ladd had talked about what they could do with the ten thousand dollars Ladd claimed he'd invested in the place: maybe buy an old cannery in Cordova, or perhaps buy back the lodge in Chitina to which they all could move.

It was all just so much talk. Then Zieger was released from jail.

The prosecutor fought his release, even though it was not clear whether he had stolen the dynamite or whether it had been sold to him under the table. But it didn't matter; the prosecutor said there was no way of knowing what Zieger planned to do with the TNT. He even presented psychiatric testimony from the ZeZe Mason murder trial that described Zieger as "immature, impulsive, aggressive, anti-social and extremely hostile with proneness to acting out his hostility."

The judge was unmoved and cut Zieger's bail from $50,000 to $1,500. Ladd and Ramey offered collateral and put down the requisite 10 percent cash bond, springing their cohort.

One wonders why a young lawyer would associate with people such as Wesley Ladd and Caye Mason. One wonders why a young lawyer, barring fear for the moment, would have any contact with Gary Zieger. One wonders, seeing what I propose by the gentle characteristics of Duncan Webb. One wonders if he received some thrill out of the macabre personalities of the three people I've mentioned. One wonders, was there a momentary adulation of the underworld? Some people read crime stories, some people go to gangster movies. Some young lawyers feel that it's kind of smart to be seen in the company of gangsters. It's all very unfortunate. You can't, of course, touch people of that ilk without something rubbing off on your own hands.
—The late San Francisco defense attorney James Martin MacInnis, in his closing arguments in the defense of his client Duncan Webb, May 21, 1975

Anchorage attorney Bob Wagstaff was the first to encounter Duncan Campbell Webb, a seasoned attorney new to Alaska who had the attitude and shaggy hair to fit right in at Wagstaff's liberal firm. Wagstaff offered to help Webb set up shop by providing temporary office space and a few referrals as a matter of professional courtesy.

Webb, thirty-seven and twice divorced, had graduated from the University of California's Hastings College of Law in San Francisco. It was a long climb up the social ladder for the former gas station attendant, coast guard enlistee, and logging truck driver. Webb practiced law for six years in San Francisco, working first for an insurance company and later as a public defender and in his own private practice. Webb had visited Alaska between college semesters, coming up initially to work as a commercial fisherman out of Ketchikan in southeast Alaska.

He moved north permanently in 1972. The move came in the middle of a professional and personal crisis—besides being in the middle of a nasty child support dispute with his second wife, he'd been cited for professional misconduct by the Disciplinary Board of the State Bar of California, which found that Webb had deceived the court and an opposing attorney in a divorce case. Webb left California several months prior to the bar association making full public disclosure of the case.

In Alaska, Webb first worked as a carpenter in Fairbanks, then as a bartender in Anchorage, while fulfilling the six-month residency required of lawyers wishing to be admitted to practice in Alaska. In February 1973, he was admitted to the Alaska bar, joined the Alaska Bar Association, and began casting about for a place to practice.

Webb eagerly accepted Wagstaff's offer, even though he had to use a desk in the waiting area. Some of the partners resented Wagstaff's generosity, but they warmed to the new arrival. The firm's attorneys began bouncing excess cases and those they didn't want to handle to the good-looking Californian.

"He was a very, very charming person. He had a gift of gab," recalled Mike Rubinstein, one of the attorneys in Wagstaff's firm. "He could make himself very likable in a very short period of time. He really had a talent for entering people's lives very, very quickly and getting right down close to them."

As likable and as bright as Webb appeared, there were some troubling aspects to the eager young attorney. He tended to mix too closely with his criminal clients. Some attorneys who knew Webb believed his close association with those he defended stemmed from a deep sense of commitment, however misguided, to serving his clients well. More seasoned defense attorneys, including Rubinstein, considered Webb's actions unwise and even dangerous conduct.

"He wasn't married and he was one of these people who could stay up all night," said Rubinstein, who these days works as an assistant U.S. attorney in Florida. "He didn't just practice out of his office, because he really didn't have an office at first. But he'd go running off and go to his client's house and go to his client's place [of business], even if his client's place was a massage parlor or an after-hours gambling joint. Well, he'd be there. He'd take up business there. He was very active and his activity was very directly associating with his clients.

"In my mind's eye I can imagine him wearing a trench coat, with the collar turned up with a pair of sunglasses looking shady and mysterious and talking out of the side of his mouth. He went all the way. He started identifying with the people he was hanging out with and started to act like some kind of a hoodlum—a Mob lawyer. It seemed juvenile to me. It seemed stupid."

Duncan Webb's most important skill in Alaska might have been knowing when to move on. Within months, he left the Wagstaff firm to open his own practice with another attorney new to Alaska. In late July at the federal courthouse, Webb met Caye Mason.

Webb was defending friends of Mason's who were on trial for selling heroin. The two chatted briefly, Mason telling Webb what a terrific job she thought he was doing. She showed up a few more times during the trial, sometimes with Ladd. During one conversation, she asked Webb to meet with her to discuss some legal work she might want to send his way.

There was another link between Mason, Ladd, and Webb. One of the lawyer's first clients in Alaska had been Zieger, who had hired Webb to sue the state for abuse of prosecutorial discretion in charging him with ZeZe Mason's murder. Webb received and got a four-hundred-dollar retainer, but still hadn't filed suit when he met Mason and Ladd.

They eventually stopped by his office to talk about Mason's prospective case involving her old property in Chitina and wound up talking about Ladd's problems. During the conversation someone suggested Ladd sue my father or Cindy Bennett. If Ladd won, there would be enough money for Ladd to get back what he lost and for Mason to buy back her lodge in Chitina.

But Webb said Ladd's name couldn't appear on any lawsuits because of the notoriety from his recent trial. Instead, Webb suggested that Mason get Ladd to assign his debts to her, and they could sue in her name.

That would be no problem, Mason said. After Ladd's trial Boyko had had Ladd sign a similar assignment, transferring his claims against Cindy Bennett, Ferris Rezk, and my father to Boyko's secretary. Boyko decided the case had no merit, and dropped it. Mason was confident, however, that she could get the secretary to reassign the document over to her.

The next step, Webb said, was to find out what my father owned.

"If there's going to be any meaningful suit filed against John Rich for the debt, you're going to have to find out if he has any assets," he told them.

Over the course of the next couple of weeks, Mason and Ladd visited Webb's office a number of times. During one visit, they brought Webb a copy of Ladd's original agreement to purchase Cindy's, some paperwork involving a car he'd bought from Rezk—later repossessed—and a list of my father's holdings that filled a sheet of stationery from Boyko's law firm.

In pencil, Mason had copied a scrawled inventory that Ladd had made, neatly printing everything she and Ladd had been able to learn about what my father owned and owed. The list noted a sixty-foot trailer he'd ordered, intending to install a five-bedroom mobile home in Valdez, where he planned to open it as a third parlor to service the pipeline workers.

Mason's list seemed to outline a veritable underworld empire:

Lease for Cindy's = 605 W. 29th 274-4146
$400 monthly
FiFi: 3801 Spenard Road 272-8611
Manager: Rosie Marie Velasco
Boat: 17 ft.
Selling price $4,200.00 balance $2,900.00
payments $120.00 monthly

Land:
Area: Valdez 625 Frontage 2 mi. out of
12 × 52 Trailer Valdez
Dynamic Realty; Selling Price: $45,000.00
Down Payment $5,000.00

All Bank Business: Alaska N.B. of the North
James L. Johnston: Attorney

Car: Cadillac
Color: bg.
Year: 1971
Balance: $1,700.00
Monthly: $216.00
House: 736 E. 12th
Leased Oct. 1969, five year lease opt. to buy.
$300 monthly
50 to 60 guns assorted at 736 E. 12th
Deposit Box: at Alaska N.B. of the North

"FiFi's" and the "guns" were my father's two newest business ventures. The former was my father's second massage parlor in Anchorage. I thought the name sounded silly, but it sounded a lot better than his first idea: Kim's. There was already a parlor named Kim's, so he dropped the idea. I felt a tremendous sense of relief when my name wasn't going up on a big wooden sign that hung outside.

With its pitched roof and gabled entry, FiFi's was far more handsome than the flat-roofed Cindy's. The building had been the first Alaskan home of the Hurn family. With massage parlors as with real estate, location is everything, and FiFi's location was just as good as Cindy's. It was less than half a block from the busy intersection of Spenard Road and Minnesota Drive, a quarter mile from PJ's strip club.

The guns were part of another business my father had started. He became a federally licensed wholesale gun dealer, calling his company "Alaska Firearms Distributors."

He ran his new enterprise out of the house on 12th Avenue, and he took to it with all the gusto and enthusiasm of a beloved hobby. He'd spend hours polishing handguns and rifles, assembling gun cabinets, and gathering up boxes of each to haul down to local gun auctions. Soon he was learning everything there was to know about guns: subscribing to gun collector magazines, talking like an expert to his friends, hanging out with gun buffs, and even collecting and restoring antique guns.

Unlike those obsessed with guns for the power and violence they represent, my father loved guns—as with his past passions for cars and even sewing machines—more out of an appreciation for their history, and the craft of gunsmithing.

More than anything, the gun business represented a turning point in my father's life. He had to have a federal license to sell the guns, which involved a thorough background check, and since he had no felony convictions, he was granted a license. But for him to hang on to it, everything had to be aboveboard. Mindful of what had happened to his sewing machine business, my father was determined not to cut corners because now the feds were watching. He knew what every underworld figure knows: You don't mess with the feds. They have long institutional memories and the consequences of crossing their path can often be far more serious than any threat a half dozen Jim Vadens ever represented to my father.

But like Vaden, who had decided to check on my father's vacuum business years before, local federal agents kept a close eye on Johnny Rich—Gun Dealer. And again, like Vaden, they too eventually expressed a keen interest in my father's inventory. I wouldn't doubt that my father was expecting them. He didn't seem surprised the day they showed up on our doorstep.

I was home with my father that afternoon when several plainclothes federal marshals and FBI agents knocked on the door, armed with search warrants and a tip that my father was selling sawed-off shotguns. While they were dressed more conservatively and their manner was less menacing, they nonetheless reminded me of the gun-toting thugs who had once walked through the same door. They were brusque and pushy, and like the hoods, they ordered me to sit at the dining room table while my father escorted them through the house.

They poked around everywhere, including looking in the bathroom medicine cabinet and going through the clothes hamper. I remember thinking how I knew that the hamper contained nothing but laundry and I thought they looked silly digging around through the towels, sheets, and my dirty underwear. I also felt angry and violated having my home once again taken over by total strangers. But my father retained his usual sense of humor, and resignation, about such things.

They didn't find any sawed-off shotguns. My father didn't have any, despite rumors to the contrary that persist to this day. My father was not a stupid man and he wasn't about to intentionally foul up his latest business venture, especially since he had to know they were watching and that to run afoul of his license could result in some serious time in a federal prison.

By the time the agents were ready to leave, they were apologizing and shaking my father's hand. He just stood there with a self-satisfied grin on his face. He still loved the game and he still loved winning.

After he led them out the door, he turned to me.

"How do you like that," he said. "They come in here like gang-busters and leave like puppy dogs with their tails between their legs."

We both laughed.

As my father was fending off advances by eager federal agents, Mason, Ladd, and Webb continued their pursuit of his underworld holdings.

The idea of filing a lawsuit evaporated and a new idea emerged. It's not clear who originated the plan. It involved forming a corporation into which all of my father's assets would be transferred, using a power-of-attorney document.

During another of Ladd's and Mason's visits, on the back of an envelope Webb scribbled some notes about the corporation. He wrote "$1,000," indicating his fee, and underneath, "plus hr. rate." On the next line he wrote "DBA" for "doing business as" beside the words "Cindy's" and "FiFi's." The phrase "power of attorney" was circled with an arrow pointing to Webb's initials, which then pointed to the word "Corp" of which "Wes" and "Caye" would be officers.

It was Mason who suggested that Ladd use a power of attorney. One night, when no one was around, Mason took Ladd to Boyko's office, where they hunted for a power-of-attorney form. They found one sometimes used in real estate deals. Mason typed it up to suit Ladd's needs and brought it to Webb. Webb said it wasn't appropriate for this instance. Webb then got out a form for a general power of attorney and gave it to Mason. On August 10, Ladd brought it back, retyped but rife with errors.

It was close to quitting time and Webb's secretary, Leslye Langla, was getting ready to leave when Webb asked her to work a little overtime.

"Can you type me up a power of attorney?" he asked.

New to the job and eager to please, she agreed. Webb handed her a general power of attorney prepared for an earlier probate case and told her to copy it, except for the names.

Langla assembled a Dagwood sandwich of three legal-size sheets interspersed with carbons, put it into her typewriter, and began to work.

"KNOW ALL MEN BY THESE PREMISES," she typed, "that John F. Rich, Jr., has made, constituted and appointed, and by these presents does make, constitute and appoint DUNCAN C. WEBB true and lawful attorney for himself and in his name, place and stead, and for his use and benefit to have all right, title and interest in the estate of John F. Rich, Jr."

The rest was a single-spaced paragraph taking up most of the 8½ × 14 sheet. Dense with legalisms like "hereditaments," "hypothecate," and "bottomreis," it carefully but arcanely explained that in signing the power of attorney my father would be transferring to Webb all his mortgages, leases, merchandise, real estate, goods, and wares—in short, everything he owned.

Webb would later say that it was his client's idea to have his name placed on the document. He would also say that Mason claimed that my father was cooperating with them in developing the corporation as a way to pay off his "debt" to Ladd. Webb said Mason kept promising that my father would come by the office. He said he trusted her because she worked for Boyko, a prominent attorney.

The power-of-attorney document was standard boilerplate material and Langla made quick work of it, hurrying because Wesley Ladd was leaning over her while she typed, making her nervous.

When she was finished, Webb told her to give the original, plus one copy, to Ladd. The other copy was to stay in the office for Webb's files. Before she got up to leave, Ladd thanked her and handed her a ten-dollar bill for her trouble.

Over the next couple of weeks, Ladd and Mason came to see Webb about a dozen times. Their last visit was on August 21, when Boyko's secretary reassigned Ladd's claims over to Mason. That day, Mason delivered the document to Webb. This was the final legal maneuver they thought they needed to take over Johnny Rich's underworld "empire."

August 5, 1973

Hi

This will probably seem kind of strange getting a letter
from me, but I have a problem.
First of all, I want to say I'm sorry for some of the things
I said at your trial. I also don't feel too good about beating
you out of your massage parlor. However, I would like to make
things right with you if you are interested.
I am going to have to leave town. Not just the town but the
state. So I am going to offer you a deal on everything I own,
a real good deal.
Will you contact me as soon as possible?

PLAINTIFF'S EXHIBIT

PLAINTIFF'S EXHIBIT

STATE'S EXHIBIT

The "Hi Wes" letter. The "Wes" was deleted for trial purposes.

CHAPTER FOURTEEN

THE PERFECT CRIME

Well, the conversation again picked up concerning John Rich and the massage parlor . . . we were all seriously talking 'bout doing away, one way or another, with John Rich, and we'd get in on the massage parlor. I don't think it had actually been, at this point, I don't think it had actually been anybody committed themselves exactly how we was going to get rid of Rich, but the fact was there, that we was going to do something to recover that massage parlor, and getting him out of there would be one of the necessary moves.

So I told Caye Mason what I was doing and Caye Mason did not object to it, in fact she started to say what she could do with the books. She is a bookkeeper by trade and apparently she is a pretty good bookkeeper. And she said she would do the book work. Well, the pace really picked up then. In the conversations, let's do something to get rid of John Rich. Well, at this time I had made several efforts to contact John Rich, but I had not contacted him. I had not seen him at all no where. And, uh, I mean, this went on for a period of, it must have been four or five weeks; just talking about doing something. And finally Gary says, "Well, if you can't find him, uh, take Benny and I. We'll find him. We know him better than you do anyway."

Well, they did accompany me on two or three trips. The first two was unsuccessful in locating him. The third time we did locate John Rich. . . .

—From Wesley Ladd's confession to Jim Vaden

That August, my father had bought the *Cindy,* a handsome, seventeen-foot fiberglass Chris-Craft. The name was painted across the stern in big cursive letters, white against the boat's green hull. My father kept the boat, on its trailer, parked at its namesake massage parlor.

The boat wasn't as sexy or as fast as his old speedboat, but then, my father was getting older. On May 5, he'd turned forty, and a change seemed to overtake him; the new boat was the most obvious sign that he was entering middle age. We fought less often. He was more tolerant of me. For the first time in many years, things were looking up. He seemed happy. He was enjoying modest financial success, talking of taking vacations and planning to build a new house, maybe in Sand Lake, something designed by an architect— big, with several levels, high ceilings, decks, a heated garage—something that sounded a whole lot like the house he rented in Muldoon when I'd first returned to Alaska.

The boat also represented a new financial credibility. Done with the bankruptcy, he was able to walk into Alaska Marine Sales & Service to buy the boat and list a real occupation, one that provided a legitimate income, on which to base a loan.

He was managing well; he had to. He owned two massage parlors and the gun wholesale business. He had to pay licensing fees, insurance premiums, quarterly taxes—on time and in full. John Rich had gotten as conventional—and as legitimate—as he was ever going to get. And he'd remarried.

His latest girlfriend, Bridgette Burns, had gotten pregnant. He'd met her when she was seventeen; by the time they wed, she was eighteen. I'm not sure where my father met Bridgette, a short woman with short black hair and an enormous bustline. Having grown up in Anchorage, she'd been on the streets since she was in her early teens and looked every bit as old, if not older, than the topless dancers in their twenties who my father normally dated. My father was on the brink of middle age, and Bridgette might have started out as nothing more than an aging man's fling with a much younger woman. Bridgette and I got along until I learned her age, after which we fought all the time. I was out-raged that my father was living with, then married to, a teenager. He wanted her to stay at the house on 12th to keep me company; when that didn't work out, he had Al and Shannon move in and he moved Bridgette to Cindy's, where she also worked.

My father told one friend that he'd married Bridgette because of the pregnancy. They married in January, and for reasons that were not entirely clear, my father insisted on having the civil ceremony per-formed in Palmer, fifty miles north of Anchorage. Despite whatever pressures might have pushed my father into the marriage, not long afterward he began talking about his hopes for a son.

One reason for the easing of tensions between my father and me was that we didn't see much of one another. In addition to practically living at Cindy's, he was spending a lot of time at FiFi's.

Besides spending more time on my own, I was making more of my own decisions. I still had a midnight curfew and at least had to tele-phone my father—at whichever parlor he was working—to say where I was going and with whom. He rarely vetoed any of my plans until one day in early August.

There was a dance at Shaky Acres and I asked to go. He refused, and insisted that I spend the weekend with him at Cindy's. Furious, I packed an overnight bag, called a cab, and went to the parlor. I stormed in, demanding to know why I had to stay there.

"Because I said so," he snapped back. "That's reason enough."

Not for me it wasn't. I badgered him to let me go. He didn't get angry; he mostly tried to ignore me as he sat at a table doing paperwork, nodding and occasionally trying to tease me by mimicking my whining. After nearly an hour, exasperated, he told me why he wanted me nearby.

"Wesley Ladd is back in town," he said. "I'm afraid he may try to get at me by doing something to you."

I knew the name, but little more. I'd heard Ladd had been in-volved in a killing, but didn't know it had happened within feet of where my father and I were arguing. Wesley Ladd was a name from the evening news, nothing more, and I couldn't understand what it had to do with me. I was mad that this Ladd character, whoever he was, had ruined my plans.

My father then warned me to stay away from parked cars with people in them, and even more so than in the past, to let him know where I was going.

He should have been as careful when it came to himself.

Around six P.M. on Wednesday, August 22, Wesley Ladd pulled into the parking lot at the Pacific Auction House. Accompanied by Benny Ramey and Virginia Pinnick, he was driving an AMC Matador that Caye Mason had rented for the day. They wanted a vehicle my father wouldn't recognize.

They'd left Mason's house in Eagle River in two cars—Ladd and Ramey in the rental car with Pinnick following in her pickup. At the Sears parking lot, Pinnick parked her truck and joined the men for the ride to the auction house.

The auction hadn't started and they didn't see my father's Cadillac, so they drove around and returned about fifteen minutes later. By then my father had arrived. It was the first break they'd had in weeks of trying to track him.

Several times Ladd, Ramey, Gary Zieger, and sometimes Mason had cruised town trying to find my father. Once, Ladd had Mason call three motels in Valdez because he'd heard my father was there looking to buy land. They'd even concocted a plan to have Pinnick pose as a job applicant and ask my father to meet her somewhere for an interview. Caye Mason made the initial call to Cindy's and was told to call back later, but never did.

They got lucky Wednesday night.

The auction had started and Ramey went inside and walked up to my father, planning to say he knew someone who wanted to buy two shotguns and to ask if they could meet somewhere. Ramey was carrying four hundred dollars that Mason had given him and he showed my father the money. The two chatted, but it was too difficult to hear above the crowd and the auctioneer's cry. They agreed to meet once the auction was over, at eleven at PJ's.

When the auction ended, my father asked his friend Ed Pipkin, a local pawnshop owner, to join him for a drink at PJ's. Ed declined. Until then, Ladd, Pinnick, and Ramey drove around, picking up Zieger at the last minute.

. . .

It was raining by the time Ladd steered into PJ's dirt parking lot, dark except for the glow of the streetlights. Ladd parked well out of sight of the front door.

My father drove up soon after and went into the bar. As soon as the door closed behind him, Zieger and Ramey, both armed, climbed out of the Matador.

My father was well inside the bar by the time Ramey caught up with him and suggested they speak outside. My father followed him out and the two went and stood by his Cadillac. Ramey said the buyer was in Eagle River; could they go out there? My father said no, his gun sales license barred him from selling weapons outside the city limits. At this, Ramey pulled his gun and Zieger stepped from behind the Cadillac.

They forced my father to get inside. Zieger got behind the wheel and Ramey and my father were in the backseat. With Ramey's gun pointed squarely at his head, my father handed Zieger the keys. As Zieger steered the big car out of the parking lot, Ladd and Pinnick followed.

Not long into traffic, Ladd got lost, eventually giving up and returning Pinnick to her truck. With Pinnick leading, they began the drive to Eagle River. On the way, Ladd stopped at a bar on Eagle River's main drag and stayed long enough to have one drink.

Ramey and Zieger got to Mason's house first. They led my father to the cabin and made him sit on the corner bunk. Ladd arrived about twenty minutes later.

> John Rich was sitting on a bed there, a couch, a little three-quarter bed, a mattress built up onto a piece of plywood. We spoke. He wanted to know what this was all about. I said, "Well John," I says, "I feel that you owe me some money." I says, "You know and I know, I don't care who else knows it," but I says, "you and I know that you did tell some lies and you could have helped me by telling the truth at my trial." And he says, "Well, I got confused." He says, "I know I done wrong." At this stage of the game, I mean, the man was in fear of his life and he was almost to the begging stage. And, uh, like I said, I went out there with full intent to kill John Rich.
>
> But when I seen John Rich sitting there on that couch, I don't know, something just happened to me that, I wasn't mad at John Rich. I guess I got thinking about it and I really had not been mad

at John Rich. It was something that kind of picked up from the beginning and now the climax was about here and I really, I wasn't in the mood for any climax; not the way it was supposed to come. But John Rich was a very scart' man. He had the right to be. And he asked me, he says, "I know I beat you out of the massage parlor," he says. "I paid quite a bit through my nose myself in a roundabout way." But he says, "I will give you the massage parlor back and I'll give you $5,000 that I have got in the checking account if you will just let me go."

We had different conversation about that. "Well, if I let you go, you will just come to the police." And I mean, he convinced me that he wouldn't have went to the police. I mean, uh, the way to live . . . I don't believe he would have went to the police. In a roundabout way, I was kind of looking for an out. Something to stall; something to get out of the perdicament [sic] that I'd found myself into anyway. So I asked Gary if he would come outside where I could talk to him.

"Let's take the deal," I says. "Man, it's what we want anyway. That's all we want is the massage parlor" . . . And Gary says, "Well, we got these papers, we might as well just make him sign them."

I don't know if he used the words—make him sign them or get him to sign them—but anyway, the intent was on both of our parts to have him sign them one way or the other.

So I says, "Well, it don't matter because he has offered to make out a bill of sale in his own handwriting." But I says, "One bill's as good as another, it don't make much difference."

We didn't have the papers out there. I had to go over to the house to get the power of attorney. It was made out under Duncan Webb's name.

Ladd went to the main house to get the power of attorney, plus a copy, and a letter Mason had typed for Ladd earlier that month.

The letter was part of an elaborate ruse the pair would use to explain their sudden acquisition of everything my father owned. Should anyone ask questions, they planned to pass the letter off as something my father had written. Police eventually found the letter in Duncan Webb's office.

Ladd mailed the letter from Anchorage in a long white envelope with the return address—"605 w. [sic] 29th, Anchorage, Alaska"—for Cindy's massage parlor. The envelope was addressed to "Mr. Wes Ladd, Cordova, Alaska, 99564." The letter, a brief paragraph typed on a five-

by-eight sheet, is dated August 5, 1973, and begins with a simple
salutation:

Hi Wes
This will probably seem kind of strange getting a letter from me, but
I have a problem.
First of all, I want to say I'm sorry for some of the things I said at
your trial. I also don't feel too good about beating you out of your
massage parlor. However, I would like to make things right with you
if you are interested.
I am going to have to leave town. Not just the town but the state.
So I am going to offer you a deal on everything I own, a real good
deal.
Will you contact me as soon as possible?

When Ladd returned from the main house, he handed a copy of the
power of attorney to my father to read and sign. My father balked.

"If I sign this, you'll kill me," he said. "I'm afraid I won't walk out
of here."

"John, we talked it over, you got my word," Ladd said. "We aren't
going to hurt you."

Ladd said they had a plane waiting on an airstrip in Palmer that would
fly him out of the country after the papers were signed. My father
continued to refuse, trying to explain that even if he did, it wouldn't
work anyway. His signature wouldn't be notarized and therefore the
power of attorney would be useless. He also tried to explain that his
death would void the power of attorney. He'd used power of attorneys
in the past and knew all about them, he said.

Ladd and my father argued. Suddenly, Ramey walked over and
slammed his gun against the side of my father's head.

"Just sign the damn papers! We don't want to hear any more crap,"
he said.

Ramey raised his hand to hit my father again. Ladd told him to
stop.

I told Benny not to hit him anymore. He was bleeding. In fact, I
went outside, it had been raining and there was a bucket of some
kind there and I dipped the towel in this cold water and wrung it
out and give it to him to put on the side of his head. And I told

Benny, I says, "Hey, this ain't necessary." I really, I mean, Rich was so afraid he would have done anything. I am sure of that. . . .

My father stood and leaned against the cabin's sink counter to sign his name to the letter and power of attorney.

He'd always had an impressive signature, using tall pen strokes extending high above the tops of the consonants and capital letters. It was both graceful looking and largely unreadable. He wanted it that way, he once told me, making it a difficult signature to forge. It was a striking signature nonetheless, similar to the kind business executives use: bold, expressive, and important looking. The *J*'s on *John* and *Jr.* had great big rounded loops that slanted and drooped slightly to the left; the *F* in the middle of his name was drawn in a way that almost resembled a musical clef, leaning into and becoming one with the *R* on *Rich*. If you didn't know what his full name was, you'd have trouble separating his middle initial from his last name, the final letters which dissolve into long, sweeping strokes. Despite the fact that everybody called him Johnny, my father never signed his name that way. He always used John.

I took the papers in the house. Now, the reason I did that is because Caye Mason had previously, somewhere or another, got John Rich's signature. I'm not sure if it was out of my file or out of the traffic bureau where you get license plates and things. I think she had a, some kind of a card, I think it was an investigator's card or something; by using this she was able to get some information that had John Rich's signature on it. And uh, I took the papers and went in the house with the papers . . . Benny Ramey, John Rich and Gary was still in the cabin and I went in the house to show Caye Mason the signature. She compared the signatures and she says, "Well, it is authentic enough."

So I started to go back out the door, and uh, Virginia Pinnick was standing in the door, and I don't know. I stopped for a minute and grabbed her by her hand and she looked at me, and I could see she was about to cry. She was kind of in a state. Well, you could just read the sadness in her face. She was doing what she thought she should be doing, but she really wasn't in any mood for doing it. And I looked at her and I says, "It is going to be all right baby, because we are going to let him go. We are not going to hurt him."

She didn't say anything that I remember. She just, a relieved look came over her face, and I let go of her hand and started to walk back to the cabin, and I don't believe I had taken more than four or five steps when the first shot was heard. I was still right by the corner of the house I believe, when this shot was audible both to Virginia and I.

While Ladd was out of the cabin, Ramey claimed Zieger tried to force him to shoot my father. Ramey says he refused and drew his gun. Zieger then fired. When Ladd returned, he found my father lying on the floor.

> His head was in the closet and his body was outside the closet. The closet door doesn't have a door on it, I mean the closet is just an opening. And he was laying mostly on his back, curled up a little bit. And I went over and I said something to him, I don't know what. I have no idea what, I can't bring my mind back to know what, but I did say something . . . he looked like a dead man to me, I mean his eyes were open, I could see no breathing movements from his chest, and Gary says, "Uh, you had better put another shot into him just to make sure" . . . Gary Zieger cocked his gun, he was standing just behind me, to my left, and he cocked his gun and pointed it at me and he said, "Shoot him." He says, "We are in it, you get into it too. We are all into it." I turned back around and looked at Rich and you know, I said, "Forgive me God" and pulled the trigger.

Ramey would tell the court a different story, explaining that after the first shot, my father was very much alive. Ramey said Ladd, who carried his own .38 Cobra Featherlight, grabbed Ramey's gun, a .45, and probably hot. Ramey said Ladd didn't want to have to use his own gun.

Ramey testified that my father raised his arm as Ladd approached him.

"Don't kill me," he pleaded as Ladd stood over him. Ladd brushed his arm aside and shoved the .45's barrel into his chest. Before firing, Ramey said Ladd recited these words: "This is for snitching on me in court."

The first bullet struck my father in the lower left chest; it was non-fatal. The second, before passing all the way through his body, tore off the corner of his heart.

"It seemed like I had been kneeling down or bending over or something, I

don't even remember for sure. But I was in a crouched position, maybe. I don't really know . . . after I shot, he remained . . . he didn't make any jump. His eyes still was open staring at nothing."

After the shooting, the group went to the main house to announce that my father was dead. Pinnick offered an old sleeping bag in which to wrap the body.

They backed Mason's car up to the cabin. Ladd lined the trunk with plastic bags. Zieger then emptied my father's pockets. He kept my father's watch; Mason got five hundred dollars in cash my father was carrying. They then divided up the items in his Cadillac—a .22 automatic pistol, a couple of .22 derringers, some fishing equipment, and a painting he had bought at the auction that night.

After removing the body, Ramey noticed that a slug was embedded in the floor. He dug it out and handed it to Ladd. Later, he filled the hole with wood putty.

Mason stayed at the house to clean up. Ramey, Ladd, and Zieger got into Mason's car. Pinnick, who knew the area best, drove her truck, leading them out of Eagle River and down the Glenn Highway to Jonesville. She and Ladd had scouted the burial site a week before.

It was still raining as they took the dirt road that winds only a couple of miles to the old mine that once supplied coal to much of Alaska's railbelt region. They eventually found a wide curve in the road and parked. There, Ramey and Zieger began digging a shallow grave. Ladd stood watching with his arms around Pinnick. When they were finished, they began the drive home. Midway back on the dirt road, Ladd ran out of gas, and Pinnick had to drive off to buy some.

The morning of Thursday, August 23, Mason gave Benny Ramey a haircut. Aside from a stray fringe here and there, the cut gave Ramey a businesslike look. He took a shower and put on a cheap maroon suit, matching print shirt, and dark brown tie he and Mason had picked out together while shopping at Montgomery Ward—the old Caribou Ward's—nearly three weeks earlier. Mason paid the $91.88 bill by credit card.

Mason and Pinnick then drove the newly shorn Ramey in my father's Cadillac to the airport to catch an 11:50 A.M. Alaska Airlines flight to Seattle. On the drive Mason handed Ramey enough to cover the $108 one-way fare and a return ticket. Mason parked the Cadillac in the airport parking lot. Virginia and Mason's teenage son gave her a ride from the airport. Ladd was to pick up the Cadillac later.

Inside, Ramey bought a ticket under the name "John Rich." He was to fly to Seattle, wait a few hours, then catch a Western Airlines flight back to Anchorage under the name "Robert Stanford."

That afternoon, Mason brought the signed power of attorney to Duncan Webb's office. Webb signed his name as a witness, just below my father's signature. Mason then signed as the second witness. At around seven-thirty that same night, Ladd drove Webb to Leslye Langla's house, where Webb asked her to act as the third and final witness on the document. She hesitated, and Webb explained that he had seen my father sign the document. She signed.

Mason and Webb made a dozen or so copies of the power of attorney to deliver to my father's businesses, banks where he had accounts, and anywhere else he had assets. Mason also typed a letter to Bridgette.

The letter, similar to the one handed me at the gas station, introduced Webb as my father's attorney for the "purposes of managing his business interests and investments as described more fully in the attached copy of 'Power of Attorney' dated August 22, 1973 . . . This letter is to introduce Ms. Caye Mason who will instruct you in the procedure required under this document for accounting of the business accounts of Cindy's Massage Parlor . . . Thank you for your cooperation . . . Very Truely [sic] yours, Duncan Webb."

Another version was addressed to the manager at FiFi's.

On the following day, August 24, Webb asked Langla to type a similar letter, but addressed to me at our house on 12th Avenue. He also asked Langla to create a new file for the "Alaska Investment Corporation." She was to date the file as having been opened August 22— the day of my father's murder.

Into the file, Langla was told to place copies of the letters of introduction along with a handful of copies of the power of attorney and Mason's handwritten note concerning my father's assets. Webb then dictated a lengthy memo describing how my father had come into his office on the twenty-second, accompanied by Mason. They'd come to set up a corporation whose shares would be divided between my father and Caye. The memo noted that John Rich would be president, Mason secretary-treasurer, with a vice-president to be named later. Langla placed the memo in the file.

Later that day, while Webb was out of the office, Mason and Ladd stopped by. Langla told them that Webb was gone. They hadn't come to see him. As Mason stood by, Ladd leaned down on Langla's desk, pushed his face into hers, and gave her a poor description of how he thought my father looked.

"If anyone should ask about the document you signed last night, tell them what the man looked like," he said in a low, serious tone of voice. "He's six feet tall. Heavyset, round face, dark curly hair, dark complexed. That's all you are to say and nothing else."

Langla just stared. Ladd reached over and lightly grabbed her arm, "Do you understand?"

She silently nodded her head "yes."

That Friday, Webb, Ramey, Mason, and Ladd attempted to execute the power of attorney. With Ladd at the wheel of my father's Cadillac, they made the rounds of his businesses and our home. The first stop was the house on 12th. Al Bennett refused to let them in since the letter was addressed to me. He called Ladd a punk and the talk turned violent.

"We could whomp all over you," Ladd said.

Finally, they asked where I was; Al said I was at the Tesoro.

When they returned to the house, Webb told Al that he and Mason had put my father on a plane for Seattle where he had gone to straighten out some troubles with the IRS.

Webb said my father would be back in about a week. Until then, Webb was representing my father and was to inventory his assets and place them into a corporation for protection.

The group spent nearly forty-five minutes at the house, mostly inventorying the guns from my father's business. Before they left, Webb told Bennett he'd have to pay rent to Webb to stay in the house, and they'd be back in a few days to make the arrangements for my father's belongings.

After they left, Al called Cindy's and warned Bridgette that Ladd and company were on their way. She piled all the important paperwork and money into the *Cindy* and one of the masseuses' boyfriends towed it off. Ladd and the others arrived in time to see the boat being hauled off the lot. Webb told Ladd to catch the car. Ladd hit the gas, but gave up after the other car ran a red light.

At Cindy's, Webb told the same story he'd told Al, adding that the boat was part of the "corporation." They were to get it back as soon as possible along with all the paperwork and cash receipts, which were to be turned over to Caye Mason, who would be doing the corporation's accounting. After Cindy's, they went to FiFi's to repeat the routine.

Later Friday night, Ladd returned to Cindy's, accompanied by Mason and a couple of thugs he'd hired to help him hunt down Al Bennett, who was gone. After they left, Bridgette called my father's lawyer, Jim Johnston.

Johnston couldn't believe what he was hearing. None of it made any sense so he decided to go over to the parlor and find out himself what was going on. He was accompanied by his wife and their ten-day-old infant daughter. When he heard the story again, he called the police.

"Calling the police seemed an entirely new idea," Johnston told me, still amazed after all these years that notifying the cops hadn't even occurred to anyone at the parlor.

While waiting for a patrol car to arrive, Johnston told the parlor workers to have a locksmith change all the locks, and if Ladd and the others came back they were to get absolutely nothing. After a couple of officers arrived, Johnston, along with wife and baby, went to the station to give a statement.

At the station, in between questions, several beefy vice cops stood around cooing at the infant. Nobody seemed concerned. Even Johnston wasn't as alarmed as he thinks he should have been.

"I don't know that I thought anything was wrong. I guess I'm slow to suspect the worst."

On Saturday, Mason drove the Cadillac to Cindy's accompanied by Ramey and some muscle they'd picked up at PJ's, intending to throw everybody out. Ladd didn't go along this time. He told them to drop him off at the Gold Rush Hotel nearby.

> Something in this stage of the game, something told me to get out of it, it ain't going to work; you are done. I mean from the beginning I knew what was, I knew the end was going to come and I knew just about what the end was going to be. Anyway, I wouldn't go back, I told them just drop me off at the Gold Rush. So they did that and I went in the Gold Rush and had a drink, in fact I think I had three or four real fast like. And they went over there and when they pulled into the yard this time, they was met by two or three police cars. The police took their names, and uh, my name wasn't among them because I wasn't there and I never did go back . . . I wanted to go and hide because I knew, I just knew that it was going to come out. I knew that I had maybe a week, ten days, two weeks, two months, but I knew that this was going to end . . . there was never a doubt in my mind.

Ladd was right. After their last appearance at Cindy's, Ladd and the others dropped out of sight and the police began circling.

On August 28, a police officer questioned Duncan Webb about the power of attorney that bore his name. Webb told an elaborate tale about simultaneously representing my father's legal interests and counseling Ladd on how to sue him. Webb claimed my father had hired him to set up a corporation to settle a debt with Ladd, describing how he'd signed the power of attorney as Webb and secretary Leslye Langla looked on. The following day, Webb said, he'd driven my father to the airport. Webb claimed that my father had said he would return August 29.

Following the police interview, Webb returned to his office and told Langla to write in an August 29 appointment with my father in his datebook. When she refused, Webb did it himself. On August 29, my father didn't materialize. Ted Carlson, who was then heading the inquiry into my father's disappearance, confronted Webb, who repeated his tale.

The next day, Carlson stopped by Webb's office to see if Langla could identify my father from photographs. Webb said Langla was busy; could they meet Carlson at a restaurant in fifteen minutes? Carlson agreed. After he left, Webb, who had seen the photos, coached Langla on my father's appearance. At the restaurant, Langla hesitated over the pictures until Carlson produced a colored photograph that he said was taken more recently.

"Does this look more like the man?" Carlson asked.

Langla looked over at Webb and he smiled.

"Yes," she said.

Not long afterward, Webb told Langla he believed Ladd had killed my father. She then sought out Bob Wagstaff, who took her to the police to give a statement. With Zieger and Ladd involved, they urged Langla to get out of town. She left the following day.

But Carlson had already decided he didn't believe Webb's secretary. The day after he showed Langla the photos, he and a state trooper drove to Caye Mason's house to confiscate my father's Cadillac. Carlson knew that's where he'd find the car, since Mason had driven it to Cindy's the last time anyone had seen it. Ladd and Mason were home.

"Can I go through it first and get some of my things?" Ladd asked.

"No!" Carlson said.

Ladd followed Carlson outside and stood by as Carlson opened both of the Cadillac's doors, surveying the junk scattered across the seats. The policeman got behind the wheel. Ladd edged closer to the opened passenger door, nervously staring at the glove box. Pretending he didn't notice, Carlson continued examining the interior. Casually leaning sideways, he popped the glove box latch. It swung down, and Carlson reached inside; Ladd lunged, grabbing Carlson's hand just as the policeman got his fingers around the butt of a .45 automatic.

"Back off right now unless you want to get hurt!" Carlson yelled. Ladd drew back and didn't say another word.

Carlson had my father's car, a mystery gun with gold-painted grips, and a nervous secretary's suspicious statement. But he didn't have a body and the investigation stalled.

I entered tenth grade that fall at East High School, continuing to work evenings and weekends at the Tesoro station. Until late November, when Bridgette emptied my father's bank accounts and left the state, my only communication with her consisted of screaming fights.

On August 28, Bridgette gave birth to a boy who was not my father's son. The child was mulatto. Despite obvious evidence to the contrary—Bridgette, like my father, was white—she told everyone he was my father's child anyway and named him John Francis Rich III. Soon, she returned to an old habit, shooting heroin. After she left in early November, the state took me into custody, declaring that I was orphaned and abandoned. I went to live with the family of a friend to await word of my father's fate.

On November 27, everything changed. Gary Zieger turned up dead, sprawled beside the highway fifteen miles south of Anchorage, a twelve-gauge shotgun blast pumped into his chest. Less than twenty-four hours earlier, he'd been linked to the murder of the wife and stepson of a local nightclub owner. Zieger had been named as one of two suspects believed to have committed the crime.

About twenty thousand dollars in cash and jewels were taken from the home. At the time of the murders, Zieger was out on bail awaiting sentencing for the Cordova dynamite theft, for which he'd been tried and convicted in October. He was rumored to have committed the burglary to get money to pay for his appeal of the case.

The next day, police followed him to PJ's and served him with a warrant to impound his truck for evidence in connection with the killings. A witness said she'd seen a truck matching the description of Zieger's in the vicinity of the crime. His sentencing on the Cordova case was only a couple of days away. The officers offered to take Zieger into protective custody; there were rumors that many different people were gunning for Zieger, including some of his peers.

Nonetheless, Zieger declined the policeman's offer. Zieger was last seen alive at PJ's, looking for a ride.

Benny Ramey tripped up when he tried to pawn a gold nugget that came from the house where the nightclub owner's family was murdered. He was then pegged as the second man in the killings. This led Ramey into an underworld dragnet cast by friends and acquaintances of my father's. They wanted to solve my father's disappearance as well as prevent Wesley Ladd from rising to power in Anchorage's underworld. The unofficial search was being led by the man to whom Ramey tried to sell the nugget. He and his crew snatched Ramey and hid him out of town in a remote cabin to interrogate him. Then Zieger was shot, so Ramey decided to cooperate and face the police rather than risk the same fate as Zieger. After confessing to the vigilantes, he was handed over to Ted Carlson, who brought him into town under a heavily armed police escort. The atmosphere was so supercharged with suspicion and violence that at one point when one of the police cars got a flat tire, Carlson just kept on going, running every red light into town. There had been talk of leaks in the police department, and he couldn't be sure that the flat tire wasn't a setup that might lead to Ramey's being gunned down before being brought in.

On November 28, Ramey tried to lead Carlson to my father's burial site, but Ramey didn't know the area that well, and a heavy snow cover made it impossible to find the grave. While city police and the state troopers had been cooperating on the investigation, it became mostly a troopers' case once it was learned that the body was buried outside city limits. Trooper Jim Vaden was brought into the case.

On December 1, Vaden led a team of investigators to Mason's cabin, where they spent eight hours tearing the place to shreds, collecting everything they could get their hands on: floor scrapings, beer caps, cigarette ashes, and snippets of hair and fabric.

Two days later, Vaden visited Duncan Webb to advise him he was a suspect. Although Vaden told him both Mason and Ramey were now cooperating, Webb stuck to his original story. When Vaden pressed him, Webb cut off the interview, telling Vaden to come back if he found a body.

Two weeks later, on December 15, Ladd was taken into custody in Cordova, where he'd fled with Virginia Pinnick. Since they still didn't have a body, police could charge him only with being a felon in possession of guns. Federal agents had been investigating Ladd for gun purchases he'd made before and after Rezk's murder.

The day after Ladd and Pinnick arrived in Anchorage, Vaden began to hammer them in the interrogation room. Pinnick crumbled. On December 20, she accompanied Vaden up the old Jonesville mine road and pointed out where the body was buried. Because the ground was frozen, Vaden had to wait until the following day to bring some excavation equipment to the scene to unearth the body.

I was Christmas shopping at The Mall when I got the news.

At the end of the day, I had called a friend to ask for a ride home. She said the troopers had called the house with an emergency message for me.

For a minute I fantasized that my father wasn't dead; I'd call, and he'd be on the other end.

Standing by the bank of pay phones at The Mall's western end, I tried to think, but there were too many distractions. The place was a madhouse as last-minute shoppers scurried in and out of stores festooned in silver and gold tinsel. The lights were too bright; the tinsel, too cheap. The Christmas music made me want to scream.

I fumbled in my pocket for a dime and dialed the number.

A woman answered; I identified myself. A few seconds later an officer got on the line and spoke in a halting voice.

"I'm terribly sorry, Miss Rich . . . " he began.

He kept apologizing and pausing, as if waiting for me to break down. I just wanted him to get to the point. This last bit of news was not going to affect me. I'd been told my father was dead months ago. Everybody knew it.

"No really, it's okay," I told the trooper, feeling a little sorry for him, trying to make it easier. "I'm fine, really. Yes. That's fine. No, really. Thanks for calling."

I hung up and, without pausing, gathered up my packages and ran out to catch my ride.

PART 4

GETTING THROUGH

The mob moves in

By HOWARD WEAVER
Daily News Staff Writer
© 1974, The Anchorage Daily News

Organized crime is taking root in Anchorage.

Last year, local criminals raked off at least $22 million here, killed for business, and sold heroin on the streets. To further criminal ends, political connections were made and some legitimate businesses linked up with the criminal community.

In the process, a definable underworld structure has begun to take shape.

A fast-growing prosperous economy and the promise of an even bigger boom during the pipeline construction years have lured the Outside organizers to Anchorage.

Between 1950 and 1973, the Anchorage area population exploded from 32,060 to 150,000. Gross receipts in retail trade here more than doubled from about $172 million to nearly $400 million between 1967 and 1971.

The rise in criminal activity — and criminal prosperity — has more than matched that pace.

By conservative estimate of four main types of vice. The Daily News has placed a $22 million price tag on crime in Anchorage during 1973. That includes primarily money from drugs, gambling, prostitution and stolen property.

That works out to more than $60,000 every day of the year — more than $2,500 every hour of every day.

Underworld figures, like most Alaskans, expect a windfall from the trans-Alaska pipeline construction, which is expected to begin in a big way this spring. Construction workers are likely to hit town for rest and recreation with paychecks as big as $2,000 for a week's work.

"There's going to be a lot of bucks around, man, and somebody's gonna get them," a long-time Anchorage gambler says.

To be in position to get that money, members of the Anchorage underworld have been scrambling for the past 18 months to establish a power base from which to maneuver in the expected gold rush climate.

Representatives of criminal syndicates from Outside currently are taking the pulse of the city; their next grip may be a strangle-hold.

Here are a few indications of the organization moves now underway:

● At least eight unsolved murders or "mysterious" deaths since July 1972 — all connected with the underworld in Anchorage.

● Numerous firebombings and arsons aimed at shady businesses, criminals and police informers.

● Increasing criminal activity by persons formerly believed to be in "legitimate" business.

A special report

organized crime in Anchorage

On Page 2:
● The way it used to be in Anchorage

On Page 3:
● How crime pays off in our town — the numbers racket
● The week that panicked the local underworld
● Can the crime bonanza be stopped?

● Positive connections between local criminals and Outside syndicates, especially in Washington state and Nevada.

Murder

In the past year and a half the following persons connected with the Anchorage underworld have died:

John R. 'Punky' Gomes and Harold Lee Haynes were shotgunned to death at the Reef N Bourbon nightclub July 11, 1972. The murders, as police investigators privately concede, were the work of a professional killer. Most underworld sources believe Gomes was killed over a narcotics transaction of large proportions.

Ferris Rezk, a massage parlor operator and suspected heroin dealer, was shot in the head and killed Nov. 27, 1972 in the sitting room at Cindy's Massage. Wesley Ladd, accused of the execution, was acquitted after his attorney argued that the job was done by "an organization hit-man" who sought to take over the massage parlor-prostitution trade here.

Larry Wallace Fore, about a week after he was arrested on Jan. 17, 1973 while delivering heroin to Linda's Massage, turned up dead in an apartment shared by a musician and prostitute. His death was officially listed as "acute bronchial pneumonia." Few policemen

— and nobody who knew him — believe that was the cause of death.

Just before midnight, Aug. 22, 1973, masage parlor owner-gambler John F. 'Johnny' Rich called his wife and said he was at an auction. The next time he was seen, his decomposing body was being unearthed from a shallow grave near a coal mine 48 miles north of Anchorage. Investigators believe he was executed in a power struggle involving his "business" operations, although the plan apparently failed to net expected rewards for perpetrators.

Mrs. Margaret Sumpter, wife of long-time nightclub owner James Sumpter, and her 13-year-old son Richard Merck, were shot and killed in their home just after 2 a.m., Nov. 26, 1073—one year to the day after Ferris Rezk was gunned down.

The next day, a motorist on the Seward Highway south of town spotted the body of Gary Zieger, a police suspect in the Sumpter killings, lying face down on the roadside. He had been shotgunned to death.

These deaths and murders remain unsolved for one main reason, according to an Anchorage lawyer who watches the scene: the motives are hidden in the depths of underworld activity.

They are not "standard" killings —

done in anger or passion, or by mistake. They have been executed for more subtle reasons — to eliminate competition, to warn others in the underworld, or simply for revenge.

Arson

In a sense, the killings represent only failures in the organization attempts. Those who can be controlled by less final methods are allowed to live and operate.

But there are other methods.

Records of city fire investigators show at least 10 cases of arson or firebombings aimed at underworld figures or shady businesses.

Prostitutes, police informers, bar owners and at least one "after hours" gambling club have been scorched in past months.

Deputy Fire Marshall John Franklin says several of the cases showed a thoroughly professional approach toward this time-honored method of intimidation.

Prostitution

Control of the prostitutes — a mainstay in underworld finances — has become a prime objective of organizers.

Massage parlors, which gross about $2.6 million a year, in recent months have become increasingly organized. Of the 15 parlors now advertising, half are controlled by two persons.

Misiko Slack directs Imperial, Ruby's and Misiko's — three successful operations which are clustered fortress-like along 27th Avenue in Spenard.

An Anchorage businessman, who has "legitimate" businesses here, is believed by investigators to be involved in four other parlors. Police think he is seeking wide-spread control of the lucrative parlor business.

A representative from a Reno, Nev. syndicate is in Anchorage now, negotiating to supply all the girls who work the massage parlors now. In that way, sources who talked with the man say, the syndicate hopes to control prices, working hours and entry into the prostitution racket here.

The Reno connection — who is staying with a local massage parlor operator — reportedly was accompanied to Anchorage by girls he has offered as samples of the Reno merchandise.

Street prostitutes here say it is becoming increasingly difficult to work as an independent. Says one: "Guys come along and tell you, 'Hey it's hard to work with your face messed up'."

Police Chief Earl Hibpshman observes "there were a lot of new faces" among the fifty girls busted in police crack-downs during the past few weeks.

(Continued on Page 2)

Even the media bought into the Anchorage Mob scare.

CHAPTER FIFTEEN

THE MOB AND OTHER MYTHS

"THE MOB MOVES IN" declared the front page of the January 13, 1974, *Anchorage Daily News*. A "Special Report," illustrated with grainy black-and-white photographs of the 4th Avenue bar scene and a silhouette of a forties-vintage mobster, was divided into several parts. The stories had titles like "The Week That Panicked the Local Underworld" and "Can the Crime Bonanza Be Stopped?" One article exposed the numbers racket; another outlined "How Local Crime Pays," alleging that prostitution, drugs, gambling, loan-sharking, and the like netted $22 million a year in Anchorage. One featured old-timers waxing nostalgic about the good old days when vice was fun, prostitutes were clean, and murders were rare.

"Organized crime is taking root in Anchorage," the opening paragraph of the main story began. "A fast-growing prosperous economy and the promise of an even bigger boom during the pipeline construction years have lured the Outside organizers to Anchorage."

The stories tried to link a series of unrelated events in order to make sense of what was occurring in Anchorage's underworld, which seemed to have been turned upside down. As construction on the pipeline neared reality, violence and uncertainty became bywords in a world where things had remained largely unchanged since statehood. Everybody was trying to get a piece of the biggest oil strike in U.S. history. Men from Reno supposedly were in town trying to set up a supply of girls for the massage parlors, reviving the old rumor of attempts to organize Anchorage's skin trade. Following my father's murder, longtime Anchorage underworld figures had gone into hiding. Some left the state; others hired bodyguards. Some began sleeping with guns under their pillows.

But not since Anchorage's frontier beginnings had life been so damned exciting. Out-of-towners were landing at the airport in droves. The hotels were packed. Rents began to skyrocket. Housing prices went up. Business was good everywhere. The bars were filled with people dropping hundred-dollar bills like they were hot rocks. Cocaine was becoming the drug of choice. Once pipeline construction began, everybody was going to get rich, and the smart ones were here early. Anchorage wasn't the edge of nowhere anymore; by January 1974, it felt like the center of the universe. Rumors of the Mob only proved the point. The hysteria lent the city cachet—even the Mob was interested in Anchorage.

The paper found its most compelling proof of the Mob's arrival in the eight murders and "mysterious" deaths—including my father's—that had occurred in the previous eighteen months. One, a heroin dealer, had died from bronchial pneumonia; two men had been gunned down in a local bar. The other five deaths were tied to the activities of two men: Zieger and Wesley Ladd.

Two months after the Mob exposé appeared in the *Anchorage Daily News,* another story was played out across the front page of the rival newspaper, the *Anchorage Daily Times.*

"LADD, RAMEY INDICTED" read the March 14, 1974, banner headline of the afternoon paper's home edition. "Both Face Charges in Death of Rich" read the subhead of the article on page one, which went on to say:

> Wesley Ladd and Benny Ramey today were indicted for the kidnap and murder of massage parlor owner John F. "Johnny" Rich.
> The return of the grand jury indictments in Superior Court this

morning ended months of suspense, speculation and rumor that have been running rife in Anchorage since Rich's disappearance last Aug. 22.

The speculation and rumors were rekindled Dec. 21 with the discovery of Rich's body in a shallow grave in a mining area about 17 miles north of Palmer.

Today's indictments lifted the curtain on months of investigations by Alaska State Troopers. . . .

Once again, my father's name was in the newspapers. This time, however, instead of some inside Metro piece on just another gambling raid, the stories were front-page news. They would remain so for months. And the names were well known to newspaper reporters and readers alike.

"It was a familiar scene as the slight figure with disheveled, reddish hair sat in the courtroom," began one story that chronicled the court arraignment of Wesley Ladd.

Jim Vaden approached my father's murder with the same zeal he'd applied years earlier to shutting down his vacuum cleaner store. Aside from gathering the other necessary evidence, Vaden wanted a voluntary statement from Ladd. After waiting six weeks, he got one. On February 1, 1974, Ladd confessed to shooting my father.

Along with Ladd and Ramey, Pinnick was also indicted for first-degree murder that March. Ladd and Ramey also were charged with kidnapping. A month later, Webb was indicted.

The indictments set off years of criminal proceedings at which each conspirator blamed another. Out of six defendants, only two would go to trial—Ladd and Webb—and the rest would either plead out or cut deals with prosecutors to testify against the others. Assistant District Attorney William Mackey made up for his losses in Zieger's and Ladd's first trials and successfully prosecuted Webb and Ladd.

Caye Mason never came to trial. She was granted immunity from prosecution on the condition that she testify against the others. Defense attorney Edgar Boyko said he persuaded Mason to help the police when she sought his counsel. He provided her with another attorney in the firm and they called Jim Vaden. It was Vaden who signed her immunity agreement.

Duncan Webb was the first to be tried. As a star witness against Webb, Mason claimed she was innocent.

The late renowned Alaska criminal defense attorney Wendell P. Kay defended Webb during Webb's first trial. He had a field day with Mason during a lengthy and unrelenting cross-examination. Throughout her testimony, Mason denied any knowledge of any wrongdoing and pinned the kidnap and murder plot on the others, notably Ladd and Webb. She said she'd been led astray by the group, especially Ladd, who along with Zieger had threatened her life and the lives of her children.

"So, what you're telling me and the jury is primarily that you acted throughout this then as an accomplice to the crime of murder because of fear?" Kay asked.

"Yes sir."

Initially, Jim Vaden believed Mason was one of the least culpable in my father's death. "No one really realized the extent of her involvement. From our standpoint, we all felt like perhaps she was the least involved," he said.

But as his investigation deepened and Webb's trial wound down, Vaden began regretting his decision not to prosecute her. "You could never get the same story out of her twice. I'm not sure she even knew what the truth was."

The jury did not find Mason to be a credible witness and returned a hung verdict against Webb. Jurors told Vaden that Mason also should have been indicted. Prosecutors never used her again. Vaden said her immunity agreement was irrevocable, and while it was possible she could have been charged with perjury, this was a rare course of action in those days.

Mason remains in Alaska.

In April 1975, in part because of her age at the time of the crime— eighteen—and the assistance she eventually lent police, Virginia Pinnick was allowed to plead guilty to accessory after the fact to murder. The murder charge was dropped. She got three years, one to be served in jail, the remainder on probation. In 1976—the same year I graduated from high school—she was paroled and went on to complete an apprenticeship as an electrician. At the time she was released from jail, Pinnick indicated that she would also remain in Alaska.

Less than two weeks after he was indicted, Benny Ramey pleaded guilty to kidnapping, drawing a ten-year sentence. The murder charge was dropped in exchange for his testimony against the others. If his version of events that night in the cabin is true, and Vaden believes it is, Ramey was the most candid of all the defendants. He fully admitted his role in the kidnapping and murder. Vaden said there is no evidence that Ramey was involved with Zieger in the murder of the nightclub owner's family. Ramey may have simply been used to unload the stolen jewelry.

For security reasons, Ramey initially was jailed under a false name and would serve his sentence in various Outside state prisons. In 1978, he was paroled in Miami. Two years later he was arrested in Pennsylvania for violating the conditions of his parole when he left Florida and failed to report to his probation officer. In July 1980, the Alaska Parole Board ordered Ramey to serve an additional six months. At the end of his sentence he was released. There is no record of any further violations and in 1983 his parole was terminated. Ramey was last known to be living and working somewhere on the East Coast.

In early January 1974, Jim Vaden took Duncan Webb up on his offer, and called to say he had a body and wanted to talk. The interview wouldn't take place until April. Webb stuck by his story and was indicted.

There is no evidence that Webb knew ahead of time that Ladd and the others intended to murder my father. No one, though, knows exactly what his intentions were in getting involved with Ladd or why he included himself in the "corporation." Police and prosecutors developed two theories: One was that Ladd, et al., employing the organized crime adage that one lawyer with a briefcase is worth more than twenty guys with guns, had duped Webb and were using him as the legitimate front for their plot. The second theory is that the opposite was true and Webb was using them. Prosecutors believed that Webb lied after the fact for financial gain and to keep himself out of trouble.

Even Mike Rubinstein, who testified in Webb's defense, agrees: "I could never sort out in my mind whether Duncan was a sinister, conniving person who was in his element because he was basically like them," Rubinstein told me, "or whether he was just a flake, who really didn't know what in the hell he was doing and got himself in too deep, and just didn't have any way of getting out of it and kept on shooting off his mouth."

Webb was indicted for three charges: accessory after the fact to murder, concealing evidence, and compounding and concealing a crime. The concealing-evidence charge was eventually dismissed. All of the other charges against Webb stemmed from the numerous false statements he gave to the police. He claimed he lied because Zieger had threatened his life. There was evidence, however, that he continued to represent Zieger on other matters, up until Zieger was murdered.

After Webb's first trial ended in a hung jury, he was retried in 1975 and convicted of the accessory charge. On the stand, he repeatedly contradicted his own previous testimony, leading prosecutor Mackey to call Webb a "pathological liar." Webb's lawyer, James M. MacInnis—while arguing his client's fear defense—had no choice but to agree with Mackey's assessment of Webb.

In legal jargon, MacInnis used what's known as an "ugly duckling" defense, agreeing that his client may have been guilty of lying, but not of the crimes as charged. MacInnis's candid remarks during his closing arguments to the jury became legend in Anchorage legal circles: "Because the larger inquiry is not whether Duncan Webb tells small lies, because of course he does. If I asked him now what he had for breakfast, he would tell me something different than the actual fact, because that's the way he is . . . I've known him for years and I've always known that he was a kind of pathological liar."

In August 1975, Webb was sentenced to two years' probation. He appealed his conviction to the Alaska Supreme Court, which not only affirmed his conviction, but condemned Webb's lenient sentence: "Webb did more than simply lie," the court wrote in a near-unanimous opinion. "His criminal conduct, employing conscious dishonesty, deserves greater condemnation than if it were committed by one not obligated to adhere to high standards of honor and integrity . . . we believe that he [Webb's sentencing judge] was clearly mistaken in not requiring Webb to be placed in prison."

Disbarred in Alaska, Webb resigned his California license after the California Bar Association moved to take action against him. He left Alaska, and worked Outside for many years as a law librarian. In 1988 he applied for a pardon from the State of Alaska. His request was denied. In 1989 he applied for readmission to the California bar. The State Bar of California opposed Webb's readmission, and I was subpoenaed to testify at his hearing against his being readmitted. Edgar Boyko also testified against Webb.

After an eleven-day reinstatement trial in Los Angeles, the judge hearing the case recommended that Webb be allowed to regain his license to practice law. The judge found that Webb, who by now was fifty-six, had "demonstrated his present moral character and his rehabilitation."

Citing numerous personal and professional letters of support and Webb's involvement in youth groups and charities, the judge wrote:

> Petitioner [Webb] made an extraordinary showing of continuing successful efforts to atone for his prior misconduct and of his avoidance of any misconduct since his conviction . . . the court agrees that petitioner was convicted of a very serious crime. However, the conduct that led to petitioner's conviction was a frightening confluence of unique events which occurred almost twenty years ago, and petitioner has not been in trouble with the law since that time.

The State Bar of California did not appeal, and the Supreme Court of the State of California signed off on Webb's readmission.

Upon his arrest, Wesley Ladd called his old attorney, hoping Boyko could work his magic one more time. Boyko's response is also legend among Anchorage attorneys. Not only could he not take the case because of his former bookkeeper's involvement, but he didn't want it.

"Sorry," he told Ladd. "Only one miracle per customer."

I asked Boyko if he regretted his defending Ladd in the Rezk case. "I've never regretted Wesley Ladd," he said. "Not because I wasn't moved by what happened to your father, but I think that might have happened in any number of ways. And I have no regrets about Wesley Ladd maybe killing Ferris Rezk, who was at least as miserable a person as Wesley Ladd."

Seven attorneys turned down Ladd's case; the court finally appointed one for him. Because of pretrial publicity, Superior Court Judge James Fitzgerald moved the case to Kodiak, believing a fair and impartial jury could not be found in Anchorage.

At his trial, like Mason, Ladd claimed no knowledge of the events that led to my father's murder, recanting his confession (which had been ruled admissable evidence), and blaming the whole plot on Gary Zieger. He claimed he gave his confession under duress, and that he wasn't even in the cabin when my father was killed.

"Now the big question then, Mr. Ladd, is why you had this—why were you involved with the power of attorney?" asked Richard Collins, Ladd's defense attorney. (Collins was also the man who was the judge who presided over my father's long-ago concealed weapon case.)

"I wasn't really involved with no power of attorney," Ladd answered. "At no place was I ever involved with a power of attorney . . . the reason I was involved at all was because of Gary Zieger."

The jury didn't believe him, and on November 5, 1974, Ladd was convicted of first-degree murder and kidnapping and was later sentenced to two concurrent life terms. He appealed his case to the Alaska Supreme Court, but lost.

After serving ten years (including jail time served before going to trial) of his sentence at Leavenworth Penitentiary, Ladd was paroled in December 1983, the same year I graduated from college. I was offered the opportunity to speak against his release and declined. At the time, my decision was based on a strong desire to keep my father's death and the events surrounding it as separate from my own life as possible. That December, I was only a few months out of college, newly married, and busy trying to start a career. I do not regret my decision. I found it difficult enough as it was appearing at Webb's hearing years later. I was older and ready to face my father's death. Yet the experience stirred up a lot of emotions, none of which was easily resolved.

Ladd has remarried, is said to be a born-again Christian, and remains in Alaska. He is still on parole, having served without any violations.

· · ·

Finally, while police say the case remains open, Zieger's murder remains unsolved. Dead and unable to defend himself, he became a convenient target: the guilty party of choice for everyone involved in my father's slaying. Gary was the ringleader, the planner, and the plotter who no one dared cross or betray. Not only was Gary accused of devising the entire "corporation" and power-of-attorney scheme, he was pegged as the main kidnapper and murderer.

As for his own death, police have developed a number of theories that both include and don't include the notion of a hired hitman. The scenarios as to who actually did the killing—or the hiring, as the case may have been—include anyone from the burglary's second gunman to someone who wanted to remove Zieger as a threat to the community and/or as a favor to the bereaved family members (with or without their asking). There's even a theory that he was killed in retaliation for ZeZe Mason's murder. There were rumors that he was a marked man ever since he'd been acquitted of that crime.

Zieger was twenty at the time of his death.

I chose not to interview my father's killers.

"So, have you talked to Ladd?" I'd hear every so often. A coworker suggested I interview Ladd via videotape and produce a documentary: "Daughter of Murder Victim Confronts Her Father's Killer."

I knew if I talked to one, I'd have to talk to all of them, which meant I had to know the case better than anyone, even the police. So I acquired the evidence files, including a court file containing a lengthy index describing its contents—"Power of Attorney," "White Envelope," "Brown Envelope," "Latent Fingerprints," ".45 Cal. Pistol [photo of]," "Photos of Cabin." Everything is stamped with yellow and white stickers—"Plaintiff's Exhibit 10, 74–1734 Cr," "State's Exhibit 22, 74–1734 Cr"—and stapled neatly to sheets of crisp, white paper or wrapped in clear plastic. Another envelope, with the handwritten label *State* v. *Ladd,* contains plastic bags made brittle by the passage of time and sealed with the red tags used by troopers to describe the contents. One bag holds locks of my father's hair, others contain scrapings from the spot where he died, fragments of linoleum and wood, a beer cap, loose cigarette tobacco. The last holds one of the slugs that killed him. I examined every document, bullet, hair sample, and clothing fiber. I talked to the detectives who investigated the case, to the judges, to the lawyers. I listened to tapes of the trials, I read the transcripts. I pored over every newspaper account; I spoke with the reporters who wrote them. Finally, I read the confessions and police statements of my father's killers and coconspirators. I came to realize that the specifics of my father's murder, or why he was killed, couldn't answer the most important questions. The murderers couldn't tell me why my father loved my mother, what happened to him as a boy, why he hit me. It was not my father's murder that had haunted me all these years but the bond that never breaks between a father and a daughter.

But what of my mother?

When I look closely at the photographs taken in our home on Fireweed Lane now, I see a woman *striving* toward happiness. The closest she comes to looking truly happy is when I'm in the picture. I was the best thing that ever happened to my mother. I was easy. Like all children, I loved her unconditionally. I was the one thing that she had done right. Even her family agrees.

Undoubtedly my father was a mixed blessing for my mother. However she must have felt herself an equal partner in the life they made for themselves, she clearly sacrificed more. Gambling and grifting are one thing; prostitution another, especially for her. It was her attachment to a man that precipitated her first mental breakdown, and to build a life around wooing and being with men was perhaps the riskiest thing my mother could have done.

My father found his niche in Alaska. He made a lot of friends and he became a big shot among the nightclub crowd. He felt at home. But I don't think the same was true for my mother, no matter how hard she tried. It all looked so promising when she and my father started out. He said all the right things. He promised they were headed for the top and seemed capable of pulling it off. But after a few years in Alaska, sitting on bar stools in seedy B-joints, the reality must have set in. I realize now that I misread the look in her eyes—that look that troubled me so—to mean she wanted my help. I now know that the look had nothing to do with what she expected *from* me. It reflected, instead, how she *felt* about me.

Mental illness is a guilt-provoking disease. As a child, I know how responsible I felt. Not so much for her sickness, but for what I wrongly perceived as my responsibility to try to make her well. My father must have wondered about his role in making her sick. An uneasy truce exists between me, my mother's family, and the memory of her illness. They'd rather I not talk about it, and I try to understand how difficult it must have been for them.

When I look at my mother's only other legacy—her medical records—the words seem cold, one-sided, even cruel. The language of medicine may protect those who use it from the tragedy they deal in, and maybe in the end what the doctors and nurses wrote about my mother was all anyone could say. But they didn't know her.

They didn't know her when she had those curves, those eyes, that gypsy hair. They never saw her hourglass figure in pedal pushers and a cashmere sweater, head back, shoulders erect, hips asway. They never saw her sitting on a bar stool, one knee crossed over the other, looking out from under one immaculately painted eyebrow as she pushed her raven curls into an inviting roil atop her head.

Years after she'd died, my aunts gave me a box of her clothes. I had no idea what to do with them, especially the black knit dress with a long sleeve on one side and no sleeve on the other. The outfit went to a thrift store; I wish I hadn't let it go. What I wouldn't give to hear her laugh as she sat at a bar drinking a martini, or watch her work a room filled with her friends, drinking, laughing, and listening to Frank Sinatra on the phonograph. I wish I could have known her then—to have been in her company in 1956, when she called herself Ginger.

My father in Las Vegas in 1956, when he was full of hopes and dreams

CHAPTER SIXTEEN

PICKING UP THE PIECES

The irony of my father's death was that his "empire of vice" — as even one newspaper story called it — was only a veneer of flashy cars and expensive clothes that covered piles of virtually useless leases, debts, and rental receipts. There was no will and the estate was never probated. Everything my father appeared to own was rented, borrowed, or in somebody else's name.

The massage parlors were leased businesses furnished with a few hundred dollars' worth of rundown furniture that Bridgette sold off and turned over to new tenants. The boat and his inventory of guns went back to the bank; the Cadillac went to his old girlfriend, Stormy, since it had been in her name, and no one knows what happened to it after that. My dad's real estate holdings amounted to a couple of commercial lots near Kenai that reverted to the previous owner. Trying to hide his interest in the land, my father hadn't listed his ownership with the recorder of deeds. What Webb and the others believed to be a spacious mobile home to be used in Valdez to house the whores turned out to be a rickety, homemade utility trailer that my father had bought at auction. The Valdez lots on which Ladd and his coconspirators planned to build a thriving massage parlor enterprise never existed.

The only thing of real value my father seemed to have ever owned was the diamond ring he fought to keep during his bankruptcy proceedings. Now, reworked into a new setting and worn by the wife of the lawyer who bought it so cheaply, it was recently appraised at eleven thousand dollars.

As that first winter without my father passed, our house on 12th Avenue remained much the same as it always had. After Bridgette vanished, a woman who had worked for my father at Cindy's moved in and paid the bills. In late spring I started to dispose of the contents.

I began with the remnants of my father's auction-house bargains — surplus office equipment, gun-cleaning kits, and toolboxes. I ran a classified in the newspaper advertising a garage sale, and on a sunny June day, I piled everything onto tables in the driveway.

No sooner had I set up shop than my father's old friend Ed Pipkin parked his beat-up station wagon in front of the house. He got out and began looking over the odds and ends of my father's life. As he poked around, he told me about seeing my father at the auction just before he was kidnapped.

They'd been bidding against each other for years. Ed is a big man with a high forehead and jowly cheeks, some years older than my father. He wears a handlebar mustache and a graying ponytail. He ran pawnshops, and to this day sports a diaper pin fashioned out of gold nuggets and worn on the breast pocket of his wool shirts.

"Your father was a junkman," Ed said with a wide smile. "Just like me."

He told me how, the last night my father was alive, he'd turned down my father's offer to go have a drink at PJ's. Ed rarely if ever declined such an offer from my dad.

"If I'd gone along, your father might still be alive," he said.

"Ed, that's nonsense," I said. "You couldn't have prevented what happened."

Ed stared down at the ground.

"Yeah, well, anyway, here," he said. He reached into his hip pocket and pulled out a gold nugget money clip stuffed with a wad of greenbacks. He snapped off four hundred-dollar bills and handed them to me.

"What are you doing?" I asked.

"I want to buy everything," Ed said.

"What do you mean you want to buy everything?"

"I'll take all this stuff," he said. "I could use it at my pawnshops."

I refused. His shops were piled high with junk he hadn't been able to sell for years, but Ed wouldn't take no for an answer. The same thing had happened with another close friend of my father's when I tried to turn down his $350 payment for guns he'd "bought" before my dad was killed.

What Ed Pipkin didn't buy that day, Bridgette sold after she came back to town in the summer of 1974, putting half the money into heroin and the other half into a plane ticket out of state. I stopped by the house as the movers were hauling a few last pieces of furniture out the front door.

"Big Al" Alexander had come over from his body shop across the street. Throughout that winter, Al occasionally stopped by the house to check up on me. For my sixteenth birthday, he even brought me a present, a perfume and bath powder set, along with a card with a picture of a toy poodle that read "Happy Birthday Grandma." When he asked how old I was, he opened the card, taped a dime to the inside and said, "Call me in ten years." I was always happy to see Al.

"I can't believe it," he said as he surveyed the empty rooms. "She done sold everything. I'll be damned!"

I was stunned and relieved. Only weeks before I'd stood in the foyer wondering what I was going to do with a house full of furniture. *What sixteen-year-old owns a washer and a dryer?* I thought to myself. I also believed that everything my father had owned was stained with his blood and I wanted none of it. Bridgette solved my problems. I never saw her again. In 1987, she died in the Seattle area of massive internal injuries she received after running into traffic high on heroin.

I left the house that day and never returned, determined to sever all ties with my childhood and my father's murder. I didn't read the newspaper accounts of the capture and subsequent trials of his killers; I didn't even attend my father's funeral. I finished my high school years living with the families of friends before going to college and beginning my career as a reporter.

All I had to remind me of my father was some of his jewelry that I took with me that afternoon when I walked out of the house: a Shriner's pin (undoubtedly, some poker win) with its teardrop-size fake rubies and emeralds inlaid in the curved handle of a miniature scimitar, and a pair of dark blue topaz cuff links and matching shirt studs.

The cuff links are only dyed glass cut into a pointed spiral with a faceted crown. The back of each has been treated with the same materials used to give rhinestones their sparkle.

My father always wore them for formal occasions with his best suit and a white tuxedo shirt. They were the last thing he'd put on, just before running his shoes under the electric polisher. I remember lying in my bed in the house on 12th Avenue as he stood in the hall, next to the closet, snapping the studs into place and adjusting the cuff links. The stones caught the beam of the hallway light and reflected glints of blue and green around my darkened room. I can still remember how handsome he looked.

The pipeline was completed in 1977; the state — and Anchorage — will never be the same. Alaska's largest city now boasts 226,000 residents. Aside from a few rough edges and a scenic setting, it could be any mid-size city in the American west. A few dirt roads still traverse the fully developed mountainsides behind town. Flower beds and shrubs decorate the streets. Four-lane freeways weave north and south of a modest skyline; wooded bike paths wind through dozens of new housing developments. Newer shopping pavilions dwarf Anchorage's first indoor mall. The city has sushi bars, specialty stores, a symphony, a performing arts center, and a classical music station. Satellite technology brings dozens of channels on cable and same-day television broadcasts.

I'm not sure my father would recognize this Anchorage.

Most of my father's friends went legitimate years ago, giving up the life to sell cars or own straight businesses. A few of my father's old friends still run gambling houses. After-hours joints are as prevalent as ever, hectored constantly by a large and sophisticated police force. The topless bar trade has shrunk to a few operations heavily regulated by the state liquor board. Once the city annexed Spenard, most massage parlors went out of business; some survive as "escort" services.

. . .

My father was cremated, and for years I'd heard no one had paid for the funeral.

When I tried to find out what happened to his ashes, I learned that the mortician who handled the arrangements was indicted only a few months after handling my father's remains. The criminal charges included conducting mass cremations, withholding remains for payment, and reselling caskets. So, my father's remains had been handled by a crooked mortician. He probably would have laughed at the irony.

The mortician pleaded guilty and was run out of business. I finally learned that an old friend of my father's had gotten his ashes and scattered them in Cook Inlet, near where my father used to fish aboard the *Gray Goose*.

I was also able to uncover my father's "Record of Funeral," prepared by the parlor. Under the category of "Religion of the Deceased," somebody wrote "Jewish."

I am good friends with Jim Vaden, stopping in to see him in his office in Washington, D.C., whenever I'm in town. He retired from the state troopers and now works for an international computer company managing their police agency accounts. Last time I saw him he was headquartered in a two-story stone walk-up surrounded by embassies, working in an office painted powder blue. He said he hated the color.

One day, as we were walking down the street near his office, I asked how he felt living in a city with one of the highest homicide rates in the country. Jim stopped and turned to me.

"Makes me want to be a cop again," he said with a wide grin.

Not long after my last visit with Jim, Ted Carlson retired from the Anchorage Police Department after twenty-three years, his departure hastened by a battle with Parkinson's disease. He invited me to his party.

Fellow officers and friends by the hundreds filled a big room at the Egan Civic and Convention Center to say good-bye to the department's senior officer. Many of the policemen were too young to recall my father's era, but the crowd included an unlikely contingent of old-time gamblers, including two of my father's closest friends. They'd come to pay their respects. I sat with them clutching a gift I'd brought for Ted.

I'd spent weeks tracking down a copy of the print of dogs playing poker that Ted used to confiscate from my father's gambling joints. I gave it to him before the official program began.

"You took this off my father's walls so many times, I figured it's time you had one of your own," I said.

Without unwrapping it, Ted tucked the print under his arm and thanked me with a hug. The speeches started; policemen and citizens presented Ted with plaque after plaque. Finally he got up to give his farewell speech.

Ted moved slowly, weighed down as much by emotion as by Parkinson's. The room fell silent. At the podium, he picked up my gift and began unwrapping it, telling the audience what I had said. Without ever looking at the picture, he held it up for the crowd to see. In a quavering voice still touched by an Oklahoma accent, he said, "I don't know how many of you remember Johnny Rich . . . "

A year after Ted's retirement, I got an invitation to the commencement ceremonies for the 1991 graduating class of Chugiak High School. A small white card accompanied the white-and-gold-lettered embossed invitation. On the card was the name *John Francis Rich III*.

From the moment I looked at the handwriting on the envelope, I knew he'd sent it. A year earlier, I'd tried to find him, but without any luck. I wanted to let him know I was writing a book about my father. I needed to know what he knew about who his father was, and who he wasn't. I'd heard he was living in the Seattle area with an aunt, but I was never able to track anybody down. As it turned out, he'd been in Seattle only briefly. He'd spent most of his life in Anchorage, raised by Bridgette's mother and her stepfather. They lived near Eagle River. I found their phone number.

After making a call, I spent days wondering what he looked like. The last time I'd seen a photograph of John he was an infant. I worried about what questions he'd ask me and how I'd answer them. I knew I couldn't lie, but I didn't know how I was going to tell him the truth either.

"I have a lot of questions," he told me over the phone.

I went to pick him up a week later.

We got into my car and drove to my office. All the while, I talked about the book and all the things I'd learned about my father. Every time I said the words "my father," they resonated in my mind. *Shouldn't I say, "our father"? Isn't that what John's expecting to hear?*

But he never seemed troubled by it. By the time we got to my office, I learned why.

After we had talked, he'd gotten a copy of a story I'd written about my father for the newspaper. From looking at the photographs, he learned what he'd long suspected — that my dad wasn't his biological father. He'd never seen a photograph of my father and always assumed he was black. His family never talked about my father. I told him that's because no one ever knew much about him, including myself. John's mother died when he was too young to ask, and I don't know if she would have told him the truth.

John told me he was comfortable with the truth. He knew that his mother had worked as a prostitute. He said he might be a "trick baby." I told him he might be wrong. He said he always considered his grandparents his parents anyway.

There's something about how level-headed he was that I found familiar and comforting; his ability to be philosophical about otherwise unsettling issues. I think I must have been much like him when I was his age. He has always known his mother was a heroin addict, but he says things like, "I still loved her. She was my mother."

I told him how I had thought I was a Jew and what it felt like learning I wasn't. We talked about how such knowledge changes you — and then again, it doesn't. What it does give you is clarity. He said his learning that my father wasn't his biological father was similar.

"Yeah, I think you're right," I told him.

He's a handsome, All-American kid, tall and graceful looking; a champion diver, academically motivated. He worked on the school yearbook, he's going to college, he went to the senior prom, even renting a tuxedo that he stopped by my office to show me.

As he stood in the doorway with the tux on a hanger, explaining why he picked out one with tails, I thought to myself, *It's amazing he turned out the way he did.*

I couldn't believe what I found myself thinking. It's the same thing I've heard from people over the years about myself. And every time someone would say it, I'd want to yell at them: *"What did you expect? Why shouldn't I be okay?"*

I had a memory of meeting my grandfather as a small child, but I wasn't sure if it was real or a dream. Several of my father's friends recalled meeting a man they remembered as his father, and I began to believe he existed.

It took nearly a year to find him, using genealogical researchers who were old hands at poring over cemetery records and prying birth, marriage, and death certificates from the hands of wary state clerks. They could have traced my roots back to Adam and Eve. All I needed was a grandfather.

We followed one lead after another in hopes of finding a man who might not even be alive; so many others in my family weren't. And even if I could find him, why would he talk to me?

After months of setbacks, I got a tip that my grandfather lived in Miami. His number was listed. I put off the call for a week.

When I finally picked up the telephone, I felt light-headed. As I began dialing, I began to perspire. I had a script in front of me in case I forgot what to say; to remind me what to ask. An elderly voice, faint and distant, answered.

"May I speak with John Alexander Rich?" I asked.

"My name is John Rich," he said, sounding suspicious. "Where'd you get Alexander from?"

Please don't hang up, I thought; *give me a chance to explain.*

"I, I better explain who I am," I stammered. "My name is Kim Rich, John, umm, ahh . . . "

"Kim Rich?" he asked. *"Kim Rich?"*

"Yes sir," I answered, forgetting the script. "Umm, I'm John Rich's only daughter. John Rich who lived in Anchorage, Alaska . . . "

Before I had a chance to finish, he cried out.

"Yes! Yes!" he croaked. *"I'm the guy!"*

My search was over. We both started talking at once, each over-flowing with excitement and joy. I stuttered and fought back tears.

"I've been thinking of you all along," he said. "Wondering what happened to you. My God, you can't believe it, the last five, six, seven weeks, you kept coming to me. The only time I'd ever seen you was when I was up in Alaska and you were a tiny little girl. I brought you out to buy you some shoes. Then all of a sudden everybody disappeared and I haven't heard from nobody since. I sent letters to Alaska and they came back."

"I have a lot to tell you," I began, without even thinking over what I was about to say. "My father's dead."

"What?"

"John is dead."

He fell silent.

"Oh God, I knew something happened," he said, his voice cracking and wavering. "I had that feeling something happened because every time I got letters back, I'd go to bed and I'd think, 'Something is wrong. He would have called me. He would have come to Florida, something' . . . What he die from?"

"Umm, he died . . . he was . . . he was . . . killed."

"What for?" he asked, his voice barely a whisper.

"It's a long story," I said, struggling to find the words to explain all that had happened. "He . . . hmm . . . some people killed him . . . it's all . . . "

"In Alaska?" my grandfather asked. "Did he die in Alaska?"

"Yes," I answered.

"He shouldn't have gone there, I knew it. I knew it."

"It was a long time ago," I continued. "I was fifteen when I lost him. Ahh . . . it's a long story. I can send it all to you in a letter. Umm . . . I . . ."

"I just sent a letter about two years ago to Alaska to see if I could find him there and the letter came back," my grandfather said. "I thought maybe they'd check it up. Then another time I called phone information and I tell them about John Rich having the Safari Hotel, and they said he's not here anymore and they don't know anything about him."

"Ah, umm, the Safari went down in the earthquake."

"I was just talking to a lawyer friend of mine the other day. I said, 'How can I find out about my son?' I said I sent letters there and everything came back. I said, 'What else can I do?' So, how's your mother?"

I hadn't prepared for having to tell an old man that his only son was dead and that his daughter-in-law had died in a mental institution. Our conversation tapped a flood of feelings. I realized that all the searching, all the peeling back of layers of myth and fiction, had brought me to this moment, and suddenly I understood: To know my father was to know myself. To understand my father's imperfections and fears is to know my own. To know that my mother's illness was a failure of biology—not will—has allowed me to face my own vulnerabilities without the fear of ending up in a psychiatric ward.

As these thoughts ran through my mind, I remembered once again what a friend had told me about this whole process: *There is no way past but through . . .*

Speaking in vague, general terms, I said what I could about my mother, trying to gently break the news. I didn't have to say much.

"When I knew her she was all right. But I think it was just the difficulty with my son, you know. I won't say he was rough, he was just probably doing things he shouldn't have been doing. He was too handsome I think, that was the problem. Of course you were kind of young and you didn't know that, but she had a lot of jewelry, high-class jewelry that'd be worth a ton of money today."

My grandfather reminisced about his visit to Alaska in mid–1963, when he stayed for the summer. I have been to the circus only once in my life and I had forgotten all about it until my grandfather reminded me that he had taken me there when he was in Alaska. Instantly, I remembered sitting in the bleachers of the old Sports Arena, watching a black bear pedal around the ring on a bicycle.

He'd loved Alaska, he said; he'd never seen mountains as tall and a town so small, yet one with so many restaurants open twenty-four hours a day, all catering to the nightclub crowd. He described Anchorage as a "clean" town, where the streets and sidewalks—the few that existed—were swept and washed daily. Coming from the factory and mill towns of the northeastern United States, I guess it must have looked that way to him. My grandfather helped my father run the Safari, and among the local street crowd and prostitutes, he was affectionately known as "Pop."

My grandfather told me his life story. He spoke proudly of my Italian great-grandparents; how they raised ten children and were willing to take in my father when the family learned of his birth.

"You come from a very nice family," he said.

He told me about working the streets with the blind man, his days as a bookie and a car salesman, and being stationed in Europe during World War II. When I asked if he'd ever married, he told of going to jail for getting my grandmother pregnant, recounting details as if they'd happened last week. He didn't try to hide anything when talking about his own arrest or when my father sought him out as a teenager.

"He was so handsome. He looked just like me. Oh, he was so handsome. Anytime we walked together, everybody knew he was my son. Your grandmother was a good-looking gal too, you know. His mother was beautiful. She was gorgeous."

When I asked him if he knew my father had been a gambler, he laughed in a familiar way, a throaty chuckle that I hadn't heard in a long time. "Who didn't gamble in those days? Eh, eh, eh," he said, sounding exactly like my father: *Little girls should be seen and not heard, eh, eh, eh . . . What do I look like, I'm made out of money? eh, eh, eh . . . So what are you? Some kind of a little con artist? eh, eh, eh . . .* I wanted my grandfather to laugh again and again.

We talked for two hours during that first phone call and promised to keep in touch.

"You can come down anytime. You don't have to worry about a room or anything," he said. "Ain't that funny? I was thinking about you the other day. But I'm fine now because I heard your voice. I always wondered what happened to that little dark-haired girl."

A few weeks later, I flew to Miami and I've been back several times since. En route during the first trip, I stopped over for a weekend in Oklahoma City.

When I walked into the terminal at Oklahoma City's Will Rogers World Airport, a tall, balding man with bright blue eyes dressed in denim coveralls and a baseball cap stepped up to greet me.

"You look just like your father the last time I saw him," Ziggie said as he shook my hand.

After Ziggie drove me to his house, he walked into the attached garage and emerged carrying a cake decorated to read: *Welcome home Granddaughter.*

"That was Ziggie's idea," said his wife, Ruth, in her soft, Tennessee drawl. "He loves cakes."

It was a warm reception for someone who had come to ask him to talk about something he'd rarely mentioned in all the years he'd been married to Ruth. They had married after Ziggie was divorced from my father's mother, Helen. A dozen years of their marriage had passed before Ruth learned that Ziggie even had an adopted son. She wouldn't have minded knowing.

She is the daughter of a Tennessee mining town sheriff who sided with union organizers and was shot and killed by a drunk brandishing a .38. Ruth has reserves of patience and understanding as deep as the coal mine shaft that later took her first husband's life. When she met Ziggie, she was a widow with three children living at home, all of whom Ziggie was happy to take in and raise as his own.

Family histories have a way of repeating themselves. Ziggie's long-held secret had once been Helen's. It was several months into their relationship before Ziggie was told that Helen had a son.

Ziggie and Ruth insisted I call them "Grandma" and "Grandpa." They write all the time, beginning their letters with "Dear Grand-daughter." They keep me informed of Ruth's latest blueberry jam entries in the state fair and of Ziggie's latest find at the garage sales; he's an antiques dealer. When I was there he took me to a flea market, then he showed me his garage, stuffed to the ceiling with auction-house bargains.

In Miami, John Rich, Sr., also had no trouble picking me out at the airport. He was a slightly built man, not much taller than I and with my profile. For the occasion, he wore his best white shoes, newly polished and buffed, and a handsome straw hat.

We went to a restaurant in Miami Beach, half a block from his apartment, where we got a cup of coffee and into the wee hours of the morning, he spun tales of old Miami—his exploits in Cuba, old gambling buddies long since dead, the brothers he's been feuding with for years. He talked about all the million-dollar deals that slipped through his fingers: the lots in Miami Beach that he could have gotten for a song right after the war; the mint he would have made in Cuba had that Castro character not moved in; the real estate in the Bahamas he should have invested in when he had the chance. He talked about how he wished my father would have left Alaska.

"You see, he was king there," he said. "I opened up an automobile lot and if he'd stayed in Connecticut, we would have been very rich because he was very, very smart in automobiles. Very smart. I got him a job with a fellow by the name of Coppolo, big Ford place; he said, 'Boy your son is the best man I ever had. I'm going to have him run the place very shortly.' Then all of a sudden he left, I think because he was a nobody in Connecticut, you know.

"He'd been worth a lot of money if he stayed with me. He'd a been the richest man around."

As my grandfather spoke, I remembered something one of my father's friends said when I asked him how my father would have reacted to my writing about him. "He'd love it," the friend said. "He was always a showman. He loved the notoriety. He liked being known."

I guess I've always known that. I have never stopped loving my father; now I'm beginning to like Johnny Rich as well.